The Argument and the Action of
Plato's *Laws*

The
Argument
and the
Action of
Plato's *Laws*

Leo Strauss

The University of Chicago Press
Chicago and London

The University of Chicago Press, Chicago 60637
The University of Chicago Press, Ltd., London

© 1975 by The University of Chicago
All rights reserved. Published 1975
Midway reprint 1983
Printed in the United States of America

Library of Congress Cataloging in Publication Data

Strauss, Leo.
  The argument and the action of Plato's Laws.

  1. Plato. Leges. I. Plato. Leges. 1975.
II. Title.
JC71.P264S86   321'.07   74-16680
ISBN 0-226-77706-5

Contents

Foreword

Professor Strauss completed this study, his last major work, in the autumn of 1971, two years before his death. He wrote it with a lifetime of reflection on Plato behind him, and with a particular interest in the *Laws* that cannot have become intense more recently than the winter of 1959, when he gave a seminar on the dialogue at the University of Chicago. As the reader will perceive, this book acquires much of its inner character from its being the work of a scholar whose acquaintance with the Platonic corpus had ripened to familiarity, just as it acquires much of its external character from its being a commentary that follows its text with persistent fidelity. Coming after its author's long and serious meditation on Plato, the book will engage the attention of those who continue to entertain the question whether the *Laws* is not a sweeping recantation that expresses Plato's senescent disenchantment with Perfection. The epigraph to this volume suggests rather that the *Laws* differs from the *Republic* not in its sovereign conception but in its decisive if tacit theme.

The account of the dialogue that is offered in the following pages has three conspicuous characteristics. First, the commentary has to a high degree the appearance of a mere retelling of the discourse. This appearance will be dispelled by comparison of the commentary with the text. In the second place, the commentary emulates faithfully the reticence of the text while striving nevertheless to elucidate Plato's thought. Finally, the language of the commentary is not always prepossessing but, on the contrary, sometimes grates. Characteristically, the reason for this is that the retelling of the discourse incorporates literal renditions of the speeches. Abruptness, some inelegance, occasional ambiguity in the commentary can be traced typically through the act of translation. The transliteration of names, except where the name of a man has been given to a dialogue, adheres as closely as possible to the Greek orthography, with the result that the reader will encounter "Apollon," "Bakchic," "Kyklopes," and "Lykourgos," among others, where he would perhaps have expected Apollo, Bacchic, Cyclops, and Lycurgus. The intention was to keep to a minimum, even in little things, the distance between the reader and the text.

Professor Strauss had both the opportunity and the capacity to make any changes in the manuscript that he desired. The study as it now appears is in the state in which it existed at the time of his death in October 1973, except in one particular. Against the authority of the manuscript, I have introduced on page 174 a negative, enclosed in brackets, because the sense of the passage apparently requires it. The relevant place in the *Laws* is the first sentence of 951b.

My thanks are due to Professor Ralph Lerner, who shared equally with me in the reading of proof. We are grateful to the Earhart Foundation for the support that provided us with assistance in that task.

JOSEPH CROPSEY

The Argument and the Action of
Plato's *Laws*

In the traditional order of the Platonic dialogues the *Laws* is preceded by the *Minos*, the only Platonic dialogue in which Socrates raises the question What is law? It appears that not all laws are good or, at any rate equally good. The Cretan laws were given by Minos, who was not only a son of Zeus but the only hero educated by Zeus; no one was ever celebrated as highly by Homer and Hesiod as Minos. We are thus led to believe that the Cretan laws, and next to them the Spartan laws, are the best laws. Minos was indeed regarded by the Athenians as savage and unjust, but for no other reason than that Minos had waged victorious war against Athens. The best legislator was an enemy of Athens. The most ancient good legislator was the most ancient enemy of Athens. The quest for the best laws seems to compel the Athenians to transcend the laws of Athens and to become the pupils of an enemy of Athens—to act in a way which could appear to be unpatriotic.

The *Laws* is the most political work of Plato. One may even say that it is his only political work, for in it the chief character, the Athenian stranger, elaborates a code for a city about to be founded, i.e., he engages in political activity. In the *Republic* Socrates founds a city in speech, i.e., not in deed; accordingly the *Republic* does not in fact present the best political order but rather brings to light the limitations, the limits, and therewith the nature of politics (Cicero, *Republic* II 52). The emphatically political character of the *Laws* would seem to explain why that work is the only Platonic dialogue in which Socrates does not participate, for Socrates was prevented by his *daimonion* from engaging in political activity (*Apology of Socrates* 31c3–32a3). The absence of Socrates from the *Laws* is thus not sufficiently explained by the fact that that dialogue takes place somewhere on Crete.

1

When Aristotle discusses the *Laws* in his *Politics*, he takes it for granted that the speaker in the work is the same as the speaker in the *Republic*: Socrates. Aristotle, at any rate, saw no difference between the Athenian stranger and Socrates. Plato's *Crito* may help us to understand this. Kriton tried to persuade Socrates to escape stealthily from prison and thus to save his life. In order to refute Kriton's proposal, Socrates uses as a subsidiary argument the consideration that if he left Athens he would go either to one of the well-governed cities nearby, where he would be utterly discredited by his unlawful escape, or to Thessaly, which is utterly lawless. He does not discuss what would happen to him if he went to a well-governed city far away like Sparta or the still more remote Crete; he had mentioned both shortly before (*Crito* 53b4–6 and d2–4, 52e5–6). It thus suggests itself to us that if Socrates had escaped from prison, he would have gone to Crete, where he was wholly unknown and would have come to sight only as an Athenian stranger. In the circumstances of which his old age was no mean part, it was indeed impossible for him to act on Kriton's advice. But Plato was not bound by what is possible simply or qualifiedly. It suffices to refer to the *Menexenus*, in which his Socrates rehearses a funeral speech in honor of fallen soldiers—a speech that was allegedly elaborated by Aspasia and which celebrates the great deeds performed by Athens until about twelve years after Socrates' death. Plato invented with ease Socratic and other stories.

The only Platonic dialogue apart from the *Laws* which is located outside of Athens is the *Phaedrus*. The peculiar theme of the *Phaedrus* may be said to be writings. The laws proposed in the *Laws* are written.

The *Laws* opens with the word "god"; there is no other Platonic dialogue that opens in this manner. The *Laws* is Plato's most pious work. There is one Platonic dialogue whose last word is "god": the *Apology of Socrates*. In the *Apology of Socrates* Socrates defends himself against the charge of impiety, of not believing in the gods in whom the city believes. In the *Laws* the Athenian stranger devises a law against impiety which would have been more favorable to Socrates than the corresponding Athenian law.

Book One

At the beginning of the *Laws* the Athenian stranger asks his two interlocutors, the Cretan Kleinias and the Spartan Megillos, whether a god or some human being is responsible for the disposition of their laws. The Cretan replies: a god, stranger, a god to give what is at any rate the most just answer; with us it is Zeus—with the Spartans, they say, I believe, that it is Apollon. The most just answer is not necessarily the most true answer. Is Zeus' having been responsible for the Cretan laws known only through what the Cretans say? Are the Cretans infallible? Is their veracity beyond doubt? Be this as it may, precisely if we are entirely unsuspicious, we can imagine that the Athenian stranger has come to Crete looking for the best laws. For if the good is the old, the best is the oldest; but in order to be simply superior to what is of later origin, the oldest must be super-human, divine; the Cretan laws, however, are the work not only of a god but of the highest god, and they are apparently the only laws of this description. Accordingly the dialogue opens with the Athenian stranger inquiring with an old Cretan about the old Cretan laws. More precisely, he inquires with an old Cretan and an old Spartan about the origin of the laws of their communities: the Cretan laws are not so unqualifiedly superior to the Spartan as not to need sup-plementing in some way by the latter; the oldest, even if it is the work of the highest god, is not simply the best. The Athenian is silent about the claim raised by the Spartans on behalf of their laws. This claim is not supported, as the Cretan claim to some extent is, by the authority of the most ancient poet. Homer makes clear that if Zeus gave the Cretans their laws, he gave them through the inter-mediacy of Minos, although neither Homer nor the Cretans vouch for Minos' justice (cf. 706a7ff.).

The Athenian does not question the divine origin of the Cretan laws. On the contrary, he infers from the fact that his two interlocutors have been brought up in habits bred by laws of this kind, that they would like to discuss governments and laws while walking from Knosos to the cave and sanctuary of Zeus, i.e., while walking, as Minos had done, to the place where he had received his instruction from Zeus; they ascend to the origins of the Cretan laws; their going to the cave of Zeus is an ascent. Because of the summer heat they will seek the shade afforded by the trees and make frequent stops. Since, in addition, they will converse with one another (which Minos did not do), their walk will be agreeable despite its length.

The Athenian now approaches the question of the divine character of the Cretan laws from a different angle: if those laws are divine, their end must be the proper end. The Athenian asks Kleinias with a view to what has the Cretan law established certain institutions. According to Kleinias the Cretan legislator has established all Cretan institutions with a view to war, while considering of course the nature of the land. The Cretan legislator, not blinded by a vulgar error, had seen that all cities are engaged, as long as they are, in a continuous war against all other cities; peace is only a word; universal war is according to nature; men possess nothing good if they are not superior in war, for all good things belonging to the vanquished become the possession of the victors. As we see, Kleinias asserts spontaneously and without any preparation what the Athenian ambassadors on Melos assert after having ascended from the discussion of the case at hand to their fundamental premise. Megillos agrees with Kleinias at least up to the point that a well-ordered city is characterized by its ability to vanquish the other cities in war.

The Athenian attempts to refute the Cretan by showing that if being victorious over other cities is the best for the city, being victorious over his fellow citizens would be best for the individual. When Kleinias agrees without hesitation, the Athenian, considering that each man is not simply one, asks Kleinias whether victory will not also be best in the relations between the parts of each man. To the Athenian's surprise, Kleinias enthusiastically agrees: the individual is indeed the proper starting point for the understanding of the city; enmity, war, is supreme even within each man; how else could victory over oneself be the first and best victory? Descending at the Athenian's suggestion from the individual to the city, the Cretan observes that a city in which the better people vanquish the multitude, i.e., the inferior people, is superior to itself and most justly praised on account of that very victory. But when the Athenian thereupon suggests that if the unjust majority of the citizens overcomes and subdues a just minority, the city is inferior to itself or bad, the Cretan finds that suggestion very strange—for it implies that victory as victory is not good—but admits that it is most necessary to agree to it. The concern is no longer with superiority to outsiders but with the right kind of inner structure.

In order to convince the Cretan fully, the Athenian ascends again, not to the individual but to the family: however natural war may be, kinship is also natural. It would not be surprising if the majority of the sons of the same father and the same woman were unjust and the minority were just. (In this context the Athenian utters a timely warning against undue concern with the becoming character of words to the detriment of concern with the natural correctness of laws; both interlocutors agree; Megillos' agreement is his first spontaneous utterance.) Now the question arises who would be the best judge in settling the domestic conflict: he who destroys the bad and commands the better ones to rule over themselves, or he who keeps the inferior ones alive and makes them voluntarily obey the honest ones (the honest ones being the sole rulers), or he, the third in respect of virtue, who would establish amity among all brothers, whether just or unjust, by giving them laws (and not limiting the right to rule to the good). The first is inferior to the second, for "who would rather kill someone than use him alive and obedient?" (Xenophon, *Memorabilia* I 2.11.) The second alone establishes aristocracy strictly understood, i.e., the rule of the better over the worse. The most important, which means in the present case the best, occupies the central position. The Athenian stranger makes tacit use of the critique of law as such which another stranger develops in the *Statesman* and which is, indeed, not immediately intelligible to the two old law-bred Dorians. At any rate, Kleinias, as distinguished from the Athenian, does not have the slightest doubt that the third would be the best judge, although he had previously admitted that a community in which the better people subdue the majority consisting of unjust men, is most justly praised: the judge of the third kind would be a legislator at the same time.

One must wonder why the Athenian does not speak of the father as the natural judge of his sons. (He had silently dropped the mother in 627c4.) The answer is implied in the order of rank of the three kinds of judge. The first two are concerned with goodness rather than kinship (fraternity); the third is concerned with kinship rather than goodness. Goodness and kinship are two very different things. The disregard of this difference is the root of what is at present vociferously disapproved of as "racism."

Arguing from the Cretan's admission, the Athenian concludes that the legislator will order the city with a view not to war but to peace and amity. He thus does not yet exclude the possibility that the legislator might establish internal peace in order to enable the city to wage external war. Nevertheless, he feels entitled to conclude further that war and victory do not belong to the best things but that even a city's victory over itself belongs only to the necessary things: war is not waged for its own sake but for the sake of the fruits of victory, of the good things which one expects to obtain through victory. In other words, internal (or external) war is not the natural state of the city but, rather, comparable to disease of the body or, at best, to its cure. Is peace then the natural state of the city? There seems to be a difference on this point between the statesman and the legislator: the good legislator gives laws with a view to peace. We know already what the end higher than peace is: goodness or virtue.

Kleinias becomes aware that if, or rather since, the conclusion arrived at regarding the good legislator is correct, the Cretan and the Spartan laws are defective. The Athenian wishes to avoid a harsh fight, at least for the time being. He therefore takes issue not with the divine legislators but with a man without authority, an Athenian expatriate who had become a Spartan citizen: the poet Tyrtaios. Instead of attacking the Cretan and the Spartan, let alone their divine legislators, the Athenian attacks a fellow Athenian. He proceeds like Socrates, who prefers to take issue with the poets' stories about gods and heroes rather than with the stories embodied in public worship. It was an Athenian who found the words for the Dorian view; and the Cretans owe their knowledge of Tyrtaios' poems to the Spartans. As far as speech is concerned, the sequence is not Crete-Sparta-Athens but Athens-Sparta-Crete. As far as speech is concerned, the oldest is not the best. The Athenian, making common front with his interlocutors, engages in a kind of dialogue with Tyrtaios who, being a poet, had praised not the fruits of war but the virtue of war. The conversation thus turns from war (or peace) to virtue as choiceworthy for its own sake as the end of legislation. Tyrtaios had praised most highly courage in war against men of alien stock. Claiming to speak on behalf of his interlocutors as well, the Athenian quotes Theognis, a poet of a later age who was a colonial, as witness for the view that "the whole virtue," or justice, moderation, good sense united with courage, is better than courage alone. Since he does not take issue with Theognis, he does not engage in a dialogue with him. (The underlying reasoning can be stated as follows. We grant that excellence in war is *the* excellence;

but foreign war is milder, is much less of war than civil war; hence
the best men are those who excel in that greatest war: they need the
greatest virtue [cf. 630a2 and c3–4].) Accordingly, every legislator
who is not entirely worthless, and hence in particular the Cretan
legislator, who was instructed by Zeus, will give his laws with a view
above all to the greatest virtue, which one may call "complete justice." To the Cretan's remark, which is free from indignation, that
this demand amounts to a condemnation of the Cretan legislator,
the Athenian replies that what is at fault is not the laws of Lykourgos
and Minos but their accepted interpretation. He appeals as it were
from the accepted interpretation of revelation to revelation itself,
which discloses its true meaning only to those who never forget that,
being divine, it is supremely reasonable. On the other hand, however, he ascribes the Dorian laws to Lykourgos and Minos rather
than to Apollon and Zeus.

The Athenian delineates now what we may call the natural beginning of an inquiry into divine legislation as distinguished from
the beginning imposed on him by the opinion of his interlocutors.
The latter beginning, concerned with the origin of the Dorian laws,
led to what the Cretan regarded as the most just answer. The natural
beginning is concerned with the end with a view to which divine laws
must be supposed to have been given; it leads to an answer that is
both true and just. He praises the Cretan for having said (which he
had not said) in his interpretation of the Cretan laws that the Cretan
legislator had laid down his laws for the sake of virtue, but blames
him for having identified virtue with its lowest or smallest part,
namely, courage. He then tells the Cretan how he should have
spoken in interpreting the Cretan laws. He should have said that
the laws of the Cretans are, not undeservedly, very famous among
all Greeks, for they provide all good things. Of good things there
are two kinds, human and divine. The human goods are: health,
beauty, bodily strength, and that wealth which is enlightened by
good sense. The divine goods are also four: good sense, moderation
or temperance, justice, which is a mixture of good sense and moderation with courage, and finally courage. The order is in both cases
one of descent from the highest to the lowest. What is said about
the divine goods articulates what was previously called the greatest
virtue or complete justice. In this explanation, justice is analyzed
so that it appears as a combination of the three other virtues (good
sense, moderation, courage) with the understanding that the combination is inferior in rank to two of the virtues which are its ingredients. This inferiority seems to be due to the fact that its third

ingredient, courage, is the lowest of the virtues. What does this mean? The place occupied by courage in the order of the divine goods is occupied in the order of the human goods by wealth, an external good. Courage as the virtue of war is directed toward the external; it is a virtue of self-assertion against those without. Justice requires courage—manly self-assertion (cf. *Republic* 549c2–550a1) —because it has to do in the first place with possession and acquisition (cf. 632b1–7). The relatively low rank assigned here to justice is connected with the fact that justice as practiced in the city adumbrated in the *Laws*, in a noncommunist society, is in the first place the virtue governing mine and thine. The strangeness of what the Cretan should have said is not diminished by the fact that he should also have said that the divine goods are the necessary and sufficient conditions for the human goods, at least as far as the city is concerned; virtue guarantees happiness, which includes the well-being of the body (health, beauty, strength) and even the right kind of wealth. How strange this whole exposition was for the Cretan, we are not permitted to know, since the Athenian does not give him an opportunity to voice his views but continues in his speech, the longest speech hitherto.

The Cretan should have continued that the order of the good things just sketched is established by nature. The legislator must follow the natural order. The Cretan has said or almost said the same; but he and the Athenian understand "nature" differently. The legislator, the Athenian continues, must proclaim to the citizens that his commands have in view the good things aforementioned in such a way that the human goods are ordered toward the divine goods and the divine goods in their turn (and therewith all goods) are ordered toward the Leader Intellect. (Hence Intellect is different from and superior to good sense; see the mss readings of 631c7.) The Athenian thus tells the Cretan to say, not what the Cretan legislator has done in the past, but what every legislator, including Minos, must do in the future: the Cretan ought to have risen to the natural order, which is older than any legislation. He ought to have ascended to the origin of the Cretan laws, nay, of all laws.

Furthermore, the legislator must regulate human life from birth to grave; he must, through the very laws, correctly blame and praise the wrong and the right kind of pains, pleasures, and desires; he must teach and define what is noble and what is not in each case, as regards anger, fear, and other perturbations caused by misfortune or good fortune; thereafter he is compelled to watch the citizens' acquisitions and expenditures and the associations which they form and dissolve voluntarily or involuntarily, to observe in all these cases what is just or not, and to assign honors to the law-abiding and impose fixed penalties to the transgressors: finally, surveying his laws, he will establish guardians of all laws—some of these guardians will be guided by good sense while others proceed through true opinion—so that Intellect, having bound all these things together, will reveal them as subservient to justice and moderation and not to wealth and ambition. (Many laws can reasonably be suspected of being in the service of wealth and ambition.)

The Athenian seems to have given a comprehensive if extremely succinct summary of the task of the legislator. Yet he did not mention the two highest themes: the gods and the regime (*politeia*). As for the latter, one might say that the regime which he has in mind is not, as all other regimes are, the rule of any particular kind of men or of any man, but the rule of law; the human rulers are only the executors of the law. As for the gods, the divine goods are the human virtues (cf. 626c6), but they are ordered toward the Leader Intellect. Yet the Athenian calls death the end of the whole polity (*politeia*): what is deathless transcends politics. From this we understand that the whole legal order must, according to the Athenian, be subservient to justice and moderation, i.e., not to good sense, let alone Intellect. Good sense and Intellect must be effective in legislation and to some extent even in the execution of the laws, but they are not that to which legislation is ordered. In legislation the higher is in the service of the lower, and this is strictly speaking against nature. This is a fundamental crux of the city. The Athenian avoids in his summary the term "education" (*paideia*). Above all, he is silent on piety or the divine things proper in his summary of the natural order of the laws.

He concludes his summary by expressing the wish that his interlocutors set forth how all things that he has mentioned are contained and arranged in the laws, said to be of Zeus and the Pythian Apollon, which Minos and Lykourgos have given: the old Dorians must know this in one way or another; for "us others" it is in no way clear. The Dorians must show, beginning with courage, that every kind of virtue is properly provided for by the two codes. This suggestion does not entirely agree with that transmitted through the Athenian's summary, for the latter did not, surely not clearly, begin with courage. The Athenian returns from what he has presented as the natural order to the order most intelligible to the Dorians, who must, in the spirit of their laws, begin with courage, i.e., ascend from it. Megillos proposes that the Athenian should examine Kleinias

first, but having thus come into the open he is exposed to the Athenian's attempt to make him, and thus Sparta, the prime subject of
his examination. At any rate the Athenian frames his next question,
addressed to both interlocutors, in such a manner that Megillos has
no difficulty in answering it. He has no difficulty in enumerating five
Spartan institutions invented by the legislator with a view to war
or to the promotion of endurance to pain, toil, and heat. All this
implies, but only implies, a certain understanding of courage: Megillos had not mentioned courage nor even the fighting against fear.
After having tacitly corrected this deficiency, the Athenian asks him
whether courage is nothing but the fighting against pains and fears
but not also the fighting against longings and pleasures. Megillos
replies in the affirmative, i.e., he tacitly admits that courage rightly
understood includes moderation; courage is the praiseworthy habitual
posture not only toward the evils ("the left") which assail men from
within but also toward the goods ("the right") of the same kind
(cf. 634d1–2 with Aristotle, *Metaphysics* 986a22–26). Courage then
includes moderation; it has ceased to be the lowest virtue and has
become the second highest. Then the Athenian reminds Megillos
that, as the Cretan had stated formerly, one is blamed for being
inferior to oneself, which means, as the Cretan now makes clear,
for being overcome by pleasure rather than by pain. The two divinely
inspired lawgivers must have provided for courage in the two respects. Which institutions then did they establish in order to make
the citizens taste pleasures and prove themselves masters of them?
The Dorians are embarrassed for an answer.

The Athenian seems now to be compelled to question the ade-
quacy, the goodness of the Dorian laws without using any subter-
fuge, and thus to hurt the feelings of his interlocutors. He therefore
proceeds with special circumspection. Everyone, including the Athenian himself, especially if he is an old man, must listen with gentleness to criticism of the laws of his community if such criticism is
brought forward by someone who wishes to see both the truth and
the best (the truth about the laws of the city in question and the
best which may differ from those laws). When Kleinias approves
of this sentiment, the Athenian addresses him for the first time by
name. Leaving it open whether the Dorian regimes are correctly
blamed by anyone, everyone must admit that one of their finest laws
is the one which forbids the young to criticize any of their institutions but stipulates that all should say with one voice that all their
laws are fine since they were given by gods, and should not tolerate
dissent on this point; yet one of their old men may make speeches

of this sort when speaking to a ruler and men of his own age, provided no one young is present. We see here that the answers given
by the two Dorians at the very beginning were "most just" in the
precise sense of being legal or in full agreement with the Dorian
laws. We see above all that the Athenian speaks now of what he
had previously only done—that he makes explicit the principle on
which he had previously only acted, namely, the questionable premise of the divine origin of the Dorian laws, which allegedly makes
certain the goodness of those laws. After this has been understood,
he can safely continue to speak from time to time in the old manner.

Kleinias praises the Athenian more highly than ever before, comparing him to a soothsayer who has correctly divined what went on
in the mind of the legislator of the remote past—he compares him
as it were to the Cretan soothsayer Epimenides, who was famous for
prophesying not about future things but about things which had
happened yet were immanifest (cf. Aristotle, *Rhetoric* 1418a24–26).
He admits, in other words, that Minos himself ascribed his laws to
Zeus in order to protect them against hasty blame. The Athenian's
retrospective prophecy is not surprising since his thought extended
much beyond Minos to the natural order itself.

The Athenian's high praise and deep understanding of the Dorian
law of laws is bound to mitigate the displeasure which he can no
longer avoid causing to his interlocutors. He first makes sure that
the strictly private conversation of the three old men—from which
no corruption of the young can be apprehended—about the Dorian
laws is unobjectionable in the legislator's view; while being a stranger he regards himself as subject to the Dorian law of laws and even
authorized by it to examine the other Dorian laws. He thus gives a
legal (as distinguished from a rational or philosophic) justification
for his criticism of those laws. Encouraged by the Cretan, he expresses his perplexity about the fact that the Dorians' legislator has
commanded them to abstain from tasting the greatest pleasures and
kinds of play, while in the case of pains and fears the legislator
knew very well that only by being exposed to them from childhood
can one learn to endure and to overcome them, and enacted laws
in accordance with this insight. Dropping the somewhat forced (cf.
710a6) interpretation of moderation as the better half of courage—
an interpretation which can be understood as a concession, no longer
necessary, to the Dorian prejudice—the Athenian asks how the legislator has provided for the promotion of moderation as distinguished from courage. According to the natural order, justice, not
moderation, should come next after courage. But justice is the most

complex or complicated of the virtues and moderation is one of its ingredients. The two virtues which come first in the order not of rank but of coming into being are courage and moderation (cf. Aristotle, *Rhetoric* 1361a3–4). Their primacy is the consequence of the primacy of pain and pleasure as the natural sources of ill-being and well-being. (In the context, the concentration on moderation as moderation intimates that that virtue is to become the theme until the end of Book Two; this intimation was foreshadowed by the fact that, in the Athenian's summary of the natural order of goods, a higher rank was assigned to moderation than to justice. Compare the cooperation of courage and moderation as articulated in Book Three of the *Republic*.) Somewhat hesitatingly, Megillos, who has used the intervening time for doing some recollecting, replies now that the common meals and the gymnasia seem to serve well in regard to both virtues. Yet these institutions, the Athenian objects, and especially the gymnasia seem to have corrupted what is according to nature regarding the aphrodisiac pleasures of all animals; for the pleasure deriving from the intercourse of males and females, which serves procreation, seems to be in accordance with nature, whereas homosexual acts are against nature. These practices can be traced to the Dorian cities. The Cretans went so far as to invent the myth of Zeus' homosexual relations with Ganymede in order to give their practice the highest possible sanction. (What they say about the divine origin of their code has no greater credibility than that myth, since it too has no other foundation than that they assert it.) It could seem then that the Dorians do permit their citizens to taste pleasures, if also very questionable ones, but apparently not with the intention of making them control the desire for those pleasures.

Megillos does not deny the facts to which the Athenian has referred, but he insists politely that in spite of them the Spartan legislator has correctly commanded avoidance of pleasures. He leaves it to Kleinias to come, if he wishes, to the Cretan legislator's assistance. Kleinias fails to do so: the issue from now on is exclusively the goodness of the Spartan laws. Megillos extols the Spartan law for prohibiting symposia with all their attendant evils (i.e., pleasures) and for arranging that drunkenness be severely punished, whereas the Athenians among others indulge this evil, using the celebrations in honor of Dionysos as pretexts (just as the Cretans use the myth of Ganymede as a pretext for their self-indulgence). Megillos responds to the Athenian's blame of the Spartan syssitia by a blame of the Athenian symposia; he acts the part of a patriotic defender of his city. He thus compels the Athenian to act in the same manner: to come to the defense of his native city, mentioning in passing another defect of the Spartans (the looseness of their women). Ordinary people may be content to say that "this is customary with us but you perhaps have a different custom regarding this matter." But one cannot be content with an appeal to the established laws when the established law itself and therewith the badness or goodness of the legislator has become the theme. The Athenian is prepared to defend not just wine drinking but drunkenness, i.e., to recommend to the Dorians the Athenian institution of symposia, not indeed as Athenian but as sound. This subject came up in a sense by chance, but by dramatic necessity will prove to be the chief subject of the first two Books of the *Laws*. Of the Athenians one might perhaps say that their indulgence in this respect is only the reverse side of their being not very warlike. To counter this, the Athenian mentions six warlike nations—all of them barbarian—which do not refrain from drunkenness. Could barbarian institutions conceivably be superior to Dorian ones? When Megillos replies that the Spartans defeat all of these nations in the field, the Athenian warns him that victory in war does not prove the superior nobility of the institutions of the victors. This applies of course also to the cases in which the Athenians were victorious. The divine goods are not evidently the sufficient condition of the human goods broadly or loosely understood. In order to judge reasonably of the nobility of institutions, one must use a different criterion.

The Athenian wishes to make clear, using drunkenness as an example, the correct way of inquiry regarding all institutions, for are not all Dorian institutions debatable? It is clearly irrelevant whether a given pursuit is accepted by people who are habitually victorious in war, as irrelevant as whether it is accepted by myriads of nations. What one must consider is whether it is good if used in the right way, in the right circumstances. One must consider in particular what kind of men supervise the practice or are the rulers over it. One cannot judge fairly of symposia if one has seen only symposia not ruled by anyone or ruled only by bad rulers. The ruler in any activity must have the specific knowledge or science required and in addition the specific strength needed for quelling the specific disturbance accompanying the activity in question. For instance, in order to be a good pilot it is not sufficient that one possess the art of piloting; one must also be immune to seasickness. Or a military commander must not be a coward. It seems that the opposite of cowardice, courage, is as little knowledge or science as immunity to seasickness (cf. 963e).

The Athenian might have gone on to say at once that the ruler of a symposion must possess the specific knowledge or science required and the specific strength (immunity to drunkenness) required. But he has not yet completed his exposition of the correct way of inquiry —of praising and blaming—regarding all institutions. Must the competent praiser or blamer of institutions not also possess the specific science required and the specific strength, the latter being perhaps immunity to the passions aroused by antiquity or novelty, familiarity or foreignness? The Athenian says, however, that someone who has never seen a well-ruled association of the kind which is by nature in need of a ruler, cannot praise or blame it properly; and that this applies to wine drinking in particular, a practice alien to the Dorians and not legal with them and hence unknown to them from experience, as Megillos at any rate asserts (cf. 637e2). He adds that he himself has come across many symposia in many places and in addition has investigated by questioning, so to speak, all, yet has hardly seen or heard of a single one which was altogether as it should be. It could seem that either no one possesses knowledge of a perfect symposion or else that such knowledge is not experience. The perfect symposion is the symposion "itself" (640e1); the many symposia of various degrees and kinds of imperfections are distortions or dilutions of the symposion "itself." The perfect symposion, one is tempted to say, is the "idea" of the symposion. The perfect city of the *Republic* is not the "idea" of the city, for that city owes its being to human making. One could say that both the perfect city of the *Republic* and the perfect symposion of the *Laws* are utopias —blueprints of what one would wish or pray for and at the same time of what is possible—and accordingly that the *Laws* obscures the difference between an "idea" and a "utopia." This difference between the *Laws* and the *Republic* corresponds to the difference between Kleinias-Megillos and Glaukon-Adeimantos, between the manifest absence and the manifest presence of philosophy.

But how can there be knowledge of an association which is utopian? Is the Athenian a kind of diviner (634e7)? Megillos is altogether silent. The Cretan sees this much, that owing to the Dorians' lack of experience of a well-ruled symposion they might not be able, if they came across a symposion, to judge correctly of it. He realizes that before attempting to judge he must learn from the Athenian.

The Athenian begins his teaching as follows. All meetings and associations for the purpose of actions of whatever kind and in whatever place need a ruler in order to be correct: there are associations which are not in need of a ruler and are even incompatible with rule (cf. 639c1–2; *Protagoras* 338b2–c6). Symposia, like armies, need rulers. If possible, the ruler of an army must be altogether fearless and imperturbable. But armies are led to battle with enemies, while symposia are peaceful gatherings of friends in friendliness and for friendliness. In a way symposia abound as much in disturbance as fighting armies. Hence the ruler of a symposion must, if possible, also be altogether imperturbable; he must be the sober ruler of drunken people. In addition, he must, just as the general, possess knowledge but the knowledge required of him is not described as science (*episteme*) but as good sense (*phronesis*) regarding associations and even as wisdom (*sophia*); he must preserve the available friendship and take care that it is increased by the symposion. Wisdom is so important that if the ruler is wise, it is not necessary that he be old. (We recall that in the law of laws the only difference that counted was that of old men and young, not that of wise and unwise.) Sobriety is required of every ruler: the symposion is an example illustrating the city; it is therefore more than an institution promoting moderation, one virtue among others. This comes out in the immediate sequel when the Athenian replies to a question.

Granting what the Athenian had just said, Kleinias wishes to know what great good—comparable to the great good produced by a well-ruled army—would come from a well-ruled (*orthos paidogogethen*) symposion for private citizens or the city. He thus gives the Athenian the cue for his reply: a well-ruled symposion makes a major contribution to education (*paideia*), a much less ambiguous good for the city than victory, which may well breed *hybris*, the opposite of moderation. Kleinias is highly pleased with this answer: he addresses the Athenian for the first time as "friend" instead of as "stranger"; is this due to his concern with an improvement in education or to his concern with making symposia respectable? He is surely eager to hear whether the Athenian can prove that what he said is true. The Athenian hesitates to reply in the affirmative, but the subject of the discussion on which they have embarked—"laws and regime" —entitles him to state his opinion on the usefulness of symposia. If Kleinias were firmly opposed to symposia, he could easily have used the Athenian's hesitation in order to reject the proposal altogether on the ground that even the proponent lacks evident knowledge of the usefulness of that institution. Kleinias seems to desire symposia. Hitherto the Athenian had appealed to certain opinions inherent in the Dorian laws—opinions which might induce the Dorians to doubt the wisdom of their laws; now, it seems, he can appeal to a forbidden desire. Kleinias speaks also for Megillos without having been authorized by him to do so.

The Athenian now appeals again to the benevolence of his interlocutors. He does not have to worry any more about the propriety or permissibility of questioning the wisdom of the divine laws; he had disposed of this difficulty quite some time ago when he appealed to the highest of those laws, the law of laws. Still, symposia are foreign to the Dorians. By defending symposia the Athenian defends an Athenian institution. He thus underlines the deep difference, not to say hostility, between Dorians and Athenians. But not only is the subject Athenian; his manner of speaking about it is likewise Athenian. Athens is known and perhaps also disliked for her love of speech and her abundance of speech, while Sparta is known for her brevity of speech and Crete for being concerned with abundance of meaning rather than of speech. The Athenian must now make a very extensive speech on a very small subject (drunkenness), for symposia cannot be regulated according to nature without the correctness of Music (singing accompanied by the playing of musical instruments), and this in its turn cannot be achieved without the correctness of the whole of education. (The introduction of the whole of education for the purpose of correctly regulating symposia recalls the introduction, in the *Republic*, of philosophy as required for making possible the actualization of communism and equality of the sexes.) Should they not drop the subject therefore and turn to another discussion of laws?

The Dorians assure the Athenian of their friendliness, not so much toward Athenian love of speech and abundance of speech, as toward Athens. They have such friendly feelings not because of what Athens has done for Sparta and Crete but because of what Sparta and Crete have done for Athens: Kleinias and Megillos are magnanimous (cf. Aristotle, *Eth. Nic.* 1124b9–10). For good reasons Megillos (who now discloses his name) does not refer to what Sparta had done for Athens in the Persian war (cf. 698d5–e5). He refers to what he, the scion of a family of Athenian *proxenoi*, felt as such from childhood for Athens as his second fatherland, and what he did in defending Athens against her critics among his fellow citizens. He adds that the good men among the Athenians are outstanding in goodness because they alone are good without coercion, by their very nature, by divine allotment. He divines that absence or near-absence of coercion by laws is bad in most cases but not in all. Kleinias speaks exclusively of what Crete did for Athens at the time of the Persian war. He does not expect the Athenian to know of this through Athenian tradition. Epimenides, a kinsman of Kleinias, a divine man, went to Athens at the behest of a divine oracle ten years before the Persian war, offered certain sacrifices which the god had ordained, and gave the Athenians true and comforting predictions regarding the Persian war. The antiquity or remoteness of the Cretan benefaction is more than compensated by its divinity. In both cases not the cities but individual families are claimed to be friendly to Athens.

The Athenian can now begin to make clear "what education is and what power it possesses" with a view to, or within the limits of, the discussion in which they are engaged. Education will be, if not their theme, at least the way through which their discussion will move until it has arrived "at the god." Their discussion will have reached its end when their walk to the cave of Zeus has reached its end. If this is so, the whole *Laws* is devoted to education, in the first place of the two old Dorians, in a way comparable to that in which Xenophon's *Cyropaedia*, and not only its first Book, is devoted to the education of Cyrus.

The What is . . . ? question had not been raised with the same explicitness regarding the virtues at whose promotion education is directed. And even the question, What is education? is not, strictly speaking, discussed, i.e., discussed through questioning of the interlocutors, but the Athenian answers the question which he had raised: he teaches. The level of the discussion is sub-Socratic.

Education (*paideia*) is guidance of children (*paides*) through play (*paidia*) to the things in which they are to be good when they have reached manhood; the playing must include the serious study of preliminary subjects without the command of which the very playing is impossible. Education must lead the soul of the child at play to passionate desire (*eros*) for that in which he must be perfect when he has reached manhood, i.e., in virtue, in being a perfect citizen who knows both how to rule and how to obey in accordance with right. The Athenian will have to show that education, as he delineated it, is greatly assisted by symposia and that symposia have this effect by promoting moderation.

Moderation, self-control, implies that man while being one, is twofold, nay, manifold. He has in himself irrational counselors opposed to one another, in the first place, pleasure and pain, and then opinions or expectations of future evil or good. Superimposed upon all these is reasoning or calculation as to what is better or worse; when that reasoning has become the common decrees of the city, it is called the law. The Dorians have great difficulty in following the Athenian: the reasoning precedes its acceptance as law by the city; what change does it undergo through that acceptance? does it become more reasonable through it? or if the law instills some reasonableness into the city, the citizen body, it is obviously salutary, the reasonable man will obey it but he does not need it for his own guidance. On the other hand, if we admit all "laws" which are anywhere in force to be laws, can all of them be said to be reasonable?

The Athenian tries to lead the Dorians to an understanding of the relation between reasoning and law by proposing that they should conceive of every living being as a puppet of the gods, leaving it open whether the gods put it together as a plaything or with some seriousness. One could find that the comparison of living beings, including men, to puppets is a strange way of explaining self-mastery. In fact the Athenian at once silently drops the mythical (cf. 636d4–5) explanation and limits himself to what "we know"; he does not, however, drop the image of puppets. The aforementioned affections are like sinews or cords which drag us in opposite directions, to opposite actions. In order to be virtuous, we must always follow one of the cords that drag us (hence we are not simply dragged like puppets), namely, the single golden and holy guidance of reasoning which is called the common law of the city. Are then the reason and the law identical? Far from it. Reasoning is indeed noble but soft, gentle, and not violent, and therefore it cannot rule if it is not assisted by tough and steely sinews: the guidance by the law is not only noble but most noble. The law thus seems to be of higher dignity than the reasoning as such, and virtue would be simply identical with obedience to the law. Yet the things through whose assistance law acquires its superiority are far from being "golden"; do they differ at all from the irrational affections which should be simply subservient to reasoning? Accordingly, after having formally concluded "the myth regarding virtue," the Athenian declares that the private man must take hold of the true account (*logos*) within him regarding those things that drag us, and must live in obedience to it, whereas the city must take over an account from some god or from him who has acquired knowledge regarding the things mentioned and, having made it a law, converse with itself and other cities. It would be wrong but not entirely misleading to say that the reasonable individual is autonomous and the city is not. Those who are guided merely by the law, however reasonable, without knowing (knowing through themselves) that it is reasonable, are as much puppets as those who are dragged only by their passions, although they are of course superior to the latter.

After having intimated rather than set forth the complex relation of law and reason, the Athenian concludes that, having reached greater clarity on vice and virtue, they are likely to arrive at a better understanding of education and therefore of the usefulness of symposia. To that conclusion Kleinias assents.

Wine, especially if indulged in to excess, we are told, increases the power of pleasure, pain, and the passions while it weakens the perceptions, memories, opinions, and reasonable thoughts; it makes men childish or childlike just as old age does; it leads men into every kind of degradation. To understand why wine drinking or drunkenness can nevertheless have a salutary effect, we have only to remind ourselves of the degradations of the body which people voluntarily undergo for the sake of future health and strength. The degradation of the soul which is brought about by wine drinking has this advantage over the degradation of the body through medicine or gymnastics, that the former is not painful at least in its initial stage. But which defect of the soul is cured by symposia? We know from what went before that courage and moderation are closely akin. Since courage is the right posture toward fear, let us see whether there is not a kind of fear the right posture toward which could be, or could take the place of, moderation. That kind of fear is fear of bad reputation or sense of shame. Sense of shame however opposes the surrender not only to the most frequent and greatest pleasures but also to pain and fear. Sense of shame can then take the place of both courage and moderation. It does take their place especially for the legislator who calls it *aidos* (reverence or awe) and pays it the highest honor. The peculiar kind of fear called *aidos* fulfills for a short while the function formerly fulfilled for a short while by courage (cf. 633b8–634b6); it takes the place of courage. The reason is this. Victory in war and hence courage as the virtue of war are at first glance the end at which the Dorian laws aim; but these laws owe their power not simply to desire for victory or its fruits but to the discipline engendered by the laws believed to be divine; even here and precisely here the divine goods are necessary and sufficient for procuring the human goods (cf. 631b6–c1). Therefore one can say that the virtue or habit produced by the Dorian laws is in the first place not courage but *aidos*. Yet the subordination of courage to *aidos* must not make us oblivious of the fact that courage as courage is a habit of fearlessness and *aidos* is a habit of fear. One must remember this fact in order to understand the peculiarity of *aidos* and therewith the possible usefulness of symposia.

In retrospect it appears that in answering the Athenian's initial questions, Kleinias has forgotten *aidos*, i.e., has severed the connection between the divine origin of the Cretan laws and the end to which they are devoted (victory in war) and thus has weakened the hold of those divine laws. As can be seen from the Athenian's silence on *aidos* in his summary of the natural order of laws and their ends (631b3–632b1), Kleinias' oblivion enables him to become a partner in the Athenian's inquiry.

Returning to the difference between courage and moderation and modifying his earlier statement in the light of what he has said about *aidos*, the Athenian says that just as one promotes courage by exposing the young and the mature to ordinary fear, one promotes moderation by exposing them to whatever could tempt them to be shameless. Promoting moderation requires, indeed, a much more varied effort on the part of the legislator than promoting courage. The Athenian now instructs the legislator of any society by putting questions to him which Kleinias answers.

If there were a potion producing extreme fear and depression without doing serious harm, so that by being forced to overcome that fear one would become courageous, that potion could replace the cumbersome training commonly used for promoting courage; the fear drink would of course not be permitted to induce a degree of fear which no human being could overcome. But the comparison of wine with the fear drink makes us expect that participation in properly regulated symposia will constitute the complete training in moderation. In what sense can this be true? Wine exhilarates, increases one's self-confidence, hopefulness, daring, and finally makes him able and willing to say as well as to do everything with utmost freedom. We infer that in a well-ordered society which does not permit symposia, there will be no *parrhesia* whatever. This inference agrees with what we have learned about the Dorian law of laws. It is true that that law permits frank discussion of the defects of the old laws by old men who converse in the strictest privacy. But will not precisely old men be to the highest degree under the influence of ingrained, inveterate, law-bred reverence for the old-established which is traced to the gods? Does not precisely old age have its peculiar defects obstructing reasonable criticism and change of laws (cf. 646a4)? Old age may be an image of wisdom—just as law is an image of right reason—but it is not wisdom. Will the old men then not need, in addition to the legal freedom or authority to criticize the laws, a medicine which will make them truly free to do that? Could not wine, or at any rate the vicarious enjoyment of wine through a conversation about wine, have this rejuvenating effect (cf. 645e3–8)? At any rate, a temporary suspense of *aidos* is required for the change of ancient laws.

Apart from this, it is undeniable that wine loosens the tongue and weakens all restraints and hence that common wine drinking affords the cheapest and least dangerous opportunity for knowing the natures and habits of one's fellow citizens and in particular of the vices which they can conceal when sober. Such knowledge belongs to the same art whose task it is to treat these natures and habits—the political art. The treatment consists above all in making the citizens immune to shamelessness by means of symposia.

Book Two

When the Athenian had first suggested that symposia make a major contribution to education, he had hesitated to assert the truth of this suggestion; only a god could do that (641c8–d7). In comparing wine to the postulated fear drink, he had addressed questions to the legislator which Kleinias answered (648a8–649a7); the answers were not given by the Athenian. Now when he raises the question whether symposia entail some great advantage in addition to enabling one to know "our natures"—he is here silent on our habits —he says that, "as the *logos* seems to hint," they do, and that as for the manner in which they do it, "we" must listen to the *logos* attentively, lest "we" be ensnared by the *logos*. Since it is not—not merely—the Athenian's speech, the *logos* is mysterious, enigmatic, and hence likely to be a trap. The Cretan is not for a moment afraid of being trapped.

We were led to expect that symposia are eminently useful for treating or tending the natures and dispositions of the souls, in other words, for education. Our expectation is now considerably reduced: symposia are useful for the safeguarding of education, i.e., they do not form part of education itself. To justify this change, the Athenian repeats, i.e., changes, his definition of education. The crucial changes are these. First, education is now clearly understood to be not more than the habituation of the subrational part of the soul. Second, the end of education is now said to be the perfect human being, and not the perfect man (*aner*) or the perfect citizen. The virtue through which a human being is perfect is the harmony between reason and habituation—a harmony according to which reason understands and approves the likes and dislikes originally fostered only by habituation. As the Athenian had said shortly after he had given his first definition of education, reasoning, being noble but gentle and soft, needs tough helpers; in that context he had clearly distinguished between the private man who must take hold of the true *logos*, and the city which must take over the law from some god or from him who has acquired the pertinent knowledge; in the present definition or its immediate neighborhood there is no reference or allusion to the law: the perfect human being is a private man. Kleinias is not aware of the grave difference between the two definitions; according to him, both are correct, whereas, according to the Athenian, both are noble: the disregard of their difference makes them noble.

Dropping for the time being the subject of symposia, the Athenian explains briefly why education is in need of safeguarding and then, dropping for the time being the subject of its safeguarding, turns to a detailed discussion of education itself: it will be a considerable time before the discussion of symposia will be continued; it seems as if the subject of symposia has partly been used as a bait for luring the Dorians to a discussion of education. Owing to its playful character, the primary education is in danger of being corrupted in the course of the naturally toilsome life of the human race. Moved by pity, the gods have therefore instituted festivals (holy days) in which human beings, relieved from their toils, join with the Muses, Apollon, and Dionysos and thus restore the weakened education. This institution is in agreement with nature, especially the nature of the young, who cannot be quiet but always seek to move and utter sounds, and who derive pleasure from doing these things by playing with one another; human beings, as distinguished from the other animals, have a sense of order and disorder in movements and sounds; in other words, they derive pleasure from rhythm and harmony. Accordingly, the first education takes place through the Muses and Apollon, who have given us the pleasurable perception of rhythm and harmony, the necessarily common enjoyment of song and dance. Education takes place, then, primarily not through prohibition or command, punishment or reward, but through the Music things. And it does not consist in tasting pleasures in order to learn to become immune to them. The education through the Muses and Apollon is evidently not primarily safeguarding of education: it is Dionysos, the god of wine, who is responsible for the safeguarding of education.

The first education, being training in dance and song, is training in choral discipline. He who is finely educated is able to sing and dance finely, and this means in the best case that he is able to present finely through song and dance the fine (noble) things and derives pleasure from them, while he is repelled by the ugly (base) ones. There are two alternatives: he who sings noble things well but does not enjoy them but rather enjoys base ones (the good artist of bad character), and he who sings noble things poorly but derives enjoyment only from noble things (the poor artist of good character); the second seems to be preferable to the first.

In trying to elucidate what correct education is, we must not forget that this is preparatory to the understanding of the safeguarding of education. Being concerned with correct education, we are not concerned with Greek education as such; correct education may also be barbarian (cf. 648a9). This follows from the fact that we now understand by education the education of the perfect human being. It is not made clear whether or not barbarians know of Apollon and the Muses. One can say in general that there is an unambiguous relation between the virtue of the soul or of the body, or of some image of virtue, and beautiful postures and utterances on the one hand, and between vice and ugly postures and utterances on the other. Yet that relation is rendered somewhat ambiguous by the fact that "some image of virtue" may take the place of virtue itself. The kinship, yet difference, between the image of virtue and virtue corresponds to the kinship yet difference between law and reason. Just as the Athenian had only alluded to, and thus blurred, the difference between law and reason, he now disregards the difference between virtue and some image of virtue. He is therefore confronted with the question of what it is that confuses or perplexes the seemingly unambiguous relation between virtue and beautiful Music performances. Is that confusion due to the fact that noble things appear to different people in a different light? The Athenian seems to deny this: no one would say that the Music presentations of vice are more beautiful than those of virtue or that he enjoys the former. This does not prove of course that people do not feel what they do not dare to say. Yet most people say that the correctness of Music consists in its ability to produce pleasure—an unbearable and unholy view because it implies the oblivion of the noble. The Athenian admits that people necessarily enjoy and hence call beautiful (noble) the performances which agree with nature or habituation, and he traces the confusion to the fact that nature and habituation may be at variance with one another; hence people will say that presentations of vice are pleasant but degrading (cf. 662a3–6 as well as *Gorgias* 474c4–d2 and *Republic* 348e6–9) and will therefore be ashamed to own their pleasures and to act on them. This would seem to mean that unqualified perversity is impossible: either nature or habit is right. But since both nature and habit can be corrupt, it is perhaps better to say that unqualified perversity is very rare. The common case is that there is disagreement between nature and habit.

Be that as it may, the enjoyment of base Music performances is as bad as the enjoyment of base company, even if that enjoyment is accompanied by some, as it were, playful disapproval of the base or shame-induced failure to praise it.

The Athenian draws a conclusion from this regarding the laws regulating Music education (this is the first time that laws are mentioned in Book Two): noble laws will not permit poets and other votaries of the Muses to teach whatever they enjoy, regardless of how it affects the character of the children and the young. What can be done in this respect is shown above all by Egypt. There, the beautiful postures and melodies have been consecrated and fixed from the oldest times for the young in the cities, and no practitioner of the imitative arts is permitted to deviate from the ancestral or to innovate. (If the good is the old and hence the best is the oldest, one must go back beyond Crete—to say nothing of Sparta—to Egypt.) However inferior other Egyptian institutions may be, the Egyptian arrangements regarding things Music are to the highest degree in accordance with the requirements of the legislative art and of the political art. The consecrated tunes, which are by nature correct, are traced by the Egyptians to the goddess Isis; if they are not the work of Isis, they are surely the work of some divine man or woman. In any case, if someone were able to lay hold of correctness regarding songs in whatever manner, he should have the courage to establish it by law against the tendency of poets and the like always to seek something new because change is pleasant and constant repetition of the same is painful, and to denigrate the consecrated choral discipline as old-fashioned. One might think that the consecration or freezing of the models provides the safeguarding of education, were it not for the fact that that safeguarding is expected from the symposia. The difficulty is that before the consecration is reasonably possible, one must possess knowledge of what is intrinsically correct. The ancestral as ancestral does not guarantee that correctness; it is at best an image of the intrinsically correct. One may say that in a good society the consecration of the intrinsically correct takes the place occupied in the Dorian societies by the law of laws.

There is no question that choral performances must be enjoyable, and this could seem to mean that the man who gives pleasure to most people and who pleases to the highest degree ought to be most highly honored. Yet different people enjoy very different things. For instance, if one competitor recited Homer, another exhibited a tragedy, another a comedy, and another a puppet show, who would deserve to win in the contest of providing the greatest pleasure? The Cretan thinks that the question cannot be answered if one has not oneself heard the various competitors. He might mean that a first-rate puppet show deserves to be preferred to a poor tragedy. But the Athenian has in mind exhibitions of the same quality. Surely the Cretan is not aware of the general or typical, which permits one to answer the question without having heard the various competitors on any given occasion. The Athenian tells him, and he cannot but agree, that very small children would give the prize to the man who exhibits the puppet show; that older children would give it to the exhibitor of comedies; that the educated women, the young men, and, so to speak, the whole multitude of citizens would prefer tragedy; and the old men would prefer the recital of Homer or Hesiod. Who then would deserve to win the contest, given the fact that each contestant has won the contest before a part of the audience? It is obviously necessary for the Athenian and his interlocutors to reply that he who has been preferred by the old men deserves to win, for their way of feeling seems to them to be far superior in all cities and everywhere to the other ways of feeling which one finds nowadays. The alternatives are the ways of feeling of sons of gods who lived in the most ancient antiquity or of another kind of man who might emerge in the future. The old must take the place of those directly instructed by gods, or of the wise. For the most noble Muse is the one that delights those who are best and who are adequately educated but especially the one man who excels in virtue as well as education (i.e., not the oldest). These men and especially the one man mentioned are the true judges of Music performances, and not the public at large; the true judge must not be the pupil but the teacher of the public, or otherwise the public would be thought, absurdly, to be the educator of the poets and hence its own educator. The true judge, the true educator of the poets and of the public, must have courage in addition to insight, for he must dare to oppose the clamor of the mob. (Courage then is not simply the lowest virtue.)

These considerations induce the Athenian to state for the third time what he had said about education and even for the fourth time if we also count what he had said about the relation between *logos* and law without explicitly referring to education (643a4–644a2, 644d2–645c1, 652b3–653c4). He says now that education is guidance of the children toward the *logos* which has been declared correct by the law and regarding which the most respectable and oldest members of the community agree on the basis of the experience that it is in truth correct. That is to say, he tries to exclude the very possibility of conflict between law and true *logos* or between the old and the wise. We are at the opposite pole of what he had said in the central statement, namely, that the right reasoning as to what is better or worse is called law when it has become the common decree of the city.

Education consists then in habituating the child to feel joy and pain in agreement with the law and with those who have been persuaded by the law, or with the old men. But since the souls of children cannot bear seriousness, they must be habituated through play, through chants which are truly enchantments. Those enchantments do to the souls of children what physicians do to the bodies of the sick; physicians give their patients wholesome nutriment in pleasant food and drink while making bad nutriment unpleasant to them. It seems that for children the noble things by themselves are something like bitter medicine while the base things attract them; the former become pleasant and the latter become unpleasant only through habituation; children cannot appreciate the noble and base things as such; they must be told.

In the immediate sequel Kleinias swears "by Zeus." This is the first oath that occurs in the *Laws*. In this way Plato indicates that he is now approaching the subject of what in the *Republic* is called "theology." In the *Laws*, education is presented as beginning with dance and song; songs have of course texts; but speeches as speeches (*logoi*) have not been mentioned hitherto in connection with the songs. In the *Republic* Socrates understands by Music education primarily the transmission of speeches or, more precisely, of untrue speeches (376e2–377a2). This difference between the two works can be traced to the difference in degree of *parrhesia* characteristic of the Athenians on the one hand and the Dorians on the other, or to the sub-Socratic character of the conversations that take place in the *Laws*.

The Athenian had asserted that the correct legislator will persuade or compel the poetic man to present, with his means, only virtuous men. Kleinias is somewhat surprised by this statement: strict supervision of Music performances is practiced only in Sparta and Crete; in all other cities lawless liberty of innovation prevails; the Music performances there are very far from producing enjoyment always in the same things and in the same respects, as, according to the Athenian, they do in Egypt. Kleinias seems to be aware of the fact that the Dorian cities do not quite live up to the Egyptian standard. The Athenian admits that what he had demanded is not

practiced nowadays; he does not make an exception in favor of the
Dorian cities. From this it would seem to follow that in a most important respect the laws are everywhere (with the possible exception
of Egypt) incorrect. Kleinias is of course tolerably satisfied with
the Dorian arrangements. The Athenian argues from this premise.
The Dorian cities compel—he does not say that they persuade—the
poets to say that the good man, being just and moderate, is happy
and blessed, regardless of whether he is tall, strong, and wealthy
or the opposite, and that the unjust man, be he ever so rich, is
wretched and lives a miserable life. This is a patent falsehood as he
makes clear by tacitly correcting the Dorians' poet Tyrtaios and as
becomes fully clear from Kleinias' rejoinder. Whereas that poet had
praised only the courageous warrior, the Athenian now makes him
praise the man who does and possesses with justice the things called
fine: he alone will be courageous; he alone will get the things called
good. He thus imputes to Tyrtaios the view which he had stated
earlier in his own name or almost in his own name, namely, that
the possession of the virtues guarantees the possession of the human
goods (631b6–d1). He then takes issue in the name of the three of
them with what is generally said about the good things; he repeats
here his earlier list of human goods but adds to it, in particular,
tyrannical rule enabling one to do as one desires and immortality
in the possession of all the good things mentioned. All these things
are excellent possessions for just and holy men but very great evils
for unjust men. The Athenian speaks in the present context of justice
and holiness as well as justice and moderation; he does not speak
of wisdom and good sense; holiness seems to take the place of these
"intellectual" virtues. Accordingly, the Dorians will cause and coerce
their poets—the Dorians do not do this now—to say what the Athenian had said and what he says now: for the unjust, the so-called
evils are good while they are bad for the just; the good things are
truly good for the good and bad for the bad. Kleinias does not think
that he and Megillos—or the Dorians generally—agree with everything that the Athenian had said. He has no doubt that the goods in
question are good also for the wicked, or that the wicked may very
well be happy. He admits that the unjust and insolent live disgrace-
fully, but he denies that they live wretchedly or unpleasantly if they
possess all the human goods in abundance. According to him, the
happy or good life is not identical with the noble life.
   The Athenian does not seem able to establish agreement with the
Dorians on how one ought to live without the help of some god.
For him the reverse of what Kleinias had said is necessary; not even

the evidence which Crete's being an island has for him is as great
as that necessity. Hence, if he were a legislator, he would try to
compel—he is not sure that he would succeed in compelling—the
poets and everyone in the city to utter the view which he had stated
and he would impose all but the heaviest penalty on anyone in the
country who would utter the view that there are some human beings
who are wicked indeed but live pleasantly or that the useful and
lucrative things differ from the things that are more just. He would
persuade his citizens—apparently he has no hope of persuading the
poets—to utter many other things different from what is nowadays
said by the Dorians and presumably the other human beings. To
settle the fundamental controversy, he proposes that he and his
interlocutors ask the gods who have given the laws to the Dorians
about the relation between the justest and the most pleasant life;
in this connection he uses his first oath. In case those gods should
say that the two ways of life are different from one another, they
would properly ask them further which sort of man is happier, those
who live the most just or those who live the most pleasant life; if
the gods would give preference to the latter kind of human beings,
their answer would be absurd. So the gods must be presumed to say
that the most just life, in contradistinction to the most pleasant one,
is the happiest life; the Athenian does not, however, say so. He may
imply that it would be absurd for the gods to give the rejected answer because the gods in question are legislating gods. The admittedly
fictitious and in addition incomplete dialogue with Zeus and Apollon
imitates the dialogues which Minos had with Zeus and Lykourgos
had with Apollon—dialogues through which they became legislators.
Hence, engaging in a quasi-dialogue with the legislating gods, the
three old men enable themselves in a way to become legislators
themselves. One wonders whether the ancient legislators' dialogues
with the gods were as monologic as the Athenian's dialogue with
them. At any rate the Athenian desists from his dialogue with the
gods, which is verging on blasphemy, and puts his question to the
legislators and fathers and even to his own father. Every father
would tell his son unceasingly, the Athenian believes, to live as justly
as possible rather than to live as pleasantly as possible. And who
means better for the son than his father? The Athenian is surely not
oblivious of the fact that there are wicked fathers, but even wicked
fathers can be assumed to wish their sons to be obedient to them to
the highest degree and to be, at least in this sense, as just as possible.
The same is true of the legislator, for the legislator is passionately
concerned with the preservation of his establishment. In making its

judgment on the right way of life, the law will presuppose that the just life contains something good and noble that is superior to pleasure. This ingredient is good repute with men and gods, which, besides being good and noble, is surely not unpleasant, while bad repute is unpleasant: not to do injustice and not to suffer it from anyone is good and noble and surely not unpleasant, as Kleinias cannot help admitting. In a word, the just and the pleasant or the noble and the good cannot be divorced from one another. The reconciliation between justice and pleasure is effected through the mediation of the pleasure deriving from fair fame and praise from men and gods. This very reconciliation is rejected as pernicious to the purity of justice by Adeimantos (*Republic* 362e4–363a7), who is indeed more austere and more exacting than the two Dorians. It would not have satisfied Kallikles for a different reason. It suffices to observe that the Athenian is silent on the case of the just man who as such refrains from doing injustice but is not for this reason immune to suffering injustice. But from whatever flaws the *logos* recommended by the Athenian might suffer, it persuades a man, if nothing else can, to be resolved to live a holy and just life. Accordingly the legislator will dispel the optical delusion regarding the just and the pleasant through persuading the citizens and especially the young by whatever means—by habituation, praise, and speech—so that the unjust things no longer appear pleasant.

The immense usefulness, even necessity, of the Athenian's *logos* has been firmly established; it has yet to be shown to be true. But this question can easily be settled: the judgment of the better soul is more authoritative than that of the worse one. The Cretan does not notice that his soul is thus tacitly qualified as rather bad. The settlement is emphatically "friendly" (662b3, 663a5, d5); the Athenian and the Dorians have reached agreement on the most important point. The possibility is therefore not completely excluded that the *logos* to which Kleinias had eventually assented is untrue. But even if it is untrue, a legislator who is not altogether useless must dare to teach an untruth for the benefit of the young; deliberately teaching a salutary untruth is an act of courage. Kleinias seems to be resigned to this necessity, because it is not easy to persuade people of the truth, noble and lasting as it is. As if Kleinias had meant that since it is so difficult to persuade people of the truth, it is still more difficult to persuade them of lies, the Athenian shows him by the example of a myth that it is easy to persuade people of very many incredible things. The example is a faint reminder of *the* noble lie recommended in the *Republic* (414b7–e1). The Athenian does not answer Kleinias' question regarding the many other incredible things which people have been induced to believe; to do this might lead very far. Instead he goes on to say that the legislator has to consider nothing but whether his invented story is salutary to the city. When he is satisfied in this respect, he must devise by all means that the whole community of this kind will utter one and the same thing at all times on the subject in question. The Dorians fully agree to this through the mouth of Kleinias. The consecration of the salutary *logos* about the good life takes the place of the Dorian law of laws. It differs from the latter inasmuch as its truth may not be questioned even by old men of the utmost respectability who converse in the strictest privacy.

As for the difference between the *Laws* and the *Republic* regarding the point under consideration, it may suffice to say that the subject on which the interlocutors of the *Laws* agree after a very brief discussion, is the theme of the *Republic* as a whole. The noble lie of the *Republic* is devoted to the belief that renders possible the best city as distinguished from the best human being.

The *logos* to be taught to all is not the Athenian's but rather that of the three old men in unison (660d11, 661d3–4, e6), or the legislator's, if not the gods'. He speaks next in his own name. He returns to the guiding subject: symposia are eminently useful for the safeguarding of education. Accordingly, he now introduces the chorus of Dionysos as distinguished from the choruses of the Muses and of Apollon. The choruses must enchant the still young and tender souls of the children with speeches about the noble things mentioned and above all with the speech asserting that the gods declare the coincidence of the most pleasant and the best life. (He tacitly substitutes the best for the most noble.) For if we say that the same way of life is said by the gods to be most pleasant and best, we shall speak at the same time most truthfully and persuasively. There will be three choruses: the Muses' chorus, i.e., the chorus of children who sing with complete seriousness, that of the older ones up to thirty years who will call upon Apollon the Healer as witness to the truth of what they declare, and pray that that god will graciously persuade the young, and that of those between thirty and sixty; those older than sixty, being no longer able to stand the strain of singing, will tell myths based on divine utterance which praise the same characters as those praised in the songs. The Dorians are somewhat bewildered by what the Athenian says about the third chorus, although, as he points out, the preceding discussion was chiefly in the service of this particular subject. Perhaps they are bewildered by the Athe-

nian's silence on the specific function of the third chorus: does it
not call on a god as witness or pray to him, as the second chorus
does? The children obviously do not need to be persuaded of the
truth of what they sing, while the older ones do need some help in
this respect; they have lost the children's simplicity or innocence;
they do need the Healer. The Athenian reminds his interlocutors of
what the three of them had said at the beginning of this discussion
(653d7–654a5). In the repetition he makes clearer than he had
done in the first statement that the very young children always make
a noise and run about without any concern for order: their enjoying
rhythm and harmony, however natural to human beings, becomes
effective only through education. Also, in the repetition he ascribes
the perception of order to human nature and not, as he had done in
the first statement, to the Muses and Apollon. Accordingly, the inability of the young to keep quiet he now traces to their fiery nature.

What then is the function of the third chorus, the chorus of
Dionysos? Is it not very strange that oldish men should dance and
sing in a chorus in honor of Dionysos? To justify this arrangement,
one must start from the fact that everyone—man and child, freeman
and slave, female and male—that the whole city should unceasingly
chant to itself the things previously stated and enchant itself with
them, and that therefore one must always vary the songs so that the
whole city will constantly enjoy the unvarying master theme. (The
Athenian silently drops the Egyptian model, for human nature craves
variety. If the slaves are to be good or obedient, they must share
the fundamental belief.) The question is, where the best part of the
city, the one most persuasive on account of age as well as of good
sense, in singing what is most beautiful, would do the most good
through its singing. The difficulty is this. With increasing age, men,
and surely men with a sense of dignity, become increasingly reluc-
tant to sing, especially in public, and would be unwilling to undergo
the fasting and other deprivations to which participants in choral
performances must submit. To make such men eager to sing, we
shall by law oblige those older than thirty first to partake of ample
common meals and then to call on the other gods and in particular
to call for the presence of Dionysos at the playful initiation of the
old men, for that god has given men wine as a medicine against
the crabbedness of old age—a medicine that rejuvenates and softens
us by making us forget our worries or depressions. Under the influence of wine the old men will become more eager, less ashamed to
sing, not indeed in public but among the small number of people
they know well. In a word, they will not be the third chorus as de-

scribed earlier nor the men older than sixty who do not sing at all but tell myths (664d1–4). They are in fact a fifth part of the city, different from the three choruses and the old men. That there are five groups in the cities was foreshadowed by what the Athenian had said earlier on the five age groups (658b7–d10). The seeming confusion has its clear reason in the complex relation between law and *logos* or the impossibility of assigning their proper place in a politically viable form to the wise as wise. Accordingly, the best part of the city is and is not identical with the old. The men whom the Athenian has in mind need wine, not to overcome their shame of singing in public, but to become able to safeguard education. Such safeguarding requires judicious allowance for variety, for variation of the old-established, for non-Egyptianism (cf. Herodotus II 77). Such variation or its supervision can be safely entrusted only to old or oldish men, i.e., to men habitually averse to innovation. Accordingly, they must be rendered flexible or rejuvenated by wine. Furthermore, they are to tell untrue, if salutary, stories; this requires "nerve," courage, daring, confidence—a state induced by wine. Yet are the old men truly the best part of the city? Wise men would not need wine in order to become able to make reasonable changes; they are flexible because they are wise. Yet they would need wine for the opposite reason: in order to participate fully in the "symphony" of the city, a "symphony" not possible in the medium of wisdom (cf. *Crito* 49d1–5); their mind must lose something—we do not know how much—of its clarity. Wine thus creates harmony between the few wise and the many unwise, the rulers and the ruled, and such harmony is moderation in the highest sense of the word.

But let us hasten back to the explicit argument. The divine men spoken of, who, as we have seen, are neither the third chorus nor simply identical with the men over sixty, must be familiar with the most noble song, the most noble Muse—a Muse nobler than that of the choruses and of common or public theaters. That Muse must become familiar to those who are ashamed of the choral or the theatrical Muse. The Dorians are wholly unfamiliar with it. As the Athenian explains, this is due to the fact that the Dorians' polity is that of an armed camp and not of inhabitants of towns; they keep their young as members of a herd of colts at grass; none of them takes his colt out of the herd, separates it from its fellow colts, however much it might fret and fume, and submits it to a private groom who takes care of it and educates it by stroking and taming it and by doing to it everything proper so that it will become not only a good warrior but a good man and citizen. Kleinias does not

like this renewed criticism of the Dorian legislators, whereupon the
Athenian tells him that his criticism of the legislators, if it is such a
criticism—for he had not just spoken of the Dorian legislators—is
not his doing but that of the *logos*, whom they should follow if this
is all right with the interlocutors: the guidance by the *logos* is not
violent but gentle.

To find out what the most noble or trans-choral Muse is or what
it achieves, the Athenian discusses three subjects or examples—
nourishment, learning and image making—with a view to three ends:
pleasure, correctness and utility. Food, drink, and all nourishment
(rearing) are followed by charm, which in this case we simply call
pleasure, but they must also be wholesome and thus possess both
usefulness and some correctness; in this case utility and correctness
coincide. Learning is closely attended by charm or pleasure, but
what produces its correctness (goodness) and its usefulness (nobility) is truth; here again it seems, correctness and usefulness coincide
but in such a way that the usefulness stems from the correctness.
The arts which produce likenesses or images and which, as such,
are not concerned with truth (667d10) should give pleasure, which
in this case surely deserves to be called charm; in these arts correctness is effected, generally speaking, by quantitative and qualitative
equality of the copy with the original. Their utility is not discussed
here. It follows that all imitation and of course all equality must not
be judged with a view to pleasure nor by false opinion, for things
are not equal because someone enjoys them or believes them to be
equal, but above all with a view to the truth. The imitative arts then
are also concerned with the truth, although in a different manner
than learning is. More precisely, the imitative or image-making arts
must provide similarity with the imitation of the beautiful or noble
(an image of virtue—655b4–5—is such an imitation). Yet this
means that those who seek the most noble song and Muse must be
concerned above all with the song which is correct, i.e., which repro-
duces the original according to quantity and quality. That is to say,
competent judges of poems and other imitative works must know
what the poem is, i.e., intends, and what the thing which it imitates
is, for otherwise they cannot judge whether the imitation is correct or
not. The Athenian illustrates this by the example of painting, i.e., of
the imitation of bodies; here the judge must obviously know whether
what is imitated is a human being or another animal, and then he
must know the number and relative position of its parts. He thus
induces us to wonder whether the judge of poetry must not possess
knowledge of the nature of the soul. We must take a further step.

Just as the good painter must possess knowledge of the human body, must the good poet not also possess knowledge of the human soul, of its nature? The imitative arts then are indeed concerned with the truth, although not merely with the truth.

Through the most noble or most beautiful Muse, which is not separable from knowledge of the What is?—of the *ousiai* (668c6) —we discern as if through a veil the truly most noble Muse, i.e., philosophy. Philosophy as philosophy, in its nakedness, would be out of place in the *Laws*, at any rate in the beginning. The most noble Muse, as explicitly spoken of, is related to philosophy as an image of virtue is to virtue itself, or as the law to the true *logos* (645b4–8), or as old age to wisdom. The triad of choruses reminds us of the triad consisting of Kleinias, Megillos, and the Athenian, a philosopher (cf. the *treis ontes* in 654d6 and 664b4); the third chorus is a dim reflection of the philosophers.

Even if poetry—to say nothing of the other image-making arts— is not possible without knowledge of the nature of the soul, it is of course not identical with philosophy or with learning, for the utility of learning coincides with its correctness, with its being true, while the utility of poetry does not consist in its truth. The poets, we have learned, must be compelled to be useful or to keep within the limits of the noble. To keep the poets within the proper limits is the chief task of the third chorus who are to be the teachers of the poets. This does not necessarily mean that the poets must be judged from a nonpoetic point of view, for the poets are inferior as poets to the Muses themselves, and who would dare to act as a censor of the Muses themselves? Yet paradoxically this inferiority of the human poets makes it most difficult to become aware of their blunders. The Athenian disposes of the paradox to some extent by showing that by divorcing rhythms and tunes from words, poets make it diffi- cult to discern what their rhythms and tunes signify or what model worth mentioning they reproduce. However this may be, there is no necessity that the poet should be a competent judge of what is noble and base while he is the best judge of what is poetic or not (cf. also *Republic* 387b2–5 and 389e12–390a5). The utility of poetry as poetry consists in its charm. Hence the judges must as much respect the judgment of the poets regarding poetic excellence as the poets must respect the judgment of the judges regarding nobility. The Athenian stranger would not be satisfied with pious tracts praising virtue and blaming vice which lack poetic excellence.

After having made clear or intimated the character of poetry at its best as well as at its worst, the Athenian discharges his duty by fulfilling his initial promise to prove the usefulness of symposia, or rather of the chorus of Dionysos. He rehearses what he had said earlier about the effect of wine drinking, while making two things clearer than he had done before. First, under the influence of wine everyone is filled, not only with the ability and willingness to say everything but also with unwillingness to listen to what others, any others, say: he does not listen to authority. Second, the participants in the right kind of symposia, who must no longer be young, are themselves through these symposia being educated by the legislator; in other words, education lasts as long as life. The commanders at the banquets are to be sober men older than sixty.

While wine drinking has now been sufficiently vindicated, one hesitates to declare to the many the greatest boon due to Dionysos' gift, because human beings misconceive that boon to the point of regarding it as a curse. That human misconception expresses itself in the *logos* and tradition according to which Dionysos was stricken with madness by his stepmother Hera, and in order to avenge himself has given men wine to make them mad too. The Athenian does not directly deny this account as far as it concerns gods but opposes what he knows to the mythical account of the relation of wine and madness (cf. 636d4–5 and 644d9–e1). He knows that no living being is born in possession of good sense but is in a state of madness in which it is given to disorderly sounds and motions; wine has not been given to men in order to make them mad, for their punishment, but in the last analysis as a cure for their natural madness: man's defective condition is not a punishment but is by nature; man's original state is naturally defective. And rhythm and harmony are of human origin (673c9–d5). The greatest boon due to wine is a specific *parrhesia* and a specific refusal to listen to traditional stories. The Athenian does not speak of the blessings of madness, the highest of which is philosophy; there is a madness which precedes order and there is a madness which transcends order, i.e., the legal order.

With the criticism of the myth of Dionysos and Hera the discussion of Music has been completed. The Athenian claims untruthfully that he and his interlocutor(s) had said before that the primary disorder is the origin not only of music but of gymnastics as well. The Dorians are much more familiar with gymnastics than with music; this is the reason why Kleinias fails to perceive the parallelism of the two arts. The parallelism of the two arts corresponds to the parallelism of courage and moderation (cf. 635e4–636a3). When Kleinias answers to a question with a question, the Athenian almost goes out of his way to state that Kleinias' question is an answer: all questions are answers, contain answers, to prior questions. As he goes on to say, the discussion of music having been completed, they will turn immediately afterward to the discussion of gymnastics. In fact, they turn immediately to a discussion of the city. Gymnastics and the city are interchangeable inasmuch as the city must be able to wage war and wars have their ground in the body and its desires (*Phaedo* 66c5–d2). In other words, the true city is the city called by Glaukon the city of pigs, the city which has no higher purpose than to satisfy the needs of the body (*Republic* 372e6–7, 374a5, 433a2–6).

Before turning to the new subject, the Athenian formally concludes the speech about wine. He approves of the use of drunkenness and similarly of the use of all other pleasures, provided such use is in the service of acquiring self-control. As for the unregulated use of drunkenness, he would prefer to the Cretan and Spartan laws the Carthaginian law, which forbids the use of wine altogether to all men on campaigns; he also would forbid the use of wine to female slaves, to male slaves, to magistrates, to pilots, to judges, and to those participating in important deliberations—in fact to everyone at daytime except for medicinal purposes and at night to men or women who are about to procreate children. The Dorian abstention from wine seems to have been less strict than earlier statements might have led us to believe.

Book Three

We have learned what the ends of legislation and their natural order are. These ends are above all the various virtues according to their rank. The investigation which begins now presupposes that that knowledge is insufficient for guiding a legislator. For the virtues cannot be understood properly without consideration of the city which they serve even when they transcend it.

In the *Republic*, Socrates begins his investigation of justice by inviting his interlocutors to look with him at the coming-into-being of a city. But that coming-into-being, which they merely seem to behold, is in fact their making or founding, not only of a city but of a good city in speech. The bad or imperfect cities prove to emerge through the decay of the good city. In the *Republic*, reason or intellect guides the foundation of the city from the beginning, and eventually rules the city in broad daylight without any dilution or disguise. Such a city is something to be prayed or wished for rather than something which can arouse the spontaneous and passionate concern of experienced political men. Accordingly, the Athenian stranger deals with the city very differently than does Socrates conversing with Glaukon and Adeimantos.

He also begins his political inquiry with a consideration of the coming-into-being of the city or rather of cities. Without such a consideration one might misconceive the context within which political life is possible or, more precisely, the condition or limitation of political life. In other words, one must study the genesis of the city because the city is essentially a derivative phenomenon, derivative from man, proceeding from man.

The political investigation proper begins with the beginning of political life. Since the end of political life is death (632c1, cf. 801e7–8), its beginning would seem to be birth or the state of initial madness (672c1–5). But the beginning of political life which the

Athenian now has in mind is the beginning not of the individual man but of the city. Will it also be characterized by complete irrationality?

The Athenian looks at the beginnings in the light of the grievous defects of human life as we know it. Viewed in that light, the beginnings appear to be rather good. This is in conformity with the belief, which suffuses the conversation of the three old men, that the good is the old and hence the best is the oldest. Yet the Athenian does not fail to intimate the great shortcomings of the beginning. The kind of beginning of cities which the Athenian has in mind is not what one would call a mythical but a natural beginning. It is the starting point of their increase toward virtue and at the same time toward vice. In that beginning men were then neither virtuous nor vicious. There were many, innumerably many such beginnings, for time has no beginning that we know of and the human race has no beginning that we know of, but cities are known to come into being and to perish. By going back to the beginning of political life, we go back, of course, beyond the time of Minos, to say nothing of Lykourgos; we ascend or descend to a point long before Minos. Still, the ancient, traditional speeches about the beginnings contain some truth. One can learn through them that there have been many destructions of human beings through floods, plagues, and many other things with the consequence that only some small part of mankind survived. Nothing is said to the effect that these destructions were acts of divine punishment. On the other hand, the fact that the destruction was never total could seem to show that some superhuman providence watches over the human race. It is sufficient to consider only one of these destructions, namely, that which occurred through a flood. The selection of a destruction of this kind is somewhat arbitrary (cf. *Timaeus* 22a7–d5) but convincing to Kleinias; it is justified by the use to which the Athenian puts it.

The sparse survivors of the flood in question lived on mountains as herdsmen. They had lost all arts and tools and in particular the artifices by which city dwellers do mischief to one another. This is proved to some extent by the fact that we know the inventors of the various arts by name. Seven such inventors are mentioned by name, the central one being Marsyas, one of the two inventors of music who was said to have contended with Apollon in wisdom (Xenophon, *Anabasis* I 2.8). At any rate, in the beginning men lived in solitude, fear, and great poverty. Political life emerged not suddenly but in small steps over a very long time. Owing to their fear and solitude men were glad at the beginning to see other men:

owing to their simplicity they did not distrust one another; there was
no war of everybody against everybody. Nor did poverty compel
men to fight with one another, for they had plenty of herds to live
from. It is true that at the time preceding the one about which the
Athenian speaks, i.e., for a very long time, some men might perhaps
have been in dire need and hence, we must add, have been compelled
to fight with one another for the scanty food. But thereafter men
were neither poor nor rich and hence likely to be kind and good.
Their goodness was also due to their simplicity, inasmuch as their
simplicity induced them to accept as most true whatever they were
told is noble and base; their goodness did not proceed from knowledge. A god had given them the arts of the potter and the weaver.
They also had fire, but the Athenian does not say that it had been
given to them by a god; is he thinking of Prometheus' theft of fire?
They were more virtuous than present-day men except that they
lacked wisdom in every form but had simplicity instead. Their epoch
was not the golden age, the age of Kronos, if it is indeed characteristic of the age of Kronos that philosophy is possible in it (cf.
Statesman 272b8–c5). This view of early man may be said to result
from a comparison between present-day Athens and ancient Athens
(or old-fashioned Sparta) or from the observation of the amazingly
quick change that had occurred after the Persian war, contrasted
with the extremely slow changes that had taken place in the much
longer earlier times.

All that the Athenian had stated before about early men must be
considered to have been said for the purpose of making us understand why they needed law and who their lawgiver was. They did
not have laws proper, i.e., written laws, but they lived in obedience
to customs and so-called ancestral laws. Yet their way of life, antedating law proper, was already a kind of polity, the kind called
"dynasty" and ascribed by Homer to the Kyklopes. Megillos, who
speaks here again after being silent for a very long time, understands
Homer and the Athenian to mean that the first polity was characterized by savagery; the Kyklopes were most inhospitable—in no
way glad to see other men—and were cannibals. Connected with
the Kyklopean polities arising from them are those in which the
oldest rules over the other descendants of the same father and
mother; those families form, as it were, natural herds, as distinguished from herds of cattle or horses whose composition depends
on human action; they are held together by fraternity without any
invidious distinction between the just and the unjust members (cf.
627c3–6). Rule in these families or clans is kingship, the kind of

kingship which is the most just of all: all later kingship, however
good, is less just. In this respect at any rate the best is the oldest.

This way of life was profoundly changed when a number of
families settled together in walled towns, each family having its own
ruler and its own customs regulating its conduct toward gods and
one another; whether, how, and when the belief in gods or rather
the worship of gods arose, is not said (cf. *Odyssey* 9.269–276); the
belief in gods may have been a survival from prediluvian times: the
belief in gods survived the loss of all arts and every kind of wisdom
(cf. *Republic* 372b7–8 and 607a4). We have now reached, without
being aware of it, the beginning of legislation and of the deliberate
making of laws. For after a number of clans had come to live together, men were compelled to choose some from their midst who,
after having considered the private customs of each clan, selected
the customs which they liked best and submitted them for approval
to the rulers of the clan; these men, not bound to any prior ancestral customs, were the first legislators. The regime which they established was no longer a "dynasty" but an aristocracy (the *patres
conscripti*) or some sort of kingship (differing of course from the
most just kingship of all, which is the Kyklopean "dynasty").

The third kind of regime—next to dynasty-kingship and aristocracy—is a kind in which all kinds and characteristics of regimes,
and hence simultaneously of cities, occur. This kind too is mentioned
by Homer, who presented or intimated all three kinds (the Kyklopean, the cities on the slopes of mountains [681a1], the cities
in the plain). The Athenian uses this occasion for praising Homer
and the divinely inspired poets in general who seize many of the
things which truly happen with the help of some Graces and Muses.
Homer properly read is a better guide to the beginnings than what,
for instance, the Cretans say. Homer enables the Athenian to make
a graceful transition from the earliest times to the Trojan war, or
from men in general to Greeks. This is one reason why the account
is now called a myth. At the time of the Trojan war, men amazingly
had forgotten the destruction of almost all men through the flood
and had lost all fear of water, not only of rivers but even of the sea.
Oblivion of the cataclysms is indispensable in the third stage, in
which men must be certain that what they live in and live for lasts
forever, for otherwise it would be hard for them to dedicate themselves fully to their cities; oblivion of the initial (and final) terror
is necessary for political felicity, for one cannot act on a grand scale
without hope. But since, from time to time, profound changes are
necessary, one must enlarge the horizon which is most of the time

sufficient for action; one must enlarge that horizon by the true *logos* or by the right kind of myth.

Through a succinct survey of the events that happened after the Trojan war and that set beyond dispute the autochthony of the Spartans, the Athenian has reached the point beyond which the Spartans' own accounts (*mythoi*), as distinguished in particular from Homer's, supply the required information; the terrible deeds of Aigisthos and Orestes are barely alluded to. Accordingly, Megillos becomes now the interlocutor of the Athenian for a considerable time. As if by a divine dispensation, i.e., by the Athenian's providence for his interlocutors (although not "according to nature"—682a2), they have returned to the subject from which they turned away in order to discuss music and the symposia, namely, to the originating beginnings of the Dorian legislation, for they have now arrived at the settlement of Sparta. The settlement of Crete is passed over in silence. The silence on Crete has been prepared in various ways. It is justified in the present context by the fact that Sparta and her sister cities held out the promise that Crete never held out: the promise of the protection of the whole of Greece against the barbarians. Sparta, founded in the remote past and lasting up to the present, is a specimen of the fourth city, the preceding ones being, to repeat, the Kyklopean, the city on the mountain slope, and the city in the plain (681e1–682a2). We may be reminded of the four cities of the *Republic* and the *Timaeus*, where the fourth city is ancient Athens, not, as in the *Laws*, ancient Sparta. But the four cities of the *Republic* and the *Timaeus* are cities "in speech" while those of the *Laws* are cities "in deed."

The Athenian proposes that they now begin a detailed examination of the Spartan arrangements without apologizing for the fact that some of these arrangements may prove to be defective. Megillos agrees with some enthusiasm: the whole day, perhaps the longest day of the year, will seem to be short if it is spent on a second consideration of legislation. Taking into account the *Laws* as a whole, we may observe that, since the day is very long, it is sufficient for elaborating a complete code of law; a complete code of law can be elaborated by a competent man in a single day of sufficient length.

The Peloponnesian Dorians established originally Argos, Messene, and Sparta; Messene moves for obvious reasons into the center. Argos and Messene each had one king; Sparta had two kings. The three kingships swore that they would rule according to common laws regulating ruling and being ruled, and the citizens swore that they would preserve the kings' rule as long as the kings kept their oath; furthermore, the three kingships swore that they would come to the assistance of a king and of a people who were being wronged and the three people swore that they would come to the assistance of a people and a king who were being wronged. If this order was destroyed, it must have been due to a fault of the rulers (cf. 631b1–c1). In this context the Athenian swears by Zeus (this oath is the third occurring in the *Laws*); in the context the oath could induce one to think that no god presided at the establishment of the Peloponnesian confederacy.

That confederacy was established by legislators who may have been kings. Ordinarily the peoples demand from the legislators that they lay down such laws as the multitudes voluntarily accept. This is about as reasonable as if one were to demand from gymnastic trainers or physicians that they tend and cure bodies so as to cause pleasure to bodies. This illustrates the Athenian's statement that the first kingship was the justest of all; in that early stage there was no *demos*. The context suggests that at the establishment of the Dorian confederacy the peoples did not exert pressure on the legislators to lay down laws pleasing to the multitudes. The reason was this. In old established cities the peoples sometimes demand redistribution of land and remission of debts, but at the time of the Dorian establishment the land was being distributed for the first time and there were no large and old debts; it seems that the Athenian regards the demands for redistribution of land and remission of debts as reasonable in certain circumstances. Despite many favorable circumstances the Dorian establishment failed in Argos and Messene. Megillos, who is none too pleased at the implied criticism of Dorian institutions, is at a loss to say how this happened. Although they have to tell a sad story, the Athenian suggests, what happened in a rather remote past should not prevent them from continuing painlessly in their wandering, their sober play befitting old men; that play consists in considering and examining laws, especially of such famous and great cities. For the men responsible for the establishment of the Peloponnesian confederacy thought of the defense of all Greeks against suffering wrong at the hands of barbarians. The order which they established was in this respect superior to that obtaining at the time of the Trojan war. The kings of the three cities, being all of them sons of Herakles, were thought to be superior to the Pelopidai, who reigned at the time of the Trojan war; and the army was thought to be superior to that which went against Troy, for the Dorians had defeated the Achaians, the destroyers of Troy. The Athenian thus retracts his earlier suggestion about the Dorians' autochthony. Furthermore, one wonders why the men who had established the Peloponnesian confederacy were so much concerned with defending the Greeks against the barbarians despite the overwhelming success of the Greeks in the Trojan war. This difficulty leads us back to the Athenian's still unanswered question as to why the Dorian establishment failed in two of the three cities, although it was so excellent in itself and, in addition, those who were responsible for it had made use of many diviners, above all of the Delphic Apollon. In rephrasing his still unanswered question, the Athenian speaks of Sparta waging war unceasingly against the two other cities. Could, which heaven forbid, Sparta be responsible for the breakdown of the Dorian settlement? Yet a most respectable contemporary scholar observes that "Plato ignores more easily than we like the later conquest of Messenia by the Spartans, and the efforts of the Spartans to extend their conquests into the territory of Argos" (Glenn Morrow, *Plato's Cretan City*, Princeton University Press, 1960, 71). It suffices to repeat that the Athenian stranger speaks "with a view to" a respectable Spartan: for a foreigner to speak of these harsh facts to a Spartan would be as unbecoming as to speak to a patriotic American of Negro slavery and the fate of the Red Indians.

In replying to the Athenian's question, Megillos calls the Dorian establishment noble (resplendent) and great. This induces the Athenian to wonder whether all men, including the three present interlocutors, judge "correctly or according to nature"—on the basis of either correct opinion or knowledge—when looking at things they believe to be resplendent and capable of marvelous achievements and forming expectations regarding them. People expect that by the noble use of a large and magnificent army one would make oneself happy. By happiness they understand freedom and empire—rule over as many, Greeks or barbarians, as one would wish, so that the rulers and their descendants can do whatever they desire. But, as the Athenian leads Megillos to admit, one should wish and pray, not that all things should proceed according to one's wish or will but rather that one's will should follow one's good sense or that one acquire understanding. The interlocutors have thus returned to the beginning of their conversation, when Kleinias and Megillos had demanded that a good legislator must make all his enactments with a view to war, whereas the Athenian had demanded that the good legislator must lay down his laws with a view to the whole of virtue and above all to the leading virtue, namely, good sense, intellect and opinion, together with passionate desire following these three (i.e., together with moderation); in this repetition the Athenian no longer says as he had said in his first statement (630d4–e2) that Zeus (Minos) and Apollon (Lykourgos) were good legislators in the sense defined. The Athenian's reminder sets it beyond doubt that Sparta was defective from her very beginning, radically, and that her defect is, to say the least, a major cause of the breakdown of the Peloponnesian confederacy. He leaves it to his interlocutors to decide whether the conclusion which he now explicitly draws and which was indeed implied in what he had said near the beginning (631b3–c1)—namely, that praying is perilous for someone who has not acquired understanding—is playful or serious, for he seems to suggest that immature people should not pray at all (cf. the *Second Alcibiades*). Above all, he draws the conclusion that the breakdown of the Peloponnesian confederacy was due to nothing but ignorance regarding the most important human things. Such ignorance is at all times the cause of political failure. Such ignorance, we remember, was characteristic of early man (679e2–3). We see now how right the Athenian was when he suggested that by understanding the first origin of regimes, one understands all later political changes (cf. 676c6–8).

The subject has ceased to be peculiarly Spartan. Hence, instead of Megillos the more talkative Kleinias becomes the interlocutor again. He promises to praise the Athenian by deed rather than by speech—by eagerly listening to what he is going to say, "if god wills"; he had never before used that pious expression which is here a reasonable response to what the Athenian had said about the prayers of most people. One would justly call it the greatest ignorance, we learn now, if someone does not love but hates what seems to him to be noble or good; it is the greatest ignorance because it resides in the largest part of the soul, its experiencing pain and pleasure being like the *demos* and multitude in the city. If pleasure and pain oppose that which is by nature fit to rule, namely, opinions, or, in the case of the city, if the multitude does not obey the rulers and the laws, we have the most outrageous kind of ignorance. (Ignorance is not the absence but the powerlessness of opinion.) In other words, the greatest ignorance is incontinence. The Athenian does not suggest here, as he had suggested near the beginning, that the greatest ignorance is ignorance regarding the natural order of the goods (cf. 631b6–d). Instead he seems to correct the Socratic assertion, according to which it is impossible to know what is to be preferred and yet to choose the worst, or according to which virtue is simply knowledge. But knowledge is one thing, opinion is another.

By disregarding here the crucial difference between knowledge and opinion ("knowledge or opinion or *logos*"), he gains the full sympathy of Kleinias who apostrophizes him here for the first time as friend. Harmony between opinions and likes, the Athenian continues, is the indispensable condition for even the most exiguous kind of good sense, i.e., even for that kind which is at present in the center of consideration, as distinguished from the most noble and greatest harmony, which would most justly be called wisdom. This amounts to saying that moderation would most justly be called wisdom. It implies that virtue is not identical with knowledge but requires in addition the right kind of habituation (653b1–6). It follows that the wise ought to rule in the cities. But how can those who have only opinion and therefore are, strictly speaking, unwise, obey the wise? How can they recognize the wise as wise?

The Athenian approaches this question by literally enumerating the various admitted titles to rule. There are seven of them: rule of parents over their offspring, of the well-born over the baseborn, of the older over the younger, of masters over slaves, of the stronger over the weaker, of the men of good sense over the men lacking knowledge, and of him who is chosen by lot over him who is not chosen. The only kind of rule which the Athenian calls according to nature is the sixth, the greatest of all; it is identified, as it has been previously identified, with the rule of law over willing subjects or citizens. (The first three titles, which are closely linked with one another, reflect the principle of wisdom, while the fourth, which occupies the center, reflects the principle of superior strength. The fourth title is the only one regarding which nothing whatever is said as to its being correct, according to nature, just, or even necessary. Only in the discussion of the fourth and the sixth titles are the ruled mentioned before the rulers: the true slaves are the ignorant. The omission of wealth as a title is noteworthy.) The fifth title is called according to nature by Pindar, whom the Athenian does not clearly contradict at this point. It would seem that the most important titles are those of the wise and of the stronger. Surely of these two titles it is true that they are in opposition to one another.

The enumeration of the seven titles circumscribes the fundamental political predicament. That predicament consists in the first place in the tension between the common (good) and the private (good). Because of that tension, government—the concern with the common —must be not only wise but strong as well. Yet wisdom and strength are very unlikely to coincide; wisdom may reside in a single man, while strength by nature resides in the majority, the multitude who are brachially by far superior to the small minority of the men of sense (*Republic* 327c7–9): the rule of the stronger is democracy (*Gorgias* 488d5–10). (Hence the justest kingdom of all is the one in which there is no *demos.*) Brachial superiority is superiority in bodily strength; the body is that which is by nature private, each man's own by nature (739c7–d1; *Republic* 464d8–9) whereas the intellect cannot be private. The relation between kingship and democracy reflects, therefore, the relationship between the intellect and the body. One must keep all this in mind in order to do full justice to the Athenian's later remark according to which monarchy and democracy are, as it were, the two mothers of regimes (693d2–5). Since both the intellect and the body are ingredients of the city, since in other words the highest title to rule is only one among many, the political problem consists in reconciling that highest title with the other titles which conflict with it, and this means above all with the title based on superior strength: the rule of the intellect must be modified by the rule of the stronger, i.e., it must be diluted. As was indicated earlier (632c6–7), while good sense and intellect must be effective in legislation, legislation cannot be ordered toward good sense and intellect but only toward justice and moderation; in legislation the higher is in the service of the lower, and this is, strictly speaking, against nature. In other words, wisdom must become the ingredient of a mixture. Since wisdom is extremely rare, one may be compelled to rest satisfied with a mixture of which wisdom is not an ingredient but which may be the closest approximation to wisdom that is politically feasible. We are prepared for this conclusion also by what had been said on the "three or four" definitions of education, which intimated the difference between *logos* and law—a difference alluded to by the Athenian's omitting "law" from his Pindar quotation (cf. *Gorgias* 484b1–9): rule of law is a kind of rule of the stronger while the rule of wisdom is not (cf. 645a3).

The discussion of the various titles to rule must be put to use for the explanation of the failure of the Peloponnesian confederacy. For reasons of common decency the Athenian lays the responsibility entirely on Argos and Messene, or more precisely on their kings. But the responsibility rests in the first place with the then legislators, who, as we may add, could only blasphemously be called gods. This remark, in which the Athenian's third oath occurs, induces Megillos again to step forth. While no god presided at the establishment of the Peloponnesian confederacy, a god was watching over Sparta and, by bringing about the birth of twins in the royal family, made royal power more moderate; from that time Sparta always had two kings. Thereafter some human nature with the admixture of some divine power mixed the sober (*sophron*) power of the twenty-eight elders with the still too strong power of the kings. A third savior added the ephors, whose mode of election comes close to election by lot. Thus the Spartan regime became properly mixed (out of kingship, aristocracy, and democracy); its ingredients are strength on the basis of birth, sobriety (moderation) of the old, and election by lot; all seven titles to rule, with the exception of course of the rule of masters over slaves, seem to have been used for the mixture. The Athenian does not hesitate to assert that the god had shown the Spartans the most lasting form of government. No such guidance assisted Argos and Messene. The most important effect was the disgraceful conduct of these two cities in the Persian war, in which only the united efforts of Athens and Sparta saved Greece from enslavement and from the destruction of the peculiarity of each Greek tribe and of course of the Greek nation as a whole. (During the discussion of the Persian war and a considerable part of the discussion of Persia, Kleinias is again the interlocutor: the conduct of Sparta in respect to Persia was not altogether admirable—cf. 698e3 and *Menexenus* 240c6–8, 243b.) But to return to the cause —the error of ancient statesmen and legislators so-called—they did not lay down the laws with a view to the city's being free, sensible, and in friendship with itself. (Morrow, *l.c.*, 561n, reasonably contrasts this triad with the triad "freedom, equality, fraternity" propounded by the French Revolution: the French Revolution replaced being sensible by equality. Cf. also England on *Laws* 701d7.) Or, which means the same thing, the legislator's aim must be moderation or good sense or friendship, for all these terms point to the same. Kleinias reminds the Athenian of freedom; he does not wish to have freedom absorbed into, or replaced by, moderation. Yet is not moderation, as adaptation of wisdom to the opinions of the citizen body or to consent, the same as (rational) freedom?

The Spartan regime is mixed. It contains two opposite ingredients, kingship and democracy (the ephorate), which are brought into harmony by the aristocratic ingredient (the *gerousia*). For a better understanding of the mixture one must consider each of the opposite ingredients by itself. Accordingly, the Athenian turns next to a discussion of the pure forms of kingship and democracy which we find above all in Persia and in Athens respectively. Athens loves freedom more than is meet. Persia is too much enamored of what is monarchic. These excesses did not exist in either Persia or Athens at the beginning.

Under Cyrus the Persians kept to the mean between slavery and freedom. They thus first liberated themselves from the Medes and then became the masters of many others. The rulers treated the ruled as free and equal, permitting the sensible among the ruled to speak frankly. It seems that slavery is an ingredient of the right mixture or that slavery is an ingredient of political freedom (cf. Rousseau, *Du Contrat social* I 1 first paragraph). As the Athenian divines (cf. 634e7–635a2), the decline under Cyrus' successor Kambyses was due to Cyrus' complete ignorance of correct education, an ignorance which showed itself in the manner in which he brought up his sons. Owing to his almost constant absence on campaigns, his sons were completely spoiled by his women, who were new to royal wealth and who lived and "educated" accordingly. As we learn from Aristotle (*Politics* 1269b39–1270a3), Sparta also suffered from the frequent absence of her men on campaigns and the ensuing gynecocracy, but this was obviously trivial compared to what happened in Persia. Cyrus himself had been brought up in the severe Persian way; but his sons, without his knowing it or sufficiently caring about it, received the Median education through women and eunuchs with the final consequence that Kambyses lost his throne and life through the Medes themselves. Dareios, not being the son of a king, restored Persian rule and governed as successfully as Cyrus. But he too neglected the education of his son (Xerxes) with disastrous consequences for Persia. (Kambyses' conduct toward Apis is paralleled by Xerxes' conduct in regard to the Greek gods.) Here the Athenian goes so far in his divining of the past as to address a timely warning to Dareios, which was disregarded. He draws a conclusion which is emphatically his and not, perchance, of a god who inspired him— the conclusion that the decline of Persia was due not to chance but to the bad life which the sons of the exceedingly rich and of tyrants lead as a rule; this insight must be considered by the legislator and hence also by the three old men now conversing about legislation. This leads him to praise, not indeed the Spartan legislator, but the city of Sparta, which does not assign different honors and upbringing to poverty or wealth, to private station or royalty, with the exception of what the divine had told it at the beginning through oracles stemming from some god; for in a city, at any rate, outstanding honor must be assigned only on the ground of virtue accompanied by moderation. There is an obvious tension between this principle and the Spartan arrangement, especially the kingship, however limited. Accordingly, there are no kings in the regime recommended by the Athenian later in the dialogue.

The Spartan has some difficulty in understanding what the Athenian just said: Was it meant as a critique of hereditary kingship? Are there associations in which outstanding honors are assigned on the ground of virtue accompanied by *mania*, an opposite of moderation? The Athenian takes Megillos to mean that there cannot be virtue that is not accompanied by moderation. Yet it is obvious that a man may be of outstanding courage but at the same time dissolute. Megillos would not wish to have such a man as his housemate or his neighbor: might he not find him acceptable as a leader of an army (cf. Aristotle, *Politics* 1309b1–6)? Not only courage can be unaccompanied by moderation; wisdom of a certain kind—the wisdom possessed by the practitioners of the arts—also can; wise men of this kind may very well be unjust, and injustice is by nature inseparable from dissoluteness of one kind or another (cf. *Republic* 485e3 and Xenophon, *Memorabilia* I 5.6); dissolute artisans are most undesirable as housemates or neighbors, and yet they may be useful to the city (cf. Aristotle, *l.c.* 1260a36–40). On the other hand, the wise man as the three interlocutors understand him, the man whose pleasures and pains are in perfect harmony with the correct *logoi*, the perfect human being (653a9–b6; but cf. 689b and 688b1–4), is of course moderate. This leads to the further question, raised by the Athenian, whether moderation by itself, i.e., not accompanied by any other virtue, is rightfully honored in the cities. Megillos is unable to answer it; this inability is appropriate, as the Athenian tells him, for both the affirmative and the negative answer would be out of tune. The negative answer would be shocking. The positive answer would be inappropriate because moderation in and by itself barely deserves mentioning, let alone praise or honor. Only in conjunction with other virtues does it deserve honor. Surely, moderation in and by itself is no title to rule. The Athenian repeats this devaluation of moderation while setting forth the order according to which the legislator must distribute honors and dishonors. The order is the order of the goods as stated near the beginning (631b6–d2); he does not now make a distinction between the divine and the human goods. Needless to say that the legislator whom he here instructs is not the Spartan or the Cretan legislator in particular but any legislator. He calls teachers of legislators like himself (and his two interlocutors) "men who in a manner long for laws."

This is the end of the observations occasioned by the consideration of the regime of the Persians. It is not immediately clear why the discussion of moderation is occasioned by that consideration. Moderation is never mentioned in the Athenian's account of Persia.

The most obvious lesson from the consideration of the Persian regime is that the excess of slavery of the people, or the completely
unlimited rule of their master which is characteristic of Persia, is
ruinous.

The Attic regime shows the ruinous character of complete freedom. The Athenian begins his account of the Attic regime at Athens'
finest time, the time of the Persian assault, just as he began his
account of the Persian regime at the time of Cyrus. Just as there was
some freedom under Cyrus, there was some slavery of the citizen
body in Athens at the time of the Persian assault. At that time,
Athens lived under the ancient regime in which the magistrates were
appointed from four classes distinguished from one another on the
basis of property. (Hence high honors were assigned if not on the
ground of, at least in consideration of, wealth.) The Athenians'
master was not a human being but some awe, which made them
voluntarily serve the laws then obtaining. (Awe apparently never
played a role in Persia.) Their servitude or slavery was further increased by the desperate fear caused by the impending Persian
assault—a fear which made them still more willing to obey their
rulers and the laws and made them still more united as well; they
thus were enabled to win singlehandedly the battle of Marathon.
But Marathon was only the prelude to Salamis (cf. 698c3–4). When
they feared to be assailed by sea as well as by land, they perceived
only a single slight glimmer of hope: to rely for refuge on themselves alone and on the gods. They were filled with fear of the Persians and with the preexisting fear which they had acquired through
serving the former laws—that fear which was often called awe earlier
in the *Laws*; that awe or fear enabling them to overcome the fear
of the enemy, they defended the temples, the graves, the fatherland,
and their kin and friends. Megillos spontaneously agrees, while expressing his admiration for the Athenian and for Athens. The Athenian agrees; Megillos is the right addressee of this account of the
Persian war since he shares the nature of his ancestors, who in their
way participated in that war. But the Athenian hastens to explain
Athens' decline, for only by considering that decline will one acquire
the decisive lesson that is needed for guidance of legislation and that
agrees with earlier discussions. Under the ancient laws the *demos*
was in a manner voluntarily the slave of the laws, primarily the laws
regarding Music. These laws permitted only certain kinds of songs,
and these kinds could not be mixed with one another. The audience
listened in silence. Judgment was passed by the educated. Accordingly, the multitude was ruled in an orderly manner and did not

dare to pass judgment by clamor. The ancient Athenian order was then characterized not only by awe but by the right kind of Music as well. This aristocracy was perverted into a-Music lawlessness by poets who were indeed by nature poetic but ignorant of what the Muse holds to be right and lawful. They mixed all genres and, erroneously believing that there is no correctness whatever in things Music, they believed that such things are to be judged by pleasure alone. They thus encouraged the public at large to pass noisy judgment and therewith brought about the emergence of a degraded theatrocracy. Some sort of democracy of free men in Music alone is not so terrible, but what is terrible is the opinion of everyone to be wise in everything, and this utter lawlessness and impudence had its origin in the corruption of Music. The excessive freedom destroyed all respect for all authority human and divine and thus led to interminable evils. The Athenian's indictment of excessive freedom surpasses in vehemence by far his indictment of excessive slavery in Persia: in Persia there was no Music to corrupt. He surely feels again the need for putting the rein on the *logos* or on his mouth in order not to be carried too far.

The Athenian knew that Athens' decline originated not only in the corruption of Music but also, and in the first place, in the naval victory of Salamis (707b4–c7). But the consequence of Salamis (Athenian naval power and eventually the extreme democracy) is one thing; quite another thing is the state of mind in which the Athenians went into that battle. In this respect the Athenian praises Salamis more highly than Marathon. By speaking here only of the corruption of Music and only in a different context of Athens' naval policy as the cause of her decline, the Athenian avoids the harsh conclusion that Athens' finest time and action initiated her decline.

In his account of the Attic regime and its decline, the Athenian is as silent about moderation as he was in his account of the Persian regime and its decline. The two accounts are meant to show the badness of unqualified slavery as well as of unqualified freedom. The only salvation is a mixed regime. The Spartan regime is mixed of kingship, aristocracy, and democracy. The aristocratic ingredient alone is characterized by moderation (691e1–692d1). But in the meantime we have learned that moderation by itself is not a title to honor or to rule. (The same would of course also be true of awe or reverence.) Moderation had been replaced, after some apparent vacillation, by good sense (693d7–e1; cf. 710a3–6) and then by intellect (694b6). It is this last formulation which the Athenian now repeats.

It has become clear to the reader through the discussion of the three regimes that neither the Spartan nor the original Persian regime is best and that this is at least partly due to the questionable character of hereditary kingship. Could the original Athenian regime serve as a model?

The Athenian concludes by saying that the whole previous conversation from its very beginning served the purpose of making clear how a city could dwell in the best manner and how one could lead his own life most excellently, and by asking Megillos and Kleinias how they might test their results by conversing with one another. Kleinias, who is richer in thoughts than in speeches, now reveals that, as it happens, he has been commissioned together with nine fellow citizens to prepare the sending out of a colony from the largest part of Crete and also to frame laws, regardless of whether they are Cretan or foreign, for the colony. He asks his interlocutors to join him in founding a city in speech while making a selection from what they had said. The Athenian agrees to join him provided it is not disagreeable to Megillos. Megillos has no objection whatever.

Kleinias' suggestion comes at the right moment. The speeches in the first three Books have shown that both the end of the Dorian legislation and the Dorian regime are radically inadequate. Hence one has to look for another legislation and another regime and, assuming that no other satisfactory legislation and regime is available elsewhere, for a new legislation and regime. By a stroke of good luck Kleinias is commissioned to found a new city the institutions of which do not have to be altogether Dorian.

Book Four

From here on until the end of the *Laws* a city is being founded in speech. In the *Republic* a (the) city is being founded in speech in Books Two to Seven, but there the foundation of the city was in the service of answering the question, What is justice? and of proving that the just life is so to speak infinitely superior to the unjust life (Books Two to Ten). The founding of the city in speech in the *Republic* was preceded by an examination of the wrong or half-true opinions on justice. In the *Laws*, the guiding theme of which is not simply What is justice? the founding of the city is preceded by an examination of the Dorian laws including the Spartan regime; the extensive argument regarding symposia is only a part, however important, of that examination; the results of that examination are in principle applicable as standards of judgment also to cities already founded (cf. 702a) or to every legislation past or future (631b3–632d1). From Book Four to the end of the work the Athenian speaks no longer merely as teacher of legislators in general but primarily as the adviser to a named legislator and founder "here and now."

The Athenian begins again at the beginning. But the beginning now is the beginning as it presents itself to the actual legislator-founder "here and now." Every actual city is known by its name. Accordingly the Athenian first touches briefly on the question of the name of the city to be founded. The first serious question, however, concerns the location of the future city or, more generally, the nature of its territory. That nature is satisfactory, since the city will not be too near to the sea, the land is almost completely self-sufficient, there is no other city close by, and the terrain is hilly. The city is indeed too near to the sea but sufficiently inland to prevent it from becoming commercial; owing to the hilliness of the terrain it is not likely to produce a surplus for export, and its self-sufficiency makes it independent of imports. In addition, the land is poorly equipped with timber for shipbuilding. Hence the city is not tempted to imitate certain bad examples—in this context it becomes clear that the Athenian by himself is the legislator—and in particular the bad example of Minos, the founder of Cretan thalassocracy, who harassed the Athenians so grievously and, which is worse, inculcated in his subjects the bad habits of sailors as distinguished from the noble habits of hoplites. One could have learned the superiority of hoplites to sailors from Homer or, somewhat paradoxically, from his Odysseus. (Cf. 706c4 with *Laches* 190e5–191c6. Shortly before giving his alternative account of Athens' decline, the Athenian reminds us of the wisest among the poets—776e6—whom he never attacks, and thus of the fate of Music in Athens.) A city which depends for its salvation on its navy cannot but assign honors to the practitioners of warlike arts or skills which are not the most noble—those of the pilot, the commander of rowers, and the rower. In accordance with Crete's Minoan origin, Kleinias points out that the Cretans at any rate ascribe the salvation of Greece from the barbarians to the naval battle of Salamis. The Athenian grants that this is the view of the majority of Greeks and barbarians but asserts that he and Megillos ascribe the salvation of Greece to the land battles of Marathon and Plataiai, for these alone have made the Greeks better: not salvation and mere being but the excellence of the political order, not mere living but living in the best possible way is the overriding consideration; hence the nature of the territory must be considered, as it has been considered, in the light of what it contributes to the right kind of legislation.

Aristotle, who speaks as the teacher of legislators, ascends from the discussion of the nature of the territory to that of the nature of the political multitude (*Politics* 1321b16ff.). The Athenian, who speaks as an adviser of a named legislator, does not speak of the nature of the people of the city to be founded. Those people come from all over Crete and some are Peloponnesians; their nature can be presumed to be known or perhaps is not a fitting subject. In addition, their nature is already affected or modified by the customs in which they have been brought up. If all colonists had been bred in the same laws, good or bad, and had shared the same sacred things, there would be some kind of friendship among them, but they could not easily be induced to accept new and, as one might hope, better laws. On the other hand, if different colonists have been bred in different laws, it is comparatively easy for them to obey new laws but it will take a long time until their union is, as it were, natural.

The Athenian touches here on the difficulty for which Socrates proposed the desperate solution that the founders of the best city expel
everyone older than ten, lest the children be affected by the laws
under which their parents lived (*Republic* 540e5–541a4). The Athenian seems to be content with the qualified heterogeneity of the new
citizen-body which is imposed on him by the Cretans' project.

Accordingly he is now tempted to observe that no human being
ever legislates in anything, but all kinds of chance and misfortune
legislate for us in all things: the willingness to accept new laws
is greatest in emergencies, i.e., in situations in which there is no
room for choice and hence for choice of the best. He corrects himself at once and says that the god governs all things, and next to
god chance and opportunity govern all human things, as can be seen
in seafaring, medicine and generalship, yet that in the third place art,
gentler than the first two, if it grasps the opportunity which it cannot
provide, makes a contribution that is not to be despised. This applies
of course especially to the art of the legislator. If the city to be
founded is to live in felicity, one must wish or pray that god or
chance has provided the city, not only with the right kind of territory and populace, but also with a true legislator who then would
apply his art to what no art can bring forth. Such a legislator would
wish or pray for something astonishing, as he tells the three interlocutors when the Athenian asks him; the author emphasizes in his
way that the answer is not given by the Athenian but by the only
half-present and altogether nameless legislator. That legislator then
would wish or pray for the good luck of being given a city ruled by
a tyrant—by a tyrant who possesses certain "natures": he must be
young, have a good memory, be a good learner, courageous and
magnificent; he must also possess vulgar moderation, the kind of
moderation which some children and beasts possess from birth, as
distinguished from the kind to which one refers when, in exalting
speech, one forces good sense, too, to be moderation. Good sense
does not belong to what is required of the desirable tyrant. What
the legislator requires of the tyrant reminds of what Socrates requires
of the philosophers (*Republic* 487a3–5); but Socrates requires of
the philosopher also that he be by nature graceful and a lover of,
and akin to, truth and justice. The latter qualities are not required
of the high-class tyrant, we may assume, because he is subordinate
to the legislator and hence vicariously participates in them. But this
would mean that the true legislator's nature must be the same as the
nature of the philosopher and hence that, in speaking of the nature
of the tyrant, the Athenian adumbrates the nature of the true legis-

lator: this whole section (704a–712a) is devoted to nature, to the natural conditions of excellent legislation, while the rest of Book Four is devoted to the legislator's art.

The legislator does not absolutely need support by an excellent tyrant for establishing an excellent regime; such a tyrant is merely best for that purpose: a tyrant could bring about the establishment of the best regime, that most profound change, in the quickest and best way, i.e., in the quickest and easiest way. The greatest obstacle to the establishment of an excellent city exists in an oligarchy, the regime in which the avaricious rich rule (which, however, means also that oligarchy is particularly stable). Yet even in an oligarchy the passionate desire for moderate and just pursuits might arise and thus bring about the establishment of the best regime. The strength which must combine with good sense and moderation in order to bring about the emergence of the best regime does not have to be the strength of arms; it may be the most outstanding strength of speaking, like that for which Nestor is famed: an orator of quite exceptional power might conceivably perform the function the performance of which one would expect in the first place from the right kind of tyrant. More than that. The Athenian comes close to suggesting that the greatest power and the highest wisdom must coincide in one and the same human being, i.e., that the perfect legislator would not need the support of a tyrant. He thus tacitly excludes the possibility that the cooperation between Kleinias and the Athenian would constitute the desired coincidence.

The first act of the legislator is to determine the regime of Kleinias' city. This the Athenian proceeds to do after having stated that the undertaking of the three interlocutors is a play fitting old men and after having called on the god to come to help them graciously in their undertaking. The regime should not be a simple regime, for in such a regime a part is master and the rest are slaves, but mixed like the Spartan and the Cretan. Yet from what appeared through the examination of the Persian and Attic regimes, this answer no longer suffices. The Athenian makes therefore the conditional proposal that the true master of those possessing intellect, i.e., god, should be the master of the city; where the god rules, the whole rules. Here we have, it seems, the coincidence of the greatest power and the highest wisdom. Yet if the god rules, what remains to be done by the human legislator? This question does not disturb Kleinias; he is anxious to know "which god?" The Athenian answers both Kleinias' and our questions by telling the story of how men were ruled and lived together in the oldest times, long time before

even the Kyklopean regime, under Kronos. We are free to surmise
that the rule of Kronos was destroyed by the cataclysm. The Athenian hesitates somewhat to tell the story of the age of Kronos. His
hesitation recalls the hesitation he had to voice the demand for a
tyrant. But now he does not have to entrust what he is about to say
to someone else (the legislator) since the story of the age of Kronos
has come down through a tradition of high origin. Under Kronos,
a god who loved human beings, men lived a blessed life, for they
had everything in abundance and without any effort on their part;
through Kronos' institution the cities were ruled, not by human
beings, but by beings of a higher kind who took care of them so
that men lived in peace, reverence, good order, and abundance of
right. When another stranger tells the same story to the young Athenian mathematician Socrates in much greater detail but with not
altogether dissimilar intent, he states explicitly that in the present
age, the age of Zeus, the divine caring for human beings has ceased,
men must therefore take care of themselves and have to be ruled
by human beings (*Statesman* 274d3–6); the Athenian stranger who
speaks to two old Dorian statesmen is silent on this vanishing of
divine providence. He limits himself to drawing the conclusion that
there will be no escape from evils for the cities if they are ruled by
a mortal and not by a god; therefore we must imitate the life under
Kronos by every means and obey what is immortal in us in private
and public life, giving the name of law to the disposition or dispensation effected by the intellect. The Athenian does not speak here
of the relation of law and the true *logos*; he seeks the highest possible ground of law: rule of law is rule of the god. This most powerful demand lacks, however, the clarity possessed, despite their
ambiguity, by the earlier statements about law and the true *logos*;
for it conceals completely the fact that the rule of law is the rule of
laws laid down by human beings. This much, however, seems to be
clear: the law of divine origin which the Athenian has in mind
cannot be thought to arise from a dialogue between the human legislator and a god, as in the case of the Minoan legislation that was
said to have been originated by Kronos' son.

The view that law ought to rule is challenged by some who say
that the laws are dependent on the regime (monarchy, oligarchy,
or democracy), i.e., on human beings, and therefore should be laid
down, not with a view to either of the two alternatives hitherto
considered, namely, war and the virtue of war or the whole of virtue, but with a view to the advantage and, in the first place, to the
preservation of the established regime; this, they say, is the natural

definition of justice (cf. *Republic* 359b4–5): just or right is the advantage of the stronger. We are told here, as it were in passing, that
the whole question of the end of legislation is identical with the
question of what justice is: the question guiding the *Laws* is the
same and not the same as the question guiding the *Republic*; it is
not the same since the just life in the strict sense is the philosophic
life, and the philosophic life is not a suitable subject for a conversation with Kleinias and Megillos. To return to the immediate context,
those who reject the demand that not men but the law ought to rule
try to support their view by referring to the facts that the laws are
laid down in every city by the ruling part, that the ruling part aims,
in laying down the laws in the first place, at the preservation of its
rule, and that it declares to be just only what it enacts and because it
enacts it. The men in question recognize, strictly speaking, only one
of the seven titles to rule, the title mentioned by Pindar, and disregard the others, above all the one deriving from knowledge or good
sense, i.e., the rule of law. The conflict among the recognized titles
to rule makes it all the more necessary to raise the question, which
men should rule in the city that is to be founded (for the laws themselves cannot, strictly speaking, rule). The answer is that in the first
place the laws must be given for the sake of the whole city and not
of a part, and then that those men must rule who are most obedient
to those laws or who are the best servants of the laws or of the
gods, or the slaves of the laws. This proposal causes no difficulty
whatever if the laws laid down by the founder-legislator can be
supposed to be unchangeable. In this theocratic context there occurs
Kleinias' second oath. The section concludes with Kleinias praising
the sagacity of old age, to which praise the Athenian heartily assents
(cf. 888c1–3). The difference between old age and wisdom disap-
pears from sight together with the difference between the law and
the true *logos*.

   The second act of the legislator consists in persuading the future
citizens to accept the theocracy or in producing in them the state of
mind in which they will accept it. Here the Athenian addresses primarily not so much Kleinias as the future citizens themselves; he
descends to them, as it were. He addresses them in his own and in
Kleinias' name (cf. the allocution to the future citizens in *Republic*
415a2–b3). This speech surpasses in piety the preceding ones. In
agreement with the ancient *logos* he proclaims that the god who
holds the beginning as well as the end and the middle of all beings
completes his march in a straight course according to nature; he is
always accompanied by Right, which avenges the transgressors of

the divine law and to which everyone who is to be happy must cling in humility and orderliness while he who is proud and insolent throws everything into confusion and after no long time pays a penalty to Right by ruining himself, his household, and his city. Humility is praised or recommended only here (cf. 762e8). Given this order of things, the question of what a sensible man should think or consider is virtually answered; the question of what he should do, however, requires an extensive answer. There is, indeed, a single or simple answer based on the *logos* that goes back to the origin: the like is friend or dear to the like if it has the right measure; but the god seems to the highest degree to be the measure of all things and surely to a much higher degree than some human being; hence he who wishes to be dear to the god must become as much like him as he can; hence the moderate man is dear to the god. Moderation is assimilation to the god. This rehabilitation of moderation which began shortly after it was downgraded in connection with the demand for a tyrant (cf. 710a3–8 with 711d6, e3, 7, 712a1) is as characteristic of the present speech of the Athenian as the praise of humility. All this leads up to the most noble and most true conclusion that only for the good man is it most noble and best and most fitting to sacrifice and to pray to the gods and to serve them in every other way, while the opposite is true of the bad man. After the Athenian has thus determined the aim of piety, he determines the ways in which the different venerable beings from the Olympian gods down to the parents living and dead are to be honored; he speaks most fully and most strongly of the respect due to the living parents. After he has concluded his speech to the future citizens, he mentions their relations to inferiors and equals which must be regulated by the laws: the relations to superior beings belong to a different class; not everything can be regulated by laws proper (cf. Xenophon, *Memorabilia* I 2.62).

With remarks to this effect the Athenian turns tacitly to the third and last act which precedes the legislation proper. It is an act of the teacher of legislators rather than of the legislator proper. It consists in tacitly answering the question, What is law? for his earlier statement that law is the dispensation effected by the intellect is manifestly insufficient, since it is silent on the compulsion or coercion without which there can be no law. He starts from the pertinent fact that not all men, indeed only a minority of them, are eager to become virtuous, for in front of virtue the deathless ones have put sweat, as Hesiod wisely says. He next alludes to the equally pertinent fact that the legislator's being a man of supreme knowledge cannot be taken for granted: in all legislation a human being of imperfect knowledge, who is supposed to lead men to virtue, lays down laws for human beings the majority of whom are lukewarm to the acquisition of virtue. We infer that the combination of the lack of evidence of the legislator's prescriptions and the recalcitrance of the people calls in the first place for coercion. The law as nothing but coercive command is the flooring; yet law as the dispensation effected by the intellect must remain the ceiling. Persuasion mediates between these two extremes. The most effective persuaders are the poets. The Athenian leads up to this conclusion in the following manner. He addresses the legislator in his own and in Kleinias' name (just as he did when he wished to bring up the subject of the tyrant) with two questions to which Kleinias answers. It appears that the legislator would of course state what the citizens ought to do and to say if he knew it. But does he know it? And if he does not know it, who does? In the sub-Socratic context of the *Laws*, the only kind of wise men apart from the legislators are the poets. Yet about the poets we have already heard that they do not know whether what they present poetically, i.e., what they say, is in agreement with the laws and that they are therefore subject to censorship by the legislator. This simple solution is, however, no longer sufficient (if it ever was sufficient), as we have just seen and as the Athenian makes clear by addressing to the legislator in his own and in Kleinias' name a speech on behalf of the poets and even in the name of the poets. The poet seems to be a man of knowledge, for he possesses an art, the art of imitation, but an ancient story always told by the poets and agreed to by all men says that when the poet sits on the tripod of the Muse, he is not in his senses and that he is compelled by presenting human beings of opposite dispositions to contradict himself frequently without knowing which of the contradictory statements is true; the poet is compelled to say different things on the same subject, whereas the legislator in his law must say only one thing on each subject. The legislator will prescribe and praise, for instance, the kind of burial which is neither excessive nor deficient but in the right mean. The poet, however, will praise different kinds of burial when making different kinds of human beings speak. We note that the poet, when speaking of the poets' self-contradiction, contradicts himself: the poet does not contradict himself by making different characters contradict one another; the Athenian abstracts and at the same time does not abstract from the dramatic character of the poets' works. Besides, the poet is not simply ignorant of which of the contradictory statements is true; the utmost that one could say is that he regards the question as to the truth of the contradictory statements as secondary to the question as to their fitness for human beings of contradictory dispositions. Contrary to the ancient story, originated and propagated by the poets, the poets, and especially the dramatic poets, know very well what they are doing; they present themselves as less wise than they are; they speak ironically (cf. 908e2), whereas nothing is more unbecoming for a legislator than the use of irony: he must always, to all human beings, say the same things on the same subject. (As Socrates explains in the *Phaedrus*, saying to all human beings the same things is the essential defect of writings, a defect which is presumably remedied in Plato's writings: Plato's writings, including the *Laws*, are as remote as possible from the legislator's writings.) But this does not do away with the fact that the poets are in certain respects more knowing than the legislators or that the legislators must learn certain things from the poets, especially about the great variety among the natures and habits of the souls (cf. 650b6–9).

But can one leave matters at the demand for unqualified univocity of the legislator's statements? Granted that his speech must not be manifold; it surely must be twofold. Let us look at the example supplied by the physicians. There are two kinds of physicians: slaves who ordinarily treat slaves and free men who ordinarily treat free men. The former, mere empirics, give orders to their patients like self-willed tyrants without giving their patients an account of why they command whatever they command; the latter, who possess genuine knowledge, communicate with the patients and the patients' friends, thus learning something from the sick, teach the patient as much as they are able, and do not give orders before they have persuaded him somehow. Should the physician perform his single function of healing—or for that matter the gymnastic trainer his single function of making the bodies strong and nimble—in two ways, or only in one way which is the worse and more savage of the two? Kleinias prefers the twofold procedure: slaves and free men must be treated in different ways. By bringing in the example of the gymnastic trainer, the Athenian reminds us of the question whether the legislative art does not correspond rather to gymnastics than to medicine; whether the corrective art corresponding to medicine, namely, the art of punishing, is distinct from the legislative art, or whether the legislative art necessarily includes the art of punishing (cf. *Gorgias* 464b3–c3). As appears from what follows, the last alternative is correct. In other words, there is this difference between the two kinds of medical conduct and the two kinds of legislative conduct: in legislation one and the same man must use two kinds of speeches, the tyrannical and the gentle; the legislator's speech must be in itself twofold.

The Athenian illustrates this demand by the example of the law which must form the beginning of the code. Proceeding "according to nature," the legislator will assign the first place to the marriage laws. This agrees with the Athenian's early statement on the task of the legislator (631d6) but perhaps not with what he indicated in the allocution to the future citizens, where he seemed rather to suggest that the legislator should speak first of how the gods should be honored (717a6–d4); the Athenian's fourth oath occurring now ("by the gods") might remind us of this difficulty. But perhaps that beginning of legislation would not be according to nature. (Aristotle makes the ambiguity in question rather explicit by assigning to the concern with the divine which people call priesthood the "fifth and first" place; *Politics* 1328b11–13.) Be that as it may, the Athenian first frames or, rather, outlines the simple law regarding marriage and then states at comparatively great length the twofold one. It is twofold because it contains both the reason of the law and the law. The reason why everyone ought to marry at the latest when he is thirty-five years old is that the human race partakes, in a way by nature, of immortality, for which therefore everyone has by nature every desire, for the desire to become famous and not to die without a name is the desire for immortality. The human race partakes of immortality through the generation of children. To deprive oneself of this voluntarily is never holy, but one deprives oneself of it if he does not care for children and a wife. Therefore, if he transgresses that law, he will be punished with a fine and a loss of honor in the city. But if everyone has every desire to immortalize himself by generating children, why does one need a law enjoining it? Does one need a law commanding men under the threat of a penalty to eat? The reason of the law on marriage is silent about the man who involuntarily abstains from marriage because his desire for immortality compels him to seek immortality exclusively through immortal fame. But it points to this possibility: it is in itself twofold. This possibility was actualized above all by Plato himself, who by not marrying seems to have disobeyed his own legislator, i.e., the dispensation of the intellect; yet, as we see, he did not disobey, since his action was involuntary. (He would not have objected to paying a bachelor's tax and to the inevitable diminution of respect which accompanies childlessness.) Let us go one step further. There is no reason why the admonitions to obey the various laws or the justification of the same should not be, not only twofold, but even manifold. Hence the writings of the Platonic legislator could approach in manifoldness Plato's own writings and perform the function of the latter. If one wishes, one could say that, by not marrying, Plato did what according to him the poets do: he contradicted the law and thus himself.

It is clear that the law must both persuade and threaten, that it must use both violence and persuasion, that it must speak both gently and tyrannically, although the persuasion cannot be of very great use when one has to do, as the legislator has to do, with the multitude inexperienced in education. But if this is the case, law is a mixture of a tyrannical ingredient and an ingredient which produces the consent of the multitude. Is therefore not, as Aristotle understood "Socrates" to have meant, the correct regime a mixture of tyranny and democracy? (*Politics* 1266a1–3; cf. 693d2–5 and 712d5.)

The fact that the two ingredients of law are heterogeneous does not mean that they are simply opposed to one another. When the Athenian begins to speak of the two kinds of physicians, he describes the slave physicians as servants of the free physicians who follow their masters' instruction in a low-class manner. If this is so, the law proper, the tyrannical prescription, has its ultimate or rather primary origin in genuine knowledge that is guided by the nature of the matter—it originates in the dispensation effected by the intellect —but almost completely conceals its high origin; it is an extremely crude version of the dispensation effected by the intellect.

The Athenian now proposes a correction to what he had said about the twofoldness of the law, for the uncorrected statement has fulfilled its purpose. His proposal arises from a consideration of what the three men had been saying from the beginning till now, from dawn to noon. (If we assume that about the same amount of time is needed for the conversations in V–VIII and in IX–XII as was needed for those in I–IV, we reach the conclusion that the conversations in IX–XII—they are chiefly devoted to the penal law— take place in the evening, and the discussion of the Nocturnal Council toward the end of XII takes place in the dusk, if not after nightfall. Cf. *Phaedo* 116b5–6 and e1–2. The present conversation takes place while they are sitting in the shade: for how long? Till the end of VIII?) From the beginning they have conversed about laws, but only now do they begin to pronounce laws; everything which preceded consisted of preludes or preambles of laws. All speeches need artfully composed preludes which move the audience toward the reception and acceptance of the speeches themselves. This applies in particular to laws, although hitherto no one has recognized this and acted upon it; at least no one has published preludes to laws. Accordingly, the preceding statement about laws must be corrected: the law is not twofold but simple; the prelude, which is only persuasive, is not law; the law is only the tyrannical command by itself. All laws, at least all important laws, ought to have preludes, and there ought to be a prelude to the whole code. Cutting short a possible further discussion of the subject of preludes, Kleinias proposes that they should raise what had been said about the honoring of gods and ancestors (in the allocution to the future citizens) to the status of the first part of the prelude to the whole code and now complete that prelude. The Athenian agrees and adds that the completed part of the prelude has also sufficiently dealt with honoring the living parents; he also adds that "the speakers and hearers" should ponder next the right way of treating their souls, bodies, and property and thus acquire education according to their power.

Book Five

The speaker expounds now what one may call the Second Table. That exposition is a repetition, i.e., a modification, of the statement on the legislator's task which the Athenian had made near the beginning of the conversation (631b3–632d1) and which was silent on piety. He asks everyone who has heard what had been said about the gods and the dear forefathers to listen to what he is going to say about the soul, for of all the possessions a man has, the soul is, after the gods, the most divine, being most his own. One must honor one's soul next to the gods and those following the gods. One honors one's soul by improving it. It is not clear whether one must honor one's soul next to one's parents or more than one's parents (cf. 717c3 and Aristotle, *Topics* 105b22–23). The difficulty reminds us of the earlier one, namely, of whether "according to nature" the laws concerning worship of the gods precede the marriage laws or vice versa. The speaker enumerates seven wrong ways of honoring one's soul. In the central place he mentions flinching from the toils, fears, sufferings, and pains that are praised (sc., by the legislator); surely regarding this point the three interlocutors are in as perfect agreement as possible. He mentions the soul seven times in his enumeration. He does not mention the soul explicitly when speaking of two of the seven items; in these two cases, and only in them, he speaks of the legislator or alludes to him. We are tempted to infer that it is a question whether honoring the soul consists only in obeying the laws or even whether it is always compatible with such obedience. (Cf. the silence on the soul in the *Crito*.) This inference seems to be contradicted by the speaker's summary, in which he entrusts the whole determination of the wrong and right ways of honoring one's soul to the legislator. Yet in that summary he no longer mentions "honoring the soul" and puts the emphasis on the punishment of the transgressors, especially on that punishment which

66

is not inflicted by the legislator but follows the transgression inevitably, namely, assimilation to the bad or unjust.

There follows an enumeration of the things to be honored next to what is best of all—it is not said here that what must be honored first of all is the gods and the ancestors—and to the soul: the body, wealth, children (i.e., the ordinary heirs of one's property who in a way belong to one's property), kinsfolk, friends, the city and fellow citizens, strangers, and suppliants. Gods are mentioned in connection with kinsfolk (or the family), strangers, and suppliants. When speaking of honoring the body he uses "humble" in the usual derogatory sense; the difference in the estimate of humility illuminates the difference between the Two Tables. In a final listing of those subjects of the Second Table which have been discussed hitherto, the speaker mentions the following items: the parents and the man himself, what belongs to him, the city and friends, kinsfolk, and what pertains to strangers; the order could be thought to be one of descent.

The speaker turns next to what one might call the right ways of honoring the soul, i.e., to the noble qualities of the man himself which are the work, not of law, but of praise and blame or of education. Accordingly, he does not speak in this subsection of the legislator whereas he had spoken of him repeatedly in the first two subsections: the right way of honoring the soul transcends the sphere of law. What he says on this subject reminds one of what Socrates says in Book Six of the *Republic* (485a4–487a5, 490a1–c11) on the nature of the philosopher, but he omits magnificence and gracefulness, to say nothing of good memory and aptitude to learn. Still, he mentions in the first place truth, which leads all good things among gods and men; and he says that whoever is to become "blessed and happy" must partake of truth right from the beginning; he does not apply the epithet "blessed" to the individual (cf. 718b3–5) in regard to any other particular good or virtue. But he does not, like Socrates in the *Republic*, speak of passionate love of the whole truth. There follows the praise of him who not only abstains from acting unjustly but does not permit others to do wrong by denouncing wrong doings to the authorities and even by joining them in their punitive actions; he is the great man in the city and perfect. Through the juxtaposition of "blessed and happy" and "the great man in the city and perfect," the speaker indicates the two peaks of virtue—truth and justice—which are its two poles. Similarly, regarding moderation, good sense, and all other good things which admit of being shared, the man who communicates them to others or shares them with them deserves to be honored as outstanding; it goes without saying that in this case, as distinguished from that of justice, punitive action is out of place. It should be noted, however, that the man who communicates the virtues other than justice is not praised as "the great man in the city and perfect." Furthermore, every man ought to be spirited and to the highest degree gentle; spiritedness is required for punishing unjust actions; gentleness is required for dealing with wrongdoers who can still be cured; in the case of this kind of criminal one must remember that no criminal is voluntarily a criminal (although one may not act on that insight in the case of the incurable ones). Here it is said as it were in passing that the soul is in truth, for all, that which is most worthy of honor. The statement on good sense and moderation is flanked on both sides by statements delineating the proper posture in regard to punishment. Finally, the worst of all evils inborn in most men's souls is unlimited self-love which one excuses by saying that every man is by nature dear to himself and this is as it should be. But too great love of oneself accounts for all mistakes men commit since it induces them to honor more what is their own than what is just; he who is to be a "great man" must love, not himself nor what is his, but the just things regardless whether they are done by him or by someone else. Too great a love of oneself is also at the bottom of the conceit that one knows everything while knowing nothing. This statement expresses negatively what the initial statement on truth has expressed positively. The blame of excessive self-love is appropriate in this place since it had been suggested shortly before that the soul—that which is most a man's own—is to be honored to a higher degree than friends and the city. In conclusion he speaks, not, as one might expect, of courage, but of certain "lesser things." One could say that he had implicitly spoken of courage by speaking of spiritedness but this is hardly sufficient; it is better to say that he had implicitly spoken of courage by speaking of justice, for the actions so highly praised there which are those of "the great man in the city" are actions presupposing manliness (cf. 631c5–8). The lesser things of which he speaks in conclusion are, however, no less useful than the ones mentioned before. One ought to avoid excessive laughing and weeping, and the open display of great joy and grief; every man should show equanimity in good as well as in evil fortune. And he should always hope that the god will help. This is the only reference to divine help which occurs in the statement on the virtues.

From the divine things the Athenian descends to the human things. In retrospect we recognize the plan of the section on the divine things: (1) the wrong ways of honoring the soul, (2) the things to be honored which are lower than the soul, (3) the right ways of honoring the soul, i.e., the virtues. The second subject is placed in the center, not because it is more exalted than the two others, but because it is most important in the context; it reveals the order of rank of the city compared to that of the soul. The highest of the three subjects is put at the end because it is also, from a different point of view, the theme of the statement on the human things.

The distinction between the divine and the human things reminds of the distinction which the Athenian had made in his initial statement between the divine goods and the human goods (631b6–d1). But there he understood by the divine goods the human virtues, whereas here the divine pursuits of which he speaks also include the performance of duties toward parents, the city, friends and so on, to say nothing of the gods. Above all, in the initial statement he understood by the human goods the good state of the body and of wealth; here, however, he understands by the human things pleasures, pains, and desires: he could not have stated more strongly than by this change that now the subject is still the soul or rather the honoring of the soul. He thus brings it about that the statements on the wrong and the right ways of honoring the soul surround the statement on the other things and beings lower than the gods which are to be honored.

Pleasures, pains, and desires are natural to man in the highest degree inasmuch as every mortal animal is bound to them and urged on by them of necessity in the strongest manner. One must therefore praise the most noble life as superior not only by its stateliness leading to good repute but also in regard to joy or painlessness, provided one is brought up properly from one's youth. That this is so, appears from a comparison of the noble and the base lives with regard to the question as to which of the two lives is by nature according to nature, for us, and which is against nature, from the point of view of pleasure and pain alone (733a). We wish pleasure and do not wish pain; hence we do not prefer what is neither pleasant nor painful to pleasure but prefer it to pain, and further we wish a lesser pain going with a greater pleasure but not a lesser pleasure going with a greater pain; it is unclear what we wish if pleasure and pain are equal. Our choice is also affected by the multitude, greatness, and vehemence of the pleasures and pains or their opposites. It follows that we prefer the life in which there are many and great and vehement pleasures and pains but in which the pleasure predominates, as well as the life in which there are few and small and gentle pleasures and pains but in which the pleasure preponderates. These cases circumscribe the limits of our wishes, and we must now see which of those wishes are according to nature. More precisely, we must see which life is to be preferred with special regard to pleasure, so that we shall live as blessedly as is possible for a human being. One must make the preferable the law for oneself: since the guiding consideration is pleasure, the decision cannot be left to the legislator. The Athenian raises the question among how many lives one has to choose. He answers: among four and their opposites. The four lives are the moderate, the sensible, the courageous, and the healthy; the opposites are the senseless, the cowardly, the dissolute, and the diseased; he then treats the first three as interchangeable, and he repeats this in the sequel. He asserts at comparative length that everyone who knows the moderate life, which only a few men do, will assert it to be gentle in respect of pleasures, pains, and desires, while the dissolute life is characterized by violence in all three respects; in the moderate life the pleasures predominate over the burdens, while of the dissolute life the opposite is true; hence the moderate life is of necessity by nature more pleasant than the dissolute one, and no one who wishes to live pleasantly will any longer permit himself voluntarily to live dissolutely. It is then already manifest, if what is now said is correct, that everyone is of necessity dissolute involuntarily either through ignorance or through incontinence or through both: incontinence cannot be reduced to ignorance. This would not exclude the possibility that, to a more profound searching, incontinence too would reveal itself as ignorance (cf. 689a1–e1). Similarly, the healthy life is preferable to the diseased life (although in this case it is not obvious that everyone is of necessity sick involuntarily either through ignorance or through incontinence or through both). The Athenian concludes without further argument that what is true of the moderate and dissolute man is also true of the sensible man as well as of the courageous man and the coward: the life which possesses virtue in regard to the body or to the soul is more pleasant than the one which is deficient in these respects—to say nothing of the superiority of the former in beauty, correctness, virtue, and good repute. (By a slight difference in phrasing, the Athenian indicates the unique relation of courage to pleasure; cf. 734c5–6 with Aristotle, *Nicomachean Ethics* 1117a33–b16.) The noble life is more pleasant than the base life if the former is at the same time healthy in regard to the body and the latter is at the same time diseased in regard to the body; the question whether a noble man who suffers from a most painful disease lives more pleasantly than a base man who is in perfect health, is not discussed, let alone answered.

We understand this concluding section of the prelude to the whole code—a section not free from obscurities—somewhat better if we remember the earlier discussion of what is, in a way, the same subject. In discussing the kind of speeches which the correct legislator will persuade or compel the poets to utter, the Athenian had attempted to prove, not without appealing to the legislating gods, the human legislator, and the fathers, that the good man, being moderate and just, is happy and blessed, or that the just and the pleasant (or the noble and the good) cannot be divorced from one another (660d1–663e2). In the concluding section of the prelude, the Athenian is completely silent on the pleasant character of justice. But in the statement on the poets' speeches he had proved the pleasant character of justice only by referring to the fame and praise from men and gods which attend justice, while in the present statement he is concerned with pleasure in contradistinction to good repute; he is now concerned only with that pleasure which men derive from their virtues, even if others are wholly unaware of these virtues; he is concerned only with the pleasures which are, strictly speaking, natural.

The first task after the completion of the prelude is to outline "the laws of the regime." The determination of the regime had been the first act of the legislator's art (712b–715d), but that determination (theocracy or nomocracy) was obviously insufficient. There are two classes of things involved in a regime: the conferring of the ruling offices or magistracies on the individuals, and the laws which must guide the magistrates and be enforced by them. Of the two classes the magistracies come first (cf. *Apology of Socrates* 24d11–e2; Aristotle, *Politics* 1278b8–10 and 1289a11–20). Regarding the magistracies, one must consider that there must be in a polity, corresponding to the difference of warp and woof in a web, a superior ingredient that is strong and firm and an inferior one that is softer, the former consisting of the men fit to occupy the ruling offices and the latter of those who have been but slightly educated. But the question regarding the magistracies is not the first question regarding the regime, for "the regime is a certain order of those who inhabit the city" (Aristotle, *Politics* 1274b38–1275a5). Therefore, one must first find out or determine which inhabitants of the city are citizens; one must first determine the composition of the citizen body. Since in this respect the difference between the rich and the poor is of utmost importance, one cannot sufficiently determine the composition of the citizen body without raising and answering the question regarding property in the city in general. The question regarding the composition of the citizen body and the question regarding property are the fundamental questions concerning the regime. They are the fundamental political questions and cannot be classified as social in contradistinction to political, to make use for the moment of an un-Platonic distinction. Accordingly, the Athenian devotes the rest of Book Five to these two questions.

With a view to the well-being of the new city one must first purge the future citizen body of those who have been corrupted by nature or bad upbringing regarding body or soul, i.e., character or body. Of the purges or purifications of the city, some are rather easy and others are rather difficult; the difficult ones, which are at the same time the best, can only be effected by a man who is both a tyrant and a legislator; but a legislator without tyrannical power can hardly do more than to effect a very gentle purge. The absent legislator questioned by the Athenian had wished for the support by a young tyrant of a fairly good nature in order to achieve in the quickest and best, i.e., in the quickest and easiest manner the transformation of an unsatisfactory city into a good one (710b6 and d8); but now the Athenian discusses in his own name the foundation of a new city, which therefore is not yet ruled by a tyrant; yet it is imaginable that its founder-legislator somehow possesses tyrannical power. In other words, what is very easy in one respect may be very difficult in another: the purge, if it is to be best, will be painful, hence difficult, for it will be achieved by the killing or exiling of those who are incurable (cf. 627d11–628a3). Apparently the legislator who is not a tyrant but has only the support of a tyrant cannot help making undesirable concessions to that tyrant. The more gentle purge consists in getting rid of the have-nots, who show themselves ready to attack the property of the haves, by sending them out to found a colony, for so one will call it in order not to hurt their feelings; this kind of purge is painless. It seems that the desperate poor have a status comparable to that of those who have been corrupted regarding body and soul by nature or bad upbringing. In the present circumstances neither the sending out of a colony—we do not know whether the colony for which Kleinias is commissioned to legislate is being sent out for the reason just mentioned—nor death or exile for the wicked is feasible. What can be done is to prevent, by every kind of persuasion and testing, the wicked among those who intend to become members of the new city from achieving their goal, while welcoming the good in the friendliest manner possible. The Athenian is obviously a humane man, but he appreciates the benefits which may derive from the use of harsh measures.

As for the dissensions arising in regard to land, debts, and dwellings, they have to be feared in the new city as little as in the colony founded by the sons of Herakles (684d1–e6, 685d4). How lucky this circumstance is, appears from a glance at the very cautious and time-consuming measures which old cities are compelled to take in order to get rid of this kind of dissension. In that case the changes —redistribution of land and remission of debts—must be initiated by those among the wealthy who have come to realize somehow that poverty consists, not in the decrease in wealth, but in the increase of greediness. There is no escape from this kind of civic strife except through renouncing the love of money even if such love remains within the boundaries of right. This is of course equally true of old and of new cities. The founders of a city would act monstrously if they were to excite enmity among the future citizens through the distribution of land and dwellings. The proper distribution must be a prop of the political order. The proper distribution requires in the first place the determination of the number of citizens; that number cannot be correctly determined except with a view to the available land and the neighboring cities. For there must be sufficient land, but not more, for nourishing so and so many people living temperately; there must be as many citizens as are needed for defending themselves against injury from adjoining people and as might not be wholly unable to come to the assistance of those of their neighbors who suffer wrong. The proper distribution, which must be as equal as possible, requires in the second place the division of the citizen body into parts; among those parts the land and the dwellings must be distributed as equally as possible. The final decision on these matters is obviously not possible prior to the inspection of the territory and its neighbors, but an outline of what seems to be reasonable can be risked. The Athenian suggests then that the future city should consist of 5,040 land holders and defenders of their plots and the same number of plots. This number has the advantage that it can be divided by all numbers up to ten; in fact, it is susceptible of fifty-nine different divisions. Every legislator must of course have given thought to numbers to the extent that he knows which number and what kind of number is most useful for all cities in regard to war and, as far as peace is concerned, in regard to all business transactions as well as for purposes of taxation and distributions.

The reason that the founder of a city must say "these things" is this. Regardless of whether one founds a new city or restores an old one which has become corrupt, no man of sense will attempt to change the establishments regarding the gods: the founder-legislator is not the founder of a religion. In the distribution of land he must first assign sacred precincts for the worship of gods and daimons, and regarding that worship he will abide by what Delphi or Dodona or some ancient sayings have persuaded some in whatever manner —through visions or through alleged divine inspirations—and what they through such persuasion have established in regard to sacrifices, oracles, statues, and so on. He has greater freedom in assigning a god, a daimon, or some hero to each part of the city; the division of the city into parts is thus hallowed. The cult performed by those parts in regularly recurring festivals will be most beneficial, since it enables the citizens in question to become well-acquainted with one another and thus to judge one another correctly regarding honors, magistracies, or litigation and punishment. Every man must be an open book to every one, thoroughly sincere and not a counterfeit, nor must he allow himself to be deceived by a counterfeit. It goes without saying that this warning is not meant to encourage improper suspicions regarding those who have established cults in the past; it refers only to contemporaries.

The admonition to strict adherence to the old established sacred things is followed immediately by the suggestion that they deviate from what in the game of draughts is called the sacred line. The sacred line in political matters is the best regime. This suggestion might be unacceptable to someone who is not familiar with a legislator lacking tyrannical power like the present one. Only a legislator possessing tyrannical power could establish the best regime: supreme wisdom and supreme power must coincide in the same human being (cf. 711e8–712a3). Every other legislator must be content with the second or third best regime. But every legislator ought to be aware of the three kinds of regimes so that he himself is in a position to choose wisely. The best regime is that in which all things are common to all citizens: not only women, children, and wealth but everything deemed private—the private by convention—is eliminated from all sides. More than that, even the things by nature private must, as much as possible, in one way or another, have become common. The things by nature private are the body and its parts (*Republic* 464d8–9; 416d5–6). Even those pleasures and pains which are by nature private must have become common somehow; i.e., the distinction between the pleasures which derive from the individual's noble qualities and which he has independently of others' knowing of his possessing those qualities, and the pleasures which derive from others' knowing of his possessing noble qualities, must be obfuscated. We have heard previously that the soul is in the highest degree a man's own (726a2–3); but this does not mean that the soul is private; one's own is opposed to the alien or alienable (cf. Thucydides I 70.6), while the private is opposed to the public or common. Thoughts are by nature common—as common as the truth—not private, though they may be accidentally private. The soul is not the self, i.e., the man himself; the man himself is the soul and the body (cf. the first word of the *Phaedo*). (As for the relation of character and body, cf. 735b7–c2.) The city informed by the best regime is inhabited by gods or sons of gods (853c3–7); being more than one, each of those gods or sons of gods would seem to possess things peculiar or private to him. The best regime is the only model by which one must take one's bearings; one must seek a regime which comes as close to it as possible. Previously we have been told that the model is the life under Kronos (713e6–714a1), a life of obedience to gods or demons; now we learn that the model is the divine or demonic life itself. At present we are attempting to establish a second best and later perhaps a third best regime. The second best will be the one on which Kleinias will agree with the Athenian. But Kleinias is only one of the ten men commissioned to draft the laws for the new city; the most satisfactory compromise between Kleinias and his colleagues would constitute a third best solution. In reading the present passage one must not forget that Kleinias and Megillos have not read the *Republic*. Throughout Book Five the Athenian does not encourage them to raise any questions. It should be said that in describing the character of the best regime the Athenian is silent on the rule of the philosophers; the rule of the philosophers is excluded by the character of the second best regime and it is tacitly excluded because silence on philosophy is imposed by the law which Plato imposed on himself when writing the *Laws* and which he only rarely and, as it were, surreptitiously transgresses.

In accordance with what he had said, the Athenian enacts that the land be distributed and not be tilled in common and that the dwellings will be private. Yet the plots and the dwellings will remain the common property of the whole city; the fatherland, the earth, a goddess, must be revered more than a mother since she is immortal and the common mother, just as the local gods and demons are to be revered. The 5,040 plots must forever remain intact; there must be always the one and only one heir to the plot: the son that the father prefers. If a man has a number of children, the females must be endowed in accordance with a law to be specified, while the sons who do not inherit the ancestral plot must be adopted by citizens who have no sons of their own, if need be through the action of the highest magistrate. In the case of overpopulation, the sending out of colonies may be in order; in the case of a decline in numbers owing to plagues or wars, one may be compelled to admit to citizenship foreigners with a bastard education, undesirable as this is. (How considerable is the difference between foreigners with a bastard education and the part of the citizen body that consists of those who have been but slightly educated? See 735a4.) Nothing is said to the effect that a man can be compelled to join a colony to be founded. It is helpful to compare the Athenian's suggestions as to what should be done in case of overpopulation with those of Hobbes (*Leviathan* ch. 30): according to Hobbes, the ultimate remedy is war, "which provideth for everyone, by victory, or death"; in less extreme situations colonies should be sent "into countries not sufficiently inhabited" but with due concern for the natives; the Athenian does not speak of the ultimate remedy, yet he also does not speak of concern for the aborigines (barbarians).

The preceding discourse is now presented as addressing an exhortation to the citizens concerning the same subject. Is that address a prelude, but a prelude following the law? The provisions outlined in the preceding discourse (739e8–741a5) are not called laws although they unquestionably define what should be done, and they are called laws in the subsequent exhortation or its sequel. (The exhortation does not necessarily extend beyond the point at which the speaker ceases to use the second person plural, i.e., 741b6; what follows is at least partly addressed to the magistrates only.) In accordance with this, only the exhortation or its sequel mentions punishment, whereas the preceding discussion speaks only of monitory (*nouthetikoi*) speeches (cf. Xenophon, *Memorabilia* I 2.21). The exhortation to the citizens contains both the law and the prelude. What then is the relation between the two speeches? The first speech is addressed to the legislator-founders or to the men who shall take their place in the future, while the second speech is addressed to the citizenry as a whole. The first speech is inseparable from the remark that the division of the land into plots is second best, inferior to the common possession of the land as well as of women and children; that remark and the reasoning supporting it is appropriately addressed to the legislator-founder. The speech to the citizenry, on the other hand, is appropriately silent on the inferiority of the fundamental arrangement: the thought that it is inferior would be in their case only upsetting, not to say subversive, and not enlightening; the citizens must regard that arrangement as perfectly in agreement with nature. The citizens are admonished to obey the law which commands the preservation of each plot and, in particular, forbids the buying and selling of land by threatening transgressors with condign punishment. The Athenian concludes by pointing out the great good which would come anywhere from the proposed law properly enforced, as indeed only those will appreciate who have the required experience in things noble and the required habituation (cf. 653a5–c4 and 722b7; Aristotle, *Nicomachean Ethics* 1095b4–6). In the city to be founded, there is no place for money-making from vulgar trades on the part of citizens. For the next law will forbid anyone to possess gold or silver; the money required for payment to artisans and hirelings, be they slaves or aliens, will be in a currency valuable only in the city and worthless elsewhere. The city must own money in pan-Hellenic currency for use in campaigns, embassies, and the like. If a private man should ever be compelled to go abroad and should come home with any surplus of foreign money, he must deposit it with the city in exchange for domestic money. Dowries are simply forbidden; lending at interest is entirely at the lender's peril. The citizens' concern with riches is discouraged as is the city's concern with riches, bigness, and empire. The many who also regard it as possible that a good legislator not be benevolent to the city for which he legislates, wrongly believe that men may be both very good and exceptionally rich. That belief is wrong for this reason: the bad man will acquire wealth by just and unjust means, while the good man will use only just means; hence the bad man will acquire at least twice as much wealth as the good man; and the good man will spend nobly, while the bad man will refuse to spend either nobly or ignobly; hence the bad man will possess at least four times as much wealth as the good man. More precisely, the man who abstains from noble expenditures, the thrifty or stingy man, is not a bad man, although he is assuredly not a good man. If such a man obtains wealth by just and by unjust means, he will become rich, while the one who acquires wealth by fair means or foul and is a wastrel is altogether bad and will become very poor. The good man will be neither outstandingly rich nor abjectly poor; the man who is unjust in acquiring and stingy in spending is most likely to be very rich, while the one who is unjust in acquiring and a wastrel is most likely to be very poor; the man who is just in acquiring and stingy in spending is likely to be richer than the one who is just in acquiring and liberal in spending. But will the unjust and liberal man be richer or poorer than the just and stingy one? This question is as little discussed as the case of the superlatively just man who lives in tenthousandfold poverty like Socrates, that prefiguration of the ruler in the best regime. The stingy man is naturally assigned a higher place than the wastrel (cf. *Republic* 558c11ff.).

Of the different goals at which our legislation aims, friendship rather than freedom (cf. 693b3–e1), as these terms are commonly understood, is threatened by undue concern with wealth, such concern leading to many litigations and acts of wrongdoing. We may recall here that the modern commercial republic, which fosters competition in the market, was promoted in the name of freedom rather than of friendship. For the sake of friendship the citizens in the city to be founded will derive their wealth from farming rather than from moneymaking through vulgar trade, lending at interest, and ignoble kinds of animal husbandry. Even in farming, concern with possessions must always be kept in due subordination to the care for soul and body, the two other objects of every man's serious concern or of the city's honoring. In this context the Athenian calls the virtue of the soul simply "moderation," for he thinks here above all of self-restraint regarding moneymaking (cf. *Republic* 555b7–8 and Xenophon, *Memorabilia* I 5.6).

All precautions of the legislator—precautions which in the best case will enable him to frame a code not in need of future improvement—cannot prevent the inequality of wealth which he would wish to prevent, for, of the colonists who arrive in the new city, some will have greater possessions than others. For many reasons, and in particular for the sake of rightly understood equality, it is therefore necessary to establish a number of classes (four) according to size of property so that in the assignment of offices, in the imposition of public burdens, and in distributions, citizens of different degrees of wealth will be differently treated in accordance with proportional equality; not only the virtue of ancestors and of the citizen himself, the strength and comeliness of his body, but also his wealth must be considered in the proper proportion. If a citizen becomes wealthier, he will rise to a higher class and vice versa. Having admitted private property, the Athenian cannot but admit the claim of wealth; he must modify somewhat what he had said when speaking of the theocracy (715b7–c2). The division of the citizen body into four classes according to size of property was characteristic of the ancient regime of Athens (698b2–5), as distinguished from the Spartan regime, for instance. The Athenian tries to introduce into a Dorian community, if not philosophy, at least an important ingredient of the best polity of the city which came to be the home of philosophy, just as he had tried to introduce symposia.

Precisely because there will be differences of wealth in the city, there should be, at least in the Athenian's view, legally imposed limitations on wealth. Strictly speaking, no citizen must be poor or rich. The flooring is the inalienable plot. The ceiling is the additional acquisition of the fourfold value of the plot. If someone acquires more than that through finds, gifts, trade, or in any other way, he must give the excess to the city and the gods who keep the city. Anyone who wishes may denounce transgressors of this law; the informer shall receive half of the excess, the other half shall go to the gods; the transgressor shall in addition be fined to the amount of half the excess. Information on this kind of transgression is then a perfectly legitimate way in which a man may increase his wealth and, haply, rise to the highest census class.

Next comes the determination of the location of the city and, inseparably from this, the division of the city as well as of the country and of the landholders into twelve parts; each part of the body composed of landholders is assigned one part of the country that is equal in fertility, not in size, to every other part. Each piot and dwelling place is to be divided into two parts, one near the city and the other further away; if the one part is next to the city, the other part must be furthest away, and the second nearest must go together with the second furthest, and so on. The total property of all parts, or tribes, shall be rendered as equal as possible: there shall be no poorer or richer tribes. Each tribe is to be given the name of one of the twelve gods to each of whom a plot is to be assigned. This ruling differs from an earlier one according to which each part is to be assigned to a god, a demon, or some hero (738d1–2). But the earlier ruling preceded the acceptance of the four census classes, of an Attic institution; the second ruling constitutes a further step in the adoption of Attic institutions. It is true that the Athenian citizen body consisted of ten tribes; the change from ten to twelve is silently if obviously explained by the reference to the twelve gods; but it can be explained equally well by the fact that the division of 5,040 by 12 leads to 420, which is divisible by all numbers up to 7, while the division by 10 leads to 504, which is divisible only by all the numbers up to 7 with the exception of 5: numbers have something divine.

At this point the Athenian pauses to remind himself and his interlocutors to ponder over the extreme improbability that all the things which the legislator, or they, had laid down or postulated for the well-being of the colony should ever come together. The legislator must make this reflection which he will communicate to the three interlocutors. Regarding all projects, he who exhibits the pattern must exhibit it in all its nobility and truth, in perfect agreement with itself, without making any compromises; but the acting man, his inferior, must abandon what is impossible in the circumstances but must remain as close as possible to the pattern. The exhibition of the pattern must be left to the legislator; the distinction between what is practicable in the circumstances and what is not requires the joint deliberation of the legislator and the other man. Only the possessor of the kingly art can be a legislator. But all arts owe the exactness which they possess in the first place to the art of numbering (*Philebus* 55e1–3). The legislator must regulate everything possible, without fearing the reputation of pettiness, with a view to number. He must not only himself possess the art of numbering; he also must urge all citizens to acquire that knowledge as far as they can. For there is no other single branch of educative learning of such universal utility; above all, that divine art awakens even those by nature drowsy and dull and improves their ability to learn, their memory, and their sagacity beyond what their nature has supplied them with. Knowledge of numbers must of course not be used in the service of meanness and love of money. If it is, it will promote trickery rather than wisdom. It is especially necessary to make this reservation, since knowledge of numbers tends to go together with commerce rather than with farming, the only moneymaking activity permitted to the citizens of the colony. The misuse of the knowledge of numbers can be observed among the Egyptians, the Phoenicians, and many other races. Their bad habits are due to the badness of their legislators or some great misfortune, or even some natural influence which has such an effect. Addressing now in the first place Megillos, who had so highly praised the nature of the Athenians (642c6–d1), the Athenian points out the influences which no legislator must disregard and which are of crucial importance for good or ill, the influences of winds, sunshine, waters, and the food produced by the soil. This remark cannot refer to the selection of the territory of the new city, for that territory had already been selected; the Athenian speaks here as the teacher of legislators in general, and not as the adviser of Kleinias in particular (hence he addresses Megillos and Kleinias). This is confirmed by the following fact: there is no indication that the remark under discussion refers either to the selection of the place where the city is to be built (cf. Aris-

totle, *Politics* 1330a36–b17) or to the distribution of the land among
the twelve tribes (namely, that there should be equal distribution
of the salubrious land). Most outstanding, the Athenian continues,
are the places which have a kind of divine breeze and are assigned
spheres of demons, who receive potential settlers either graciously or
ungraciously. The thoughtful legislator will examine these places as
far as is possible for a human being and will try to frame his laws
accordingly. The Athenian does not state whether and how the
examination regarding the demonic influences differs from the examination regarding the natural influences; he certainly does not advise
here the consultation of oracles. While in the case of numbers consideration of the gods and consideration of numerical properties
converged, there is at least no manifest convergence of the consideration of the natural and that of the demonic influences. It is in
this context that the Athenian addresses Kleinias alone: you too
must do what every thoughtful legislator must do; he who is about
to settle a territory must first turn to "things of this kind." Kleinias
eagerly accepts this advice. The advice is a self-criticism of the Athenian, who had not begun his founding the city in speech with a
consideration of winds, waters, and places, to say nothing of demonic influences.

Book Five ends as Book Four began, with a consideration regarding the nature of the territory. Only in Book Six does the regime
(735a5–6) properly become the theme.

Apart from Kleinias' reply at the very end, the Athenian is the
sole speaker in Book Five. This Book is the least dialogic of all
Books of the *Laws*. The connection between this fact and the argument of the Book was indicated when it became apparent. That
observation must be applied *mutatis mutandis* to the whole Book.

Book Six

Hitherto the Athenian had spoken of what the legislator or what "we" (he and his interlocutors) ought to, or will, do or say. Toward the end of the preceding Book (747d2) he had addressed "Megillos and Kleinias" (cf. 683b4–5 and 702b3 with 693a5 and 753d7). At the very end of that Book, however, after having stated what the wise legislator will do in a certain manner, he had turned to Kleinias and told him that he too must do the same (cf. 739b4). In accordance with this he assigns to Kleinias at the beginning of the present Book the task—the first political task in the strict or narrow meaning of the term that he assigns to him—of constituting the ruling offices and of regulating the manner in which the men who are to fill them are to be appointed. As he reminds him, before embarking on this task one must consider that, however well ordered a city and however well framed her laws may be, all this will even lead to ruin if the administration is put into the hands of inept magistrates. The danger is greatest at the beginning, when those who have but recently come together do not know one another sufficiently and are not yet properly educated and hence are unable to elect the right kind of people to the ruling offices. The Athenian obviously does not think highly of the education which the colonists have received in their Cretan mother-city; he mitigates the effect of his remark on Kleinias by addressing him as friend. Some way or other must be found to overcome this difficulty; otherwise their present doings will not amount to more than the telling of a myth—of a story of something that is not, or at least is not as it is told in the story, and even to the telling of a myth without a head: what the Athenian is about to do is no less than to add the head, the highest and ruling part, the initiating beginning, of the project. The question concerns, indeed, no less than the beginning of the life of the new city, and the beginning is half of the whole. The question had been answered previously by the suggestion of a good young tyrant; that answer has by now been tacitly discarded. The Athenian's doing will of course consist in speaking. To Kleinias' reply, "Let us by all means do as we say," the Athenian replies: "If god wills and we get the better of our old age so far"; for Kleinias it is reasonable to suppose that the god wills, and the Athenian agrees with this: the god's help will make it certain that they will get the better of their old age. Thereupon the Athenian restates the difficulty which they must overcome—a difficulty which, it might seem, can only be surmounted with the help of a god—or the daring, not to say foolhardy, character of their undertaking: not only do the colonists not know one another and are not bred to the new laws; we do not even know whether and how they will accept those laws; some solution must be found for the time until the laws have taken root in the second generation. The difficulty can be overcome only if the Cretans, and especially the mother-city, Knosos, do not merely take care of purification from pollution in regard to the land but elect in the first place the guardians of the laws for the new city. Addressing men of Cretan descent, the Athenian says that the Knosians must elect thirty-seven guardians of the laws, nineteen from the colonists and the rest from Knosos itself, and give the latter to the colony. Kleinias himself must become one of the citizens of the colony and one of the eighteen Knosian guardians of the laws. Thereupon, Kleinias, who is perhaps not too eager to be "given" to the colony, asks the Athenian why he and Megillos too do not become citizens of the colony. The Athenian declines for himself and Megillos on the ground of Athens' and Sparta's pride and of the vast distance between these two cities and the colony. It is not necessary to infer from this that the Athenian has any hope or desire to return to his city; he may have reasons different from those of Megillos, reasons befitting a philosopher of his age and circumstances, for declining; he may wish to continue to live as a stranger. Since it had been the Athenian's suggestion of how the magistrates and especially the guardians of the laws should be elected at the beginning which had induced Kleinias to make his unwelcome proposal, he turns now to indicating in a provisional manner how the rulers, i.e., the guardians of the laws, shall be elected later on. Everyone will participate in the election who bears arms as a knight or a hoplite or who has taken part in war so far as his age and ability permitted; the election will be conducted in circumstances which will remind everyone of the awful responsibility of his action; voting will be by written ballot (but of course not secret); the election will take place in three stages; the thirty-seven men who have been elected are to be appointed after they have been subjected to scrutiny. The regime could thus seem to be a polity as defined by Aristotle, a regime in which only those participate who are able to equip themselves with heavy arms, and of course the knights (*Politics* 1279a37–b4). But "those who have taken part in war as far as their age and ability permitted" also include the light-armed soldiers (cf. 755e7–8).

The Athenian then returns immediately to the question concerning the election of the magistrates and especially of the guardians of the laws while there are no magistrates who can preside over elections. He states again how difficult it is to answer that question. Only one thing is clear: Knosos will, or ought to, be like father and mother to the new city, which at the beginning is like a helpless child. The Knosians must choose no less than one hundred of the oldest and best colonists and one hundred Knosians. These two hundred must appoint the magistrates and submit them to scrutiny. Thereafter the Knosians will return to Knosos, i.e., they will not become, as they were to become according to the original but discredited proposal (753a1–3, 754c2–3), citizens of the new city. The Athenian reminds judicious readers implicitly of the fact that while repetition of noble things does not do any harm, the repetition need not be a statement of literally the same.

After the twofold difficulty has been disposed of, the Athenian outlines three duties of the guardians of the laws which can be determined in the present stage of the conversation. Apart from being the guardians of the laws, they are to be the keepers of the records of everyman's property, and they are to have jurisdiction regarding transgressions of the limits set to property. Understating one's worth is permitted proportionately to the four census classes (members of the highest class may fail to register as much as four minae, members of the lowest class as few as one). In this connection the Athenian, tacitly contradicting his earlier statement (745a3–6), mitigates the penalty for avarice somewhat at the expense of informers. No one younger than fifty or older than seventy may hold the office of guardian of the law.

Next comes the discussion of the election of generals and other military commanders and in particular of how they are to be elected at the beginning of the colony. The generals are to be elected by all who bear or have borne arms of whatever kind; the taxiarchs are to be elected by the infantry only, just as the cavalry commanders are to be elected by the knights only; election is by the raising of hands, i.e., not by lot.

The next magistracy discussed (cf. 758d7–9) is the Council. It would seem to be more natural to distinguish the deliberative as well as the judicial "part" of the regime from the magistracies (cf. Aristotle, *Politics* 1297b37–1298a3). The Athenian reveals his awareness of this when he speaks of the judiciary, which he also treats as a magistracy (767a5–b1 and c3–5). Yet there is this difficulty. A citizen would seem to be a man who participates in judging and ruling; he surely is a juryman and a member of the Assembly; but to say that a man who acts only as a juryman and as a member of the Assembly does not participate in ruling, i.e., is not a magistrate, is ridiculous, for men of his description are the highest authority, at least in a democracy (Aristotle, *Politics* 1275a22–29). Hence the deliberative body or bodies and the judiciary would be the magistracies par excellence. Be that as it may, it is surely remarkable that the Athenian does not discuss the Assembly, as distinguished from the Council, among the magistracies; in fact he never discusses the Assembly, although he refers to it a few times.

The Council will consist of three hundred and sixty members, ninety from each property class, to be elected by the whole citizen body. Nonvoting in elections for the Council is a punishable offense in all cases for citizens of the two highest property classes; citizens of the lowest class are not obliged to vote in the election of Council members to be elected from the two lowest classes. Seven hundred and twenty men will be elected by the raising of hands; three hundred and sixty of them will be determined by lot, and they will form the Council for a year. By treating the lowest class differently from the higher ones the Athenian kills two birds with one stone: he gives the poorer citizens greater freedom to mind their own business, and he increases the influence of the wealthy on the election of members of the lowest property class. This is to say nothing of the not unimportant fact that the prospects of reelection to the Council and hence of quasi-permanent membership in the Council are considerably greater for members of the highest property class, which is likely to be the numerically smallest, than for others.

While the guardians of the laws and the military officers were to be elected exclusively by the raising of hands, the Council is to be elected through a combination of election by the raising of hands and election by lot. The Athenian is therefore led to justify that combination by what could seem to be a digression or a belated prelude but is in fact another concise statement of the fundamental political predicament. The combination of the two kinds of election brings about a mean between a monarchic and a democratic regime, the right kind of mixed regime. In an unmixed monarchy there will be one master and the rest will be slaves; in an unmixed democracy worthless and respectable men will receive equal honors; both extreme regimes, we might say, are equally oblivious of the just claim of virtue and wisdom to supremacy. According to an old saying, which is true, equality produces friendship, but there is a great difference, not to say opposition, between two kinds of equality. One kind demands that equal honor be given to everyone; this is achieved by lot. But the demand of the truest and best equality cannot easily be discerned by everyone, for it is the judgment of Zeus, which the equality achieved by lot obviously is not; the second kind of equality gives more to the greater and less to the smaller by giving to everyone what is appropriate to his nature and accordingly by assigning greater honors to those who are greater in regard to virtue and lesser honors to those of the opposite character in regard to virtue and education. The mention of education reminds us of the earlier distinction between the men fit to be magistrates and those who have been but slightly educated (734e6–735a4), and it foreshadows the later indication regarding the inequality of education (818a). It is the second kind of inequality which gives what is by nature equal to unequal men and which is at the same time the political right, because it produces for the cities all good things. This implies that the first kind of inequality, which treats unequal men as equal, is conventional (cf. also *Du Contrat social* I 9 end). Yet in order to avoid discontent on the part of the many who are indeed deservedly disadvantaged on the ground of correct right, one must deviate from that right in the direction of the first kind of equality by using the lot, i.e., luck, which favors equally the deserving and the undeserving, for the appointment of magistrates, praying to god and good luck that they will direct the lot toward what is most just; but the lot should be used as sparingly as possible.

There are, then, not two different and conflicting roots or principles of justice, say, freedom and good government; but the single principle of justice must be diluted on account of necessity—the compelling power of the many; the dilution is a concession, a humane and expedient concession to irrationality: a rational society is not possible, unless it be the society ruled by a philosopher exercising tyrannical power. Accordingly, there is the following tacit progress in the passage under discussion. At its beginning the nondemocratic (monarchic) principle is presented as simply bad; at the end it becomes quite clear that the nondemocratic principle is good; throughout it is not questioned that the democratic principle is bad.

The best and truest kind of equality can be called monarchic, since the sole rightful ruler is the Intellect (713e3–714a2).

We have here the core of the Athenian's political suggestions. True equality, proportionate equality, is achieved by "the judgment of Zeus," while spurious equality is achieved by the lot. But, as we shall see soon, politically the alternative to the lot is election by the raising of hands, i.e., something very fallible: what is diluted by lot is not the judgment of Zeus but an already imperfect justice. This shows again the questionable character of the identification of *nomos* and *noos*. The danger to the city is averted to some extent by the division of the citizen body into four property classes and the consequent preponderance of the "non-*demos*" (759b6), i.e., of the better-educated and therefore, other things being equal, more virtuous citizens.

A Council consisting of three hundred and sixty members is too large to act with dispatch—to say nothing of secrecy—in the daily and even nightly management of public affairs. Hence, for each month, one twelfth of the Council must be in charge or act as *prytaneis* (755e4–5, 760b1). They are to be in charge of negotiations with foreign cities, of the prevention of disturbances within the city as well as of the convocation of both ordinary and extraordinary meetings of the Assembly. Nothing is said as to how the division of the Council into twelve parts is to be effected and, in particular, on how the equal participation of members of all four property classes in all twelve *prytaneis* is to be guaranteed, thirty not being divisible by four: will members of the lowest property class be excused from the time-consuming service as *prytaneis* and correspondingly members of the highest property class or classes be permitted to serve two or more months as *prytaneis*? How indeed could the poor farmers stay away from their farms day and night for a whole month, especially in the seasons of sowing and harvesting? The guardians of the laws, who are surely not elected as members of a property class and are not merely elected for a single year, are obviously of much greater importance than the Council, let alone the Assembly.

The magistrates mentioned next are those in charge of order in the country and in the town, for instance, regarding roads, dwellings, markets, and temples. The Athenian specifies, for the time being, only temple keepers, priests, priestesses, town-wardens and market-wardens. Hereditary priesthoods ought not to be changed, but at the beginning of the new city there will be few or none of them. Generally speaking, in the appointment of the magistrates just mentioned the two kinds of election must be combined, the lot being necessary for bringing about friendship between the *demos* and the others. But in the case of the priests, election by lot acquires a special dignity, not to say sanctity, for electing them by lot means leaving the decision to the god, to the divine chance (cf. 690c5–8). But even in this case election by lot must be supplemented and, if necessary, corrected, not indeed by election by the raising of hands, but by the scrutiny of those so elected with a view to the legitimacy of their birth and their ritual purity (for the god directing the lot does not, for obvious reasons, take care of these requirements). Laws regarding all divine things must be brought from Delphi, and interpreters for those laws must be appointed. Priests and priestesses are to be appointed for one year only; they must be no less than sixty years old; nothing is said to the effect that they cannot be elected when they are over seventy (cf. Aristotle, *Politics* 1329a31–34). Interpreters, on the other hand, will partly be elected by voting and partly by the Delphic oracle; they also must be sixty years of age, but they are elected for life, and when a vacancy occurs the substitute will be determined by voting, i.e., not by the Delphic oracle. Treasurers of the sacred funds are to be elected from the highest property class or classes; the procedure is to be the same as in the election of the generals.

After having concluded his statement on the Council, the Athenian had spoken in a confused or confusing way of the magistrates who are to be in charge of the country as distinguished from the city—no, also of the city; he had singled out the priests and three additional kinds of magistrates but had mentioned only two of them (town-wardens and market-wardens). He then discussed the priests and the other officers in charge of the divine things. Immediately thereafter he identifies and discusses the third kind of magistrates, the country-wardens; only thereafter does he discuss the town-wardens and the market-wardens. The discussion of the country-wardens is the most extensive section of the part devoted to the magistrates, just as the discussion of the priests is the briefest. The discussion of the priests occupies the center of the part devoted to the magistrates. The length of the discussion of the country-wardens is a sign of the fact that this kind of magistrate is the most important of the four discussed here (priests, town-wardens, market-wardens, and country-wardens). The Athenian could easily have gone over from the discussion of the Council to that of the country-wardens; through his confusing procedure he draws our attention to the importance, not so much of the priests, as of the problem of the priests, and at the same time to the contrast between the brevity of the section on the priests and the length of the section on the country-wardens.

He starts now from the consideration that, if possible, nothing should be left unguarded; the city should be guarded by the military officers, the *prytaneis*, and the town- and market-wardens, i.e., by all magistrates hitherto discussed or at least mentioned with the exception of the guardians of the laws and the priests; the reason that he is now silent on the guardians of the laws is not likely to be the same as the reason that he is now silent on the priests. He then turns to the guarding of the country. Each of the twelve tribes shall elect for a period of two years five land-wardens, and each of these groups of five (cf. Morrow, *loc. cit.* p. 186 n. 81) shall select from their tribe twelve young men not younger than twenty-five years and not older than thirty. Each group of seventeen shall be assigned by lot one-twelfth of the country for a month so that all groups of seventeen will acquire within a year a thorough knowledge of the whole country and within two years a thorough knowledge of each part of the country in each season of the year. The country-wardens have to take care in the first place of fortifications against enemy incursions but also of such things as roads, irrigation, beautification, and the building of gymnasia for the young and old and warm baths for the old and infirm. Their most serious business consists above all in guarding individuals against mutual wrongdoings by acting as judges in relatively minor matters; as all other magistrates with the exception of those who like kings pronounce final judgement, they are subject to auditing. The Athenian speaks most extensively on the penalties to which the country-wardens are subject if they are guilty of any misuse of their power: their being shifted every month from one district to another offers many temptations. During the two years they all must eat and sleep in the common mess halls of the districts; absence by day or night is subject to degrading penalties. Proper conduct in this matter will be insured by strict supervision on the part of the law guardians themselves. They must live in a humble and austere manner: being themselves servants, they may not keep servants or slaves nor use for their private service the servants or slaves of the husbandmen or villagers; heavily armed, they must explore the whole country in summer and winter; for this purpose they must practice all kinds of hunting. One may call them the secret police. Common meals and secret police were Spartan institutions (633a4–c4). The Spartan secret police was in charge of the control—and this sometimes meant the secret assassination— of helots. It is reasonable to assume that the secret police of Kleinias' city would assist citizens in recovering their runaway slaves.

As for the town-wardens and market-wardens, they are to be elected from the highest property class or classes, for otherwise they will not have the leisure to devote themselves to their public duties; the wealthy, of course, cannot escape this burden or privilege as regards the office of country-warden as well. Needless to say, the severe restrictions in regard to their daily life to which the country-wardens are subject do not apply to the town- and market-wardens: the former are an elite to a higher degree than the latter.

After he has discussed the law guardians, the military commanders, the Council, the priests, and the police magistrates, the Athenian takes up the penultimate subject, the magistrates in charge of Music and gymnastics. In either case there will be different magistrates in charge of education on the one hand and of contests on the other. As for the magistrates in charge of contests, one man, who must be no less than forty years old, will be in charge of choral contests, and one man, who must be no less than thirty years old, will be in charge of contests of soloists. Only a man experienced in choral music is eligible as magistrate in charge of choral contests; only the citizens devoted to this kind of thing are obliged to vote in his election; the tenure is for one year. The same procedure is to be followed in the election of the magistrate in charge of the contests of soloists. Those in charge of the gymnastic contests are to be chosen from the third and second property class; voting is obligatory for members of the three highest classes. It may be assumed although it is characteristically not said that the magistrates in charge of the Music contests are to be elected from the highest class or the two highest classes, i.e., from the classes which are presumably best educated. The next step marks a steep ascent: turning to those in charge of education, the Athenian speaks only of a single magistrate in charge of the whole education. He must be no less than fifty years old, the father of legitimate children, preferably of both sons and daughters. His magistracy is to be considered as by far the most important among the highest magistracies in the city, for the first shoot of every growing being, if it sprouts well, is most important for bringing it to the completion, to the excellence peculiar to its nature; this applies above all to human beings, who, if they have received a correct education and are favored by nature, are likely to become the most divine and most gentle of living beings, but, if not sufficiently or not nobly reared, are likely to become the most savage beings on earth. The goal of education then is the natural excellence of man, with due consideration for the variety of natures (cf. 757c3). Accordingly the magistrate in charge of the whole education ought to be that man in the city who is best in every respect. The most important

magistrates who are unqualifiedly magistrates—the law guardians
and the man in charge of the whole education—are discussed at the
beginning and the end of the section devoted to the magistracies
which are unqualifiedly magistracies. The man in charge of the whole
education must be a law guardian. He is to be elected for five years
by the secret vote of all magistrates with the exception of the Council, the election to take place in the temple of Apollon; certainly in
his election the lot is not used.

The Athenian adds a remark which would be suitable if he had
come to the end of the discussion of the magistracies. In fact, the
judges with whom he deals in the final section of his discussion
devoted to the magistrates are not unambiguously magistrates. The
remark in question deals with what ought to be done if a magistrate
dies before his term of office expires. By a "natural association of
ideas" the Athenian is led to state immediately afterwards what
ought to be done if a guardian of orphans dies: in a way all magistrates are guardians of orphans.

Judges are not simply magistrates, since their business is not
simply to give commands; only when they finally decide a suit by
pronouncing judgment do they act as magistrates. Only a minority
of the citizens are fit to be judges. The members of the highest court
which passes final judgment in litigation between individuals shall
be elected by the magistrates, each board of magistrates consecrating
that one of its members whom they deem best; the judges are to cast
their votes openly. Attendance at sessions of this court is obligatory
only for the members of the Council and of the other magistracies
which have elected the judges. Judges for the lower courts will be
elected by lot. If a man is accused of having wronged the city, the
multitude must participate in the judicial decision, for all are wronged
if the city is wronged (although, if an individual is wronged, he does
not ipso facto become a judge in his case, but the multitude would
resent it if it were denied that power); but the criminal investigation
shall be conducted by three of the highest magistrates upon whom
the defendant and the prosecutor have agreed. Whether Socrates
would have fared better in Kleinias' or the Athenian's city than he
fared in Athens cannot be guessed until one knows the Athenian's
law regarding impiety and the prosecution of that crime. His statements on the law courts are admittedly sketchy and provisional and
cannot be completed before the completion of the laws themselves.

The Athenian then turns to the laws themselves. In reply to
Kleinias' praise of what he had said and even greater praise of how

he had just linked up what had been said with what was to be said, the beginning and the end, he accepts the praise of what had been said, calling it the sensible play of old men; Kleinias, however, praises the noble seriousness of men who are not yet old which the Athenian reveals. Similar remarks which the Athenian had made earlier (685a7–8, 712b1–2) had not been corrected by Kleinias; it seems that by now the Athenian has won Kleinias' entire confidence. Thereupon the Athenian reminds him of the necessary limitation of what they are doing—a limitation which may be one reason why their doings should be called playful. He adduces the example of the painters who never reach the point where they no longer find anything to improve. (Kleinias has heard of this but has no experience of painting, which, according to the Athenian, is no loss for him.) Whatever may be true of painters in general, if someone intended to paint a living being of utmost beauty so that the painting could never deteriorate but would always become better as time went on, the painter, being mortal, must leave a successor who not only repairs the painting if it suffers through time but also corrects what the first painter failed to do owing to the weakness of his art. The example is applicable to the legislator, since the legislator paints the most beautiful (noble) life which he is able to paint. Measures must be taken to teach a successor to the legislator—a successor who guards the laws against deterioration and even improves them. This must be done here and now by the three interlocutors, who are in the evening of life. For it is not reasonable to expect that a man like the Athenian stranger will be available, after his demise, to the city to be founded, let alone to every generation; the triad of the interlocutors foreshadows the plurality of the legislators of the future. They have already made provisions for guardians of the laws; but the guardians of the laws must also be trained to be legislators. Accordingly, the Athenian addresses the guardians of the laws, asking them to fill the very numerous lacunae which the outline made by Megillos, himself, and Kleinias cannot help leaving, with a view to this single end: the virtue of a man who possesses that virtue of the soul which belongs to a human being and which he possesses owing to some pursuit or habit or possession or desire or opinion or some branches of learning; this end is the same for males and females, for young and old; no one must prefer any other good, not even the city, to this, but must prefer, if not subversion, surely his own exile to being ruled by worse men, i.e., to degrading slavery. We have seen earlier that the soul is to be honored more highly than the city.

The beginning of the laws proper, as distinguished from the laws determining the polity and the magistracies, is to be made with the laws concerning the sacred things. We must start from the number of landholders or plots, which is 5,040, a number divisible by twelve, and the division of the whole into twelve tribes, each tribe consisting therefore of 420 landholders, 420 also being divisible by twelve. Every section or division must be regarded as sacred, as a gift of a god. The twelveness of the tribes had already been linked up with the twelve gods (745d8–e1), i.e., the Olympian gods; now it is linked up with the twelve months and the revolution of the whole, i.e., as we may say, with cosmic gods. In one way or another every city recognizes divine sanction of its divisions, but the one proposed by the Athenian is of superior correctness because of the virtues of the number 5,040—virtues which are even greater than was previously stated. To each section—of the city and of the tribes (cf. 738d1–2 and 745d7–e2)—a god or a son of a god will be assigned with altars, and there will be periodic assemblies for sacrifices, in the first place for the sake of thanking for the god's favor or for soliciting it and in the second place for the promotion of familiarity and acquaintance among the citizens. Such acquaintance is necessary so that people will know their future spouses and their families as well as possible. This serious purpose is served by the choral plays, i.e., singing and dancing, of youths and girls who strip on these solemn occasions as far as decency permits and thus can view one another with a proper pretext—all this under the supervision of those in charge of the choruses. The details regarding such supervision have, it is true, not yet been provided for, but, as we have already learned, many small details cannot but be omitted by the legislator, and they must be filled in on the basis of experience of each succeeding year by those in charge; after ten years' experience regarding sacrifices and dances the time will have come for the final enactment of what seems to be fine, and this must remain unchanged and treated as the other laws laid down by the legislator at the beginning. Voluntarily one must never make any changes in these laws; if some necessity seems to require change, the utmost caution must be taken: all magistrates, the whole citizen body, and all oracles of the gods must agree to the change.

We have now reached the end of the laws regarding the sacred things, the laws which come first. The bulk of the statement on this subject does not deal with the sacred things as such. Having spoken of marriage in connection with the festivals in honor of the gods, the Athenian turns next to the marriage laws. He had used the marriage laws as the example for elucidating the relation between the preludes and the laws; he had selected for this purpose the marriage laws because they come first "by nature" (720e10–721a8). In considering that passage we were somewhat perplexed by the Athenian's suggestion that the legislator should speak first of how the gods are to be honored. In accordance with that suggestion he now treats the laws regarding the sacred things, or the sacred things or the gods, as first, but not by nature first (cf. 697c1–2).

When a man has become twenty-five years old, he may begin to think of marriage, and he must have married by the time he is thirty-five; he could hardly marry before he is thirty if he were drafted into the country police, in which he would have to serve for two years between the ages of twenty-five and thirty, for while on that service he must eat and sleep in the common mess hall of the district (760b7–c7; 762b6–d1). The Athenian admonishes the young man of marriageable age to consider, in choosing his future wife, not the wealth but the character traits of her family. If he is rash, he should select the daughter of slow and steady parents, and if he is steady and slow, he should make the opposite choice. Generally, one must consider in marrying what is beneficial to the city and not what is most pleasant to oneself. The pleasant is that by which everyone is attracted according to nature and hence in particular that which is most similar to oneself. Hence the rich seek to intermarry with the rich, the quick with the quick, and so on. This will lead to a polarization of the city, the opposite of friendship. To compel people by law to choose their mates according to what is best for the city would be ridiculous and in addition would provoke the anger of many. For the many are not able to discern that the right blending of the spouses is important with a view to their offspring, i.e., with a view to something that arouses their self-love more keenly than the well-being of the whole. Since law is powerless against nature in this matter, one must strive to persuade people by enchanting speeches that the quality of the offspring is to be considered more highly than wealth and by casting reproach on those concerned with wealthy matches. As we see, the Athenian has tacitly ceased to address a young man and begun to address the legislator or the magistrates. He briefly recapitulates what he had said in the first prelude to the marriage laws (721b7–c8) about everyone's duty to leave children behind. He amplifies his earlier statement about the fines to be imposed on bachelors, now making use of the distinction, not yet known then, of the citizens into the four property classes and about their loss of certain honors. He proceeds similarly in regard to the prohibition against dowries. He adds the provision that expenses and marriage fees must be kept within narrow bounds, although more may be spent on such occasions by the rich than by the poor. Drunkenness is unseemly in general; it is particularly unbecoming for the bride and for the bridegroom, for they cannot know when they will generate a child, and the state of body and soul of the parents at the time of begetting is likely to affect decisively the state of body and mind of the child. Finally, the young couple is told to reside in that one of the two houses belonging to the bridegroom's father in which the bridegroom's parents do not reside; nor should the young couple live with the bride's parents; the separation will cause longing and thus strengthen friendship.

The next subject is servants or slaves, i.e., those human beings who are part of the new household prior to the birth of children. The same order is followed by Xenophon, in his *Oeconomicus*, who completely fails to discuss the upbringing of children, whereas Plato devotes the whole of Book Seven to this subject. Xenophon does not treat the upbringing of children in his own name but reports how the Spartans and the Persians proceeded in this matter; he does discuss Socrates educating "the young" and human beings in general in his Socratic writings as a whole (see especially his *Apology of Socrates* 20). Xenophon devotes four chapters of his *Oeconomicus* to the education of a young wife by a husband; Plato is silent on this subject because the education with which he is concerned in the *Laws* is altogether public education. Slaves are troublesome possessions, and failure in the right treatment of slaves was particularly conspicuous in Sparta. (Hence, Megillos now becomes the interlocutor for a short while.) The Athenian limits himself for the time being to saying that the Spartans' treatment of their helots is praised by some and not praised by others. Generally, there are two opposite opinions and experiences regarding slaves. On the one hand we all would say that one should acquire slaves who are as well-meaning and good as possible: many slaves have proved to be superior to brothers and sons in regard to every virtue and have saved their masters and their whole households. On the other hand, it is held that slaves are utterly depraved and can in no way be trusted; this view is sanctioned by the wisest of our poets, who says (through the mouth of the swineherd Eunaios) that on the day men fall into slavery Zeus takes away half of their sense: slaves are not men who are by nature deprived of half of their sense. Zeus takes away half of men's sense when they fall into slavery probably in order to make them fit to serve as slaves or to make them slavish; the result, however, is that they become bad slaves. At any rate, those who hold this view treat their slaves like beasts and thus make their souls much more slavish than the mere fact of enslavement makes them. Those who hold the opposite opinion treat their slaves as friends. Neither way of treating them is commendable. Surely men do not wish to be slaves. In order to prevent servile rebellions, the slaves should not be of one stock nor, as far as possible, of one speech. Above all, one must treat them correctly, not only for their sake, but still more for one's own sake. One must avoid insolence and injustice toward them, if possible even more than toward one's equals: the genuinely just man will avoid injustice precisely toward those human beings whom it is easy to wrong because they are weaker than he. On the other hand, one must leave no doubt that one is a master: one must give commands, not try to persuade; familiarity is ruinous to the master-slave relation.

The Athenian turns then to the subject of buildings. Before people can live in a new colony and, in particular, marry, houses will have to be built. But the order of what is to be done "in deed" is not necessarily the order of what is to be said "in speech": the houses are for the sake of married life, and therefore the marriage laws precede the regulations regarding buildings (cf. Aristotle, *Eth. Nic.* 1112b23–24 and 1140b16). What is "by nature" first is not first in every respect. Accordingly, the laws regarding the sacred things preceded the marriage laws: there must first be sacred things before there can be marriage. Are the sacred things for the sake of marriage and other things required by nature? (Cf. *Euthyphro* 12d2–e8 and *Crito* 49c7–8.) One might expect from the context that the Athenian would speak above all of private houses; in fact he speaks above all of temples and, most extensively, of the city walls, of which he disapproves in agreement with Sparta. Yet walls might be necessary. In that case private houses must be built accordingly. This is all the Athenian has to say on private houses. The contrast with what the Xenophontic Socrates has to say on this subject is revealing: the Xenophontic Socrates is concerned with domestic, private convenience (*Memorabilia* III 8.8–10; cf. *Oeconomicus* 9.2–4); the Athenian remains as close to the regulations laid down by the Socrates of the *Republic* as the *hypothesis* of the *Laws* permits (*Republic* 416d6–7, 548a8–b2; cf. *Laws* 776a1).

Continuing to follow the lucid order of the subjects, the Athenian turns next to the life of the young couple prior to the birth of a child. What will be said on this subject is still harder to accept for the multitude than the many other hard things already said. But what seems to be correct and true must be said in all circumstances, as the Athenian here says addressing Kleinias, who of course agrees. In a kindred context Glaukon had urged Socrates to state his opinion since his listeners are neither deprived of sense nor untrustworthy nor malevolent; and Socrates had granted to him that it is safe to say the truth which one knows, about the greatest and dearest things among men who are sensible and friends (*Republic* 450d3–e1; cf. *Gorgias* 486e5ff.). The Athenian omits here all such qualifications in spite of what he had said in praise of the Dorian law of laws (635d7–e6), because what he is going to say about the way of life of men and women will be much less shocking than what Socrates said on this subject in the *Republic*. (But see 781b6–c2.)

He begins by taking issue with those legislators who think that they should regulate only the public and common life and permit everyone to lead his daily life as he wishes; they do not know that by not subjecting private life to the law, they endanger the citizen's willingness to follow the law in public matters as well: the unregulated private life acts like a cancerous growth. Accordingly, newly married men must partake of the common meals in exactly the same way as they did before they married. The common meals were a Dorian institution to which the Athenian had raised some objections in a different context (636b1–5); he is now silent on these objections because he is about to improve the Dorian institutions: both men and women must partake of the common meals. This is a surprising innovation, but common meals for men also were at the beginning a surprising innovation, dangerous to establish. Above all, common meals for men are a defective institution if they are not supplemented by common meals for women. One may grant that not everything badly ordered or not ordered at all has a deleterious effect on the things well ordered in a city. But this does not apply to the case under discussion. The Dorian legislators mistakenly refrained from establishing common meals for women. As we know, the time when the Athenian hesitated to criticize the Dorian laws has long gone. He now traces the institution of common meals for men, not to a divine legislator, but to the necessity imposed by war or some other calamity, to a legislating calamity, to "some divine necessity"—to a necessity which was divine because it was providential or because it led to something good or for both reasons. The Dorian legislators have given in to women's natural proneness to secretiveness and trickiness—a proneness stemming from their weakness. But precisely because the female nature is inferior to the male in regard to virtue, it is all the more in need of being subjected to order and law. It seems that that inferiority stems from woman's greater weakness. The Athenian and the Socrates of the *Republic* (455e1–2, 456a10–11) agree, at any rate, as to woman's greater weakness. The Athenian agrees with Socrates also as to the conclusion that it is better for the happiness of the city to order all pursuits for women and men in common. The women must then be compelled to consume food and drink within the sight of all. The compulsion is necessary because they are accustomed to live in retirement and in obscurity, and they will resist with all their power being dragged into the light; their resistance is likely to be far too strong for the legislator to overcome. Nevertheless, the speech about the whole polity must not be permitted to be a failure; therefore the Athenian is willing to say what he proposes is good and becoming if his interlocutors are willing to listen; they are naturally most eager to listen. He is silent on the question of whether what he proposes is possible as distinguished from desirable: just as Socrates, while taking up the question whether the corresponding proposal is possible as distinguished from desirable, drops it immediately (*Republic* 466d6ff.).

Having demanded a break with the habits of women everywhere, a break with a most powerful tradition, with the ancient, the Athenian turns for support to what is older than all traditions, to what antedates all political life. He refers to what he had said at the beginning of the political investigation proper, at the beginning of Book Three. He now makes clearer than he did then that the human race may always have existed and will always exist. In any case, the time during which there have been human beings is so immeasurably long that all kinds of changes in cities, including their coming into being and perishing, have taken place, that all kinds of practices, all sorts of desire for food and drink have emerged all over the earth and in all sorts of ways, and through all kinds of variations of the seasons the animals are likely to have undergone very many changes. (Presumably, therefore, common meals for women were customary at some time somewhere.) This state of things is reflected in the opinions or traditions regarding how men lived in early times. The custom of human sacrifice, which still survives in many places, reminds us of the time antedating agriculture and might suggest to us that early men were cannibals. On the other hand, we hear that men brought no bloody sacrifices at all to the gods and abstained from all animal food, and this suggests that in early times men abstained from all killing. The purpose of the Athenian's remarks on the diametrically opposed views regarding sacrifices is admittedly obscure; to say nothing of other obscurities, does he mean that both extreme views are wrong, and that the intermediate view, which approves of the sacrificing and eating of (certain) beasts, is correct? Are both cannibalism and vegetarianism perversions? (Cf. the opposition of the extremely kind and the extremely harsh views regarding slaves and the approved intermediate view in 776c1–778a6.) The Athenian tries to make clear the purport of his statement by speaking of man's basic desires, which are basic because they are common to all animals (cf. Aristotle, *Eth. Nic.* 1155b1–9), although they are modified in the case of men by the presence of the intellect. He points to the threefold need and desire which affects all things human and which, if properly guided, leads to virtue: the desire for food, drink, and procreation; these desires are diseases inasmuch as they tend toward what is called pleasant as distinguished from what is best; one must try to check them by the three greatest things: fear, law, and the true speech, using in addition the Muses and the gods of gymnastic contests. The desire which makes itself felt latest is the keenest and, in the case of human beings, the most dangerous. The Athenian fails to state that, from the facts pointed out or alluded to by him, it follows that common meals for women are good and becoming. Instead, he almost promises that in the orderly course of the argument the question of whether there shall be common meals for women will be settled.

After the Athenian has regulated weddings and what is immediately connected with them, he turns to the rules of conduct pertaining to the generation of children (783b2). In order to produce for the city the most beautiful and best children, the future parents must apply their minds to one another and to the making of children. What this means is to some extent spelled out in the rules ordained at the marriage sacrifices and rites. The future parents' compliance with these rules is to be examined by women inspectors who report in their meetings their observations about the future parents' domestic conduct. The women inspectors may enter the houses of the young people and, by instructions as well as by threats, stop them from their mistake and folly. Girls should marry when they are sixteen to twenty years old, men when they are thirty to thirty-five. Women are eligible for magistracies when they are forty, men when they are thirty. Men are liable to military service between the ages of twenty and sixty. If need be, women may have to serve in the army, after they have borne children, until they are fifty years old. These provisions illustrate what had been said about the weakness of the female sex.

Book Seven

This Book—the most extensive Book of the *Laws*—is devoted to the subject which follows next in the natural order: the rearing and education of children. To the extent to which the rearing takes place in the home, it is not properly regulated by laws but only by instruction and admonition, for laws regarding things which take place every day in the privacy of the home can easily be evaded, and the evasion fosters disobedience to the laws in general. The Athenian does not recognize a sacred right of privacy, but he sees that it is beneath the dignity of the legislator or of the magistrates to spy on how citizens arrange trivial things even if those things are not trivial when viewed in the light of their consequences. Since education aims at the excellence of the bodies and the souls, it consists of gymnastics and Music. Gymnastics comes first in time (cf. *Republic* 376e6–8). Strange as it may seem, it must begin while the child is still in the mother's womb. Since being shaken and stirred is, as such, conducive to health and growth, and even to pugnacity, the child must be exposed to motion both prior to birth and after; the pregnant women must take walks and the young children must be carried about by female servants. The legislator would make himself ridiculous by laying down laws to this effect. His admonitions must be enforced by the master of the household, who will treat them as laws. This is one way in which admonitions can be rendered effective.

The remarks on the salutary effect on the newborn child of being almost constantly moved about fall under the heading "gymnastics" or the rearing of the body. Yet they supply the rudiments of the rearing of the soul as well. When small children suffer from sleeplessness, the mothers lull them to rest by rocking them constantly in their arms and by singing tunes to them; that is to say, they treat them as one cures those who are out of their minds in Bakchic frenzy and are quieted down by dance and song. Earlier the Athenian had spoken of the initial madness of the very young, whereby they are given to disorderly sounds and motions (672c1–6); now he speaks of orderly sounds and motions as cures—for the initial madness? Is it not possible to state more precisely what that madness is? At Kleinias' request, he states the plausible cause of both kinds of disturbance and their treatment. Both little children and the frenzied are in a state of fright, and this is due in both cases to some bad disposition of the soul. The internal motion of fear and frenzy is counteracted and mastered by the motion applied from without and thus brings about calm in the soul and the cessation of the distressing palpitation of the heart. The children fall asleep and others who are awake come to their senses by means of dancing and flute playing with the help of gods whom they happen to worship by sacrifices. In the case of the little children, at any rate, the mastering of the fright in question is a first step toward the acquisition of courage, which is a part of the virtue of the soul, as well as of good temper and therewith of the virtue of the soul altogether: gymnastic serves, to say the least, the virtue of the soul as well as that of the body (cf. *Republic* 410b5–c3). In order to prevent little children from becoming ill-tempered human beings, one must not spoil them; one must not stop their weeping and crying by giving to them whatever makes them cease weeping and crying; they must learn to bear griefs, fears, and pains. To spoil children is as bad as to make them humble and nasty by harsh treatment. In their earliest years they must be directed toward the correct way of life, which consists neither in the pursuit of pleasure nor in the complete avoidance of pain but in that gracious even-temperedness which we all, following some oracular tradition, ascribe to god too. In order to be divine, one must surely be reconciled to the fact that life without pain is impossible.

While the Athenian had to overcome some resistance on the part of Kleinias, and of the taciturn Megillos, to his speech about the correct way of life, there is no disagreement whatever among the three men as to this point: everything said about the rearing of the very young belongs to what the many call unwritten customs or ancestral laws. While they cannot be laws proper, they are the bonds of every political order, connecting the laws already laid down and those to be laid down in the future. They are not, strictly speaking, ancestral or ancient: Kleinias' city is new. And the points which the Athenian had made were innovations. The so-called ancestral laws are the unchangeable customs which are the foundation and the safeguard of the laws proper. This is to say nothing of the fact that unwritten customs or ancestral laws may be bad, whereas the rules set forth by the Athenian are as good as he can make them. The ancestral laws spoken of here are the Athenian's admonitions if deferentially accepted by a city without thus acquiring the force of laws; they are those admonitions appearing in the garb of what has come down from antiquity. This procedure can be justified by the consideration that what is correct is according to nature and that nature is more ancient than any custom. Thus the appeal from custom or tradition, however venerable, to nature becomes defensible. The Athenian gives us an example of this when he takes issue with the almost universal custom of treating the right hand as stronger than the left: the two hands are by nature equally strong; the prevailing custom is against nature and has no other root than the folly of nurses and mothers. The Athenian does not stop to indicate why nurses and mothers commit this mistake: is it due to superstition? are women more superstitious than men? and why does superstition prefer the right to the left? In the city to be founded, all children, boys and girls, will be ambidextrous, for ambidexterity is an immense asset in war. Socrates had appealed from unreasonable custom to nature when demanding the equality of the sexes (*Republic* 456c1–2). The Athenian uses the demand for ambidexterity as an entering wedge or preparation for demanding a much greater degree of equality of the sexes than the cities were in the habit of allowing: the right is related to the left as the male is to the female (Aristotle, *Metaphysics* 986a34–35). But women are admittedly by nature inferior to men in regard to virtue (781b2–3; cf. 909e5 and context). Does not therefore the correspondence of male and right, on the one hand, and female and left, on the other, render questionable the asserted natural equality of right and left?

The Athenian next completes his account of gymnastics; the completion will, however, prove to be incomplete (813a7ff.). Deviating from what he had said earlier (791c5–9), he now severs the connection between gymnastics and the virtue of the soul. One of the two parts of gymnastics is dance. He recommends particularly the solemn dance procession of the young in full battle array in honor of Athena, that warlike virgin-goddess, as it formed part of the cult in Athens. The reminder of Athena is appropriate in the context in which the question regarding the two sexes, especially with a view to war, is waiting in the background.

The Athenian opens his account of Music, which has a different function from that of the discussion of the same subject in the first two Books since it does not serve the vindication of symposia as the

safeguard of education, by saying something very strange and unaccustomed, which he is apprehensive to say. All cities are altogether
ignorant about the fact that the permanence of the laws depends
on the permanence, the unchangeability, of children's games and
playthings; for only in this way can they learn from the very beginning to esteem what is old and to scorn what is new; the contempt
of antiquity is the greatest mischief for any city. The Dorians are of
course in full agreement with the end which the Athenian has in
mind, although the way which he proposes is very strange and runs
counter to the custom of all cities. Every change, he asserts, except
that of what is bad, is detrimental; as regards both bodies and souls,
what has become customary and familiar to them is conducive to
their pleasure and well-being. Hence it is a piece of divine good luck
when laws have remained unchanged for a long time so that no one
subject to them has any memory or tradition of the laws' ever having
been different from what they are now; in that case the whole soul
is filled with reverence for the established things and shudders at the
thought of changing any of them. But the legislator-founder cannot
wait for such a piece of divine good luck; he must devise something
which has the same effect. The device consists precisely in preventing
any change in children's games which hitherto have been regarded
by all as play, i.e., as not worthy of seriousness. The Athenian thus
leads up to a reassertion of what was said earlier about the legislative or political art of the Egyptians (657a4) who have consecrated
all dances and songs. He adds now the provision that determinate
dances and songs must be fixed for the different festivals of the various gods and demons and that whoever proposes any changes in
matters of this kind will be liable to be excluded from the festivals
by the priests and priestesses acting together with the law guardians
and, if he resists, can be prosecuted as long as he lives by anyone
for impiety. The right kind of piety and the right kind of education
support one another.

The definiteness with which the Athenian sets forth his quite unfamiliar suggestion is balanced by a profound hesitation which he
has, and which his interlocutors ought to have, about embarking
on a road of which one does not know whither it leads. He overcomes this hesitation to some extent by considering the fact that the
ancients have given tunes played on the lyre the name of "nomes"
(*nomoi*) and thus seem to have had some dim divination of the need
for fixing or consecrating the songs and dances of the young: the
ancients at best only divined what the Athenian clearly sees; but his
clear insight would not be sufficient, sufficiently strong, without that

weak and shaky support. He thus prepares his further suggestion that, if at all possible, no mournful, dirgelike songs should be permitted: the initial or fundamental fright must not inspire the piety of the city. This law is carried, as Kleinias says, by a unanimous vote. Also accepted is the second law regarding Music which stipulates that the sacrifices to the gods be accompanied by prayers. The difficulty regarding prayers calls for a third law: one may unwittingly pray for something bad while thinking that it is good, for instance, for moneyed wealth; the men who compose the songs, the poets, cannot be trusted to compose correct prayers; their production must therefore be examined and approved by the highest authorities in the city before they can be divulged to any man in the city who lacks authority. A fourth and a fifth law provide for hymns and praises, coupled with prayers, to gods, demons, and heroes, and for praises of deceased citizens, men or women, who have performed noble and toilsome deeds of body or soul and have been obedient to the laws. The Athenian is here, as we see, less austere and more pious than the Socrates of the *Republic*, who approves only of hymns to the gods and praises of the good (607a3–5; cf. *Laws* 687c9–688e2). He concludes this part of the argument appropriately by mentioning the fact that there are many ancient and beautiful poems and dances of the ancients from which competent men, none younger than fifty, can make selections of what is suitable to the new city. Being beautiful, those poems and dances are pleasing to well-bred people. Ancient poems which are not suitable must, if possible, be corrected by present-day poets acting under the supervision of those who execute the will of the legislator. Here, as distinguished from the first discussion of Music (665c5–7), hardly any allowance is made for spontaneous innovation in Music. The reason is the same as that for which the Athenian's novel admonitions were clothed in the garb of ancient laws and for which he had made the demand, running counter to all custom, i.e., involving the greatest change, that the children's games must never be changed and thus shall acquire the appearance of always having been the same or of never having had a beginning: the new city is to appear to its members within the limits of the possible as possessing all the splendors of the most ancient antiquity.

One of the innovations proposed by the Athenian was common meals for women (780d9–781d1), an institution particularly necessary on account of the inferiority of women in regard to virtue and for this very reason likely to be violently opposed by them. Speaking of education, he must face the question whether boys and girls should receive the same or a different education. Before turning to this question, he does two things. First, he reminds his listeners of the natural difference between the sexes as it affects Music: different kinds of song are fitting for the different sexes in accordance with their natural difference; the grand and what tends to manliness must be particular to the males and the decorous and modest to the females. This would seem to show that different kinds of education for the two sexes are according to nature. It is therefore necessary for him to reconsider the meaning of education as a whole.

Education (*paideia*), belonging together with play or game (*paidia*), came to sight as the preparation of children for the responsibilities, as we say, for the serious business of citizenship (643b1–e6, 652b3–653c4, 659c9–e5): education or play is less serious than the activity of the mature citizen, of "the serious one" (*spoudaios*) (757a2, 814e5–6). The Athenian had taken issue before with the view that children's games are just children's games and hence not to be taken too seriously (788b6–c1). Now he asserts that it is indeed an unfortunate necessity that the affairs of human beings be taken seriously but that these are not worthy of great seriousness. He explains this somewhat cryptic assertion as follows. By nature god—god alone—deserves full seriousness, but man is a plaything of god, devised as such, and being a plaything of god is the best about him. Therefore everyone, man or woman, must spend his whole life playing at the most beautiful kinds of play. Originally the Athenian had said that every living being is a divine puppet and had left it open whether it is put together as a plaything for gods or for some serious purpose (644d7–9). In the meantime he had characterized repeatedly the action of the three old men as a kind of play; when he did this for the third time, he was gently corrected by Kleinias (685a7–8, 712b1–2, 769a1–3). Above all, in the meantime we have heard that one can easily be led to believe that no human being ever legislates but that all kinds of misfortune legislate for us, or rather that god governs all human things and with him chance and opportunity, and that very little is left for human art to do (709a1–c3): the relative impotence of the legislative or political art seems to show that man is simply a plaything of god. The Athenian's view of how human beings should live is opposed to what men think now. Now they think—we expect to hear that play should be in the service of seriousness, but, he says, they believe that seriousness should be for the sake of play; for they believe that activities connected with war, which are serious, should be well-ordered for the sake of peace. What he objects to then is the belief that war is more serious than peace: the most serious thing is play and education, and play and education belong to peace rather than to war; therefore everyone must live the life of peace as much and as well as he can. The play which the Athenian has in mind consists in one's sacrificing, singing, and dancing with the result that he is able to make the gods gracious to him and to repel enemies and defeat them in battle. One is left wondering whether that result—the grace of the gods and the defeat of enemies—is not in fact the most serious end for the sake of which serious play is necessary and whether it is for this reason that human beings are not worthy of seriousness. But let us go on. What kinds of song and dance will bring about both results—the grace of the gods and victory in war—has been stated partly in outline before; as for what is still missing, one must trust Homer's—or his Athena's —words to Telemachos to this extent, at any rate, that the gods will give the future citizens the necessary guidance regarding sacrifices and choral dances. We must never forget however that men are in the main puppets, partaking of the truth only in some small points (cf. 889d1–2). Megillos, the Spartan, is thoroughly displeased with this depreciation of the human race. The Athenian apologizes, therefore, excusing his statement by the fact that he had looked away toward the god and had therefore been affected in the way he was. We recall that the goal of education is the perfect human being (653a9). But if there is no perfect human being, if no human being is simply wise but in the best case a lover of wisdom (*philosophos*), one cannot help looking away toward the simply wise being, the god. The dissension between Megillos and the Athenian is the dissension between the political man who necessarily takes the human things very seriously, and the philosopher. It was with a view to Megillos and the many like him that the Athenian had left the true end of man in the ambiguity pointed out above.

Returning to the particulars regarding education and referring to some points he may or may not have made earlier, he first lays down a demand which he clearly had not mentioned before: the teachers in matters related to war and in Music must be strangers. In the same context he stresses the fact that education is to be compulsory and public, not parental. Is this why the teachers of gymnastics and Music must be strangers? Or is the reason that citizens ought not to be teachers? Moreover, and above all, according to the Athenian's law, girls would receive the same education as boys. This demand could be thought to follow from the insight that war, that particularly virile activity, is not the most serious thing. Somewhat to our surprise, however, the Athenian's law provides that girls be trained just

as boys, precisely in horsemanship and gymnastics; he refers to innumerable ancient myths as well as to what he knows of women
living in the region of Pontos in order to show that the military
training of women is possible and hence that the exclusion of women
from military service which obtains among the Greeks is most senseless. The Athenian's law demands that the female sex must share
with the male as much as possible not only in education but in
everything else. It runs counter to custom, as Kleinias observes. But
the alternative would be that one devise a different way of life for
the women from that for the men. The various arrangements which
have been devised with this end in mind are all of them unsatisfactory. This is true even of the Spartan order, according to which girls
are to participate in gymnastics and Music and women to abstain
from wool-work but to take no part in military service, thus becoming wholly unable to fight for the city, the fatherland, and their
children and to imitate the goddess by taking shield and spear. The
Spartan order, which takes care of the men but lets the women
indulge in luxury and disorderly conduct, while preferable to the
Athenian order in particular, is then still most blameworthy. This
blame of Sparta—of the Spartan legislator—calls forth a mild protest by Megillos, who is easily appeased by Kleinias; the Athenian
does not even have to apologize, as he had to when he had "run
down" not Sparta but the human race (804b7).

Next the question arises as to what kind of life the men and
women of Kleinias' city should lead. In describing this life, which
is free from all drudgery, the Athenian mentions that there will be
common meals separately for men and for women. When he had
first reached the subject of common meals for women, it looked as
if this institution was meant to counteract sexual desire (780d9ff.).
Now it appears that it is devised for enabling them to participate in
war. The best arrangement, the Athenian reminds us, would perhaps
require community of wives, children, dwellings, and belongings;
but one must be glad if the second best city is possible and see what
kind of arrangement would fit it. The men and women of the city
are by a just law commanded to the acquisition of virtue of body
and soul; night and day are hardly long enough for this purpose.
It might be unbecoming for the legislator to state the many petty
details regarding domestic life—such prescriptions would be wholly
unnecessary in the simply best city in which there is no domestic
life—and in particular about that wakefulness at night which is
proper for those who are to guard a whole city continuously and
diligently. This much, however, must be said: no one must spend the

whole night in sleep; the master and the mistress of the house must be the first to rise in the morning, and it must be regarded as disgraceful for them to be awakened by their slaves; rulers, masters, and mistresses must devote part of the night to the performance of their duties; for much sleep is not naturally suitable to our bodies and souls and the actions of our bodies and souls: no one is worth much while he is asleep (cf. *Apology of Socrates* 40c9–e4). Apart from all other benefits which the recommended way of spending the night procures, it is likely to bestow some manliness on the souls of everyone in the cities: concern with the promotion of manliness is never absent from the Athenian's speeches about education.

In the early morning, children must be led to school by their tutors; for children must never be left to themselves, since no beast is as hard to handle, as treacherous, sly, and insolent as a child. The ultimate supervision of children and teachers has been entrusted to the law guardian who is in charge of the whole education. He must himself be educated by the law, i.e., by the Athenian. He has received sufficient guidance regarding choral songs and dances but not regarding writings without meter. He has received sufficient guidance regarding military instruction but not regarding the teaching of reading and writing, lyre playing, reckoning, and such knowledge of the courses of the divine things—namely, stars, sun, and moon—as is necessary for every city for the purpose of regulating the calendar so that seasons, sacrifices, and festivals will be observed according to nature. The list of topics of instruction will prove to be incomplete; choral songs and military instruction, whose treatment is said to have been completed, are taken up again in the sequel (cf. also 796d6–e5); nor is the order in which the subjects still to be treated are mentioned the same as the order in which they are in fact treated. What is the solution to this Platonic riddle? At the beginning, the Athenian follows to some extent the order of the subjects still to be treated by speaking first of instruction in reading and writing and then of instruction in lyre playing. Instruction in reading and writing must begin when the child is ten years old and must last for three years; thereafter three years must be devoted to instruction in lyre playing. These provisions are equally obligatory on all. But as for quickness and beauty in writing it is all right to make different demands on children of different natural gifts: not all future citizens will and can receive the same education. Some embarrassment arises concerning children's reading of writings by poets which are not meant for accompaniment by the lyre and of writings without meter, for some of these writings are harmful. The Athenian may think of the many writings in poetry and prose which foster impiety (cf. 886b10–e5, 891b2–4). He is certainly hesitant to speak against many myriads of men. Kleinias encourages him by reminding him of the fact that many of their laws previously laid down regarding weighty matters were not much to the taste of the many; he is also encouraged by his own reflection that what he is going to say is perhaps not as unpopular as he first thought. Many myriads say that the correctly educated young must have learned thoroughly and by heart the entire work of many poets or at least selected passages from them. But everyone is likely to admit that not everything said by every poet is said nobly. Hence the law guardian in charge of education is in need of a standard by which to judge what is and what is not good for the young to learn. Such a standard, the Athenian contends, is by some good fortune available in the speeches which the three men have exchanged from dawn till now; they seem to him to have been spoken altogether like a proem and to be more suitable for the young than any poetry or prose he had ever read or heard; in their light the suitability of all other writings should be judged, and they should be the prime reading matter of the young; teachers should be compelled to study them and to praise them. The Athenian's mentioning of prose writings at the beginning of his enumeration of topics still to be discussed (809b3–c1) has become fully justified. Yet Kleinias has some doubt about the whole educational scheme proposed by the Athenian; that doubt cannot be dispelled before the interlocutors have completed their legislative work. Turning next to lyre playing, the Athenian repeats what he had said in Book Two about the sixty-year-old singers of the Dionysiac chorus as judges of the propriety of musical imitations of the passions of the soul. He now omits the fertile complexities and ambiguities of the first statement; this is partly due to the fact that the Dionysiac chorus can now be presumed to be thoroughly indoctrinated with the teachings of the *Laws*.

After making some further remarks on instruction in lyre playing, and while again referring to earlier statements, he seems to put an end to his discussion of Music. He unmistakably turns again to dancing and everything else pertaining to gymnastics of the body; what he is going to say on that subject will complete the discussion of it, just as what he had said about Music had completed the discussion of Music. Boys will be instructed by dancing masters and girls by dancing mistresses. The fact that dancing is subsumed under gymnastics and his mention of the two sexes leads him to speak again of the military training of both men and women. Women must undergo thorough military training, if for no other reason at least for this: that they will be able to defend the children and the rest of the noncombatants when the whole male army has left the city in order to assail the enemy, or that when the whole armed force is attacked in the city by superior power, barbarian or Greek, the women can participate in the fighting: it would be a great disgrace if the women were brought up in such a manner that they cannot do what birds do, which without fear of death or any other danger fight for their young against the strongest beasts; but instead run straight away to temples, besetting all altars and shrines, and thus give man the reputation of being by nature the most cowardly of all beasts. Military training of women, more generally, equal education of both sexes is to counteract the misplaced or excessive piety to which the female sex is prone. Kleinias fully agrees, strengthening his agreement by an oath, his third oath, the last preceding oath having occurred in Book Four (720e10). The oath draws our attention, just as the oaths did in the former cases, to the presence of the problem of the gods.

We are now in a position to survey an important, perhaps the most important, if somewhat hidden, thread of the speeches which have hitherto occurred in Book Seven. The primary task of education consists in enabling children to overcome the initial or fundamental fright, in acquiring a fundamental manliness. The achievement of this goal is endangered by the fact that the primary educators are women, who are by nature inferior to men in regard to virtue in general and to manliness in particular, for there is a certain tension between piety and manliness: men live no longer under the rule of Kronos. Women must therefore receive the same education and especially the same military education as men. Two grave difficulties arise here. First, the proposed equality is a radical innovation, perhaps an innovation not agreeing with nature, and veneration for antiquity must permeate the whole city if it is to be healthy; this difficulty is overcome somehow by the fact that one can present this and other innovations in the garb of ancestral laws, if not as demanded by nature itself. Secondly, the more than Dorian emphasis on military training seems to support the Dorian view that the ultimate end is victory in war, which seems to depend on the grace of the gods, but is not play and education that end? The second difficulty is perhaps disposed of by the educational provisions which follow.

After a brief reference to the still unsettled details concerning wrestling, which must be understood to be strictly subservient to its use in battle, the Athenian returns to the subject of dancing. Dancing, we must not forget, belongs to the gymnastics of the body. There are two kinds of dance: the grand, which imitates the movements of beautiful bodies, and the low, which imitates the movements of ugly bodies. Each of the two kinds of dance consists in its turn of two kinds. The serious kind imitates either beautiful bodies and manly souls engaged in fighting or moderate souls being in a state of doing well and of enjoyment of temperate pleasures. The last may properly be called peaceful and the first warlike. There is a kind of dance which cannot be delineated as either peaceful or warlike and which is to be dismissed as unpolitical; it consists of Bakchic dances, in which intoxicated people imitate, as they say, Nymphs, Pans, Sileni, and Satyrs in connection with the performance of some sort of expiations and initiations. The Athenian adds a subdivision of unwarlike dances, in which men honor the gods and the children of the gods: in agreement with his earlier statement on the misplaced piety of women he had not said that in warlike dances men honor the gods and the children of the gods, although both kinds of dance form, of course, part of the worship of the gods.

After he has concluded his speech about the part played by beautiful bodies and noble souls in choric presentation, the Athenian turns to the presentation of ugly bodies and thoughts, in a word, to comedy. He does not make use of the bipartition of the dances which imitate the movements of ugly bodies, perhaps because he has already disposed of satyr plays. It is at least equally likely, however, that in speaking of comedy he, as it were, forgets about that bipartition because the consideration of comedy leads him with a kind of necessity to the consideration of tragedy. In considering comedy and tragedy he is still dealing with dances and hence with gymnastics; we have stressed, and not unduly stressed, what seems to be the high point of his speech on gymnastics. That thought is subterraneously continued in his speech on comedy and tragedy.

One must know the ridiculous in order to know the serious (and vice versa), i.e., in order to become sensible. But one must not do and say ridiculous things (except where it is appropriate). Hence comedies must be the work of slaves and hired foreigners: no male or female citizen must be seen devoting himself to this kind of imitation; and comic performances must always abound in novel conceits: the fact that in this unique case innovation is required underlines the undesirable character of comedy; and the ridiculous loses its character to some extent by repetition, while the noble cannot be repeated often enough. The Athenian discusses tragedy by addressing tragic poets who might come to the new city and ask whether they will be permitted to enter it and its territory in order to present their works. He implies that no citizen would be a tragic poet or act in tragedies. He would respectfully reply to those divine men in the name of the founders-legislators that the latter themselves are the authors of the most noble and best tragedies possible, for their whole polity is an imitation of the noblest and best life—it is an imitation of the life under Kronos' benign rule (713e6–7)—and such an imitation they assert to be the truest tragedy (tragedy as such meaning to be an imitation of the noblest and best life); hence they and the tragic poets are rival composers of the noblest drama, which, as they expect, only the true law is by nature able to achieve; in addition, tragedians are likely to contradict the teachings of the laws in most points; the tragic poets will therefore not be given permission to present their works before the magistrates have passed judgment on whether those works are suitable for the city: if what the tragedians say is the same as, or better than, what the legislators say, they will be granted the requested permission, but if not, the permission will be denied. That is to say, tragedy may or may not be admitted to the city, but comedy surely will be admitted.

We have now reached what is in fact the end of the discussion of both gymnastics and Music. But the Athenian does not say so; this is in accordance with his obfuscation of the difference between gymnastics and Music and with the purpose which that obfuscation serves. Kleinias' earlier doubt (812a5–6) has now been removed.

The Athenian turns next to three branches of learning which are emphatically proper to free men: (1) reckoning and knowledge of numbers, (2) the art of measuring length, surface, and depth, and (3) the course of the stars and how they naturally travel in relation to one another. In his initial enumeration of topics still to be discussed (809c4–d1) he had not mentioned the topic that appears now as the central item.

Only a few must study all these subjects thoroughly and exactly; the many must learn of them only as much as is necessary, for the exact study of these subjects would not be easy or even possible for all; education cannot simply be equal education. "Necessary" must be rightly understood. It may mean the necessary as distinguished from the noble; in this sense it was said that the many must study of mathematics only as much as is necessary. "Necessary" is rightly understood in the light of the rightly understood proverbial saying that not even the god could ever be seen fighting against necessity: the necessities, or compulsions, in question are the divine ones, not the human ones like erotic desires (*Republic* 458d5–8) to which no god is subject. The divine necessities are, as it seems to the Athenian, the necessities with which one must willingly comply and which one must understand if one is ever to become for human beings a god or a daimon or hero capable of taking care of human beings in a serious manner: one could not become a divine human being if he does not know the numbers and their kinds or if he does not understand how to count nor how to mark off night and day and is ignorant of the revolution of moon, sun, and stars. It would be very foolish to think that all these branches of learning are not necessary for him who wishes to go on to know anything of the noblest branches of learning: the mathematical sciences are not the noblest branches of learning. The Athenian, as distinguished from the Socrates of the *Republic*, does not state what the noblest science is for which mathematics is only the preparation: Kleinias and Megillos are too inexperienced in mathematics to be led toward the transmathematical. As for the teaching of the free-born in reckoning and counting, the Athenian recommends the Egyptians' manner of doing it by which the children learn those things with play and pleasure along with reading and writing. The Egyptians thereafter proceed to the teaching of the art of measuring. There they prevent a common Greek error from arising—the error that all lengths, all widths and depths are commensurable with one another and all lengths are commensurable with all widths and all depths; of the commonness of that error among the Greeks the Athenian until lately was quite unaware. At this point (819e3) the conversation comes to resemble a Socratic dialogue to a higher degree than usually in the *Laws*: geometry is the central item. The Greeks' ignorance of this matter is disgraceful; knowledge of it is indeed, to repeat, necessary, although not noble. After he has provisionally settled the question whether the young should study geometry as a legal issue, the Athenian turns to the question of whether the young should study astronomy. In the case of astronomy one is confronted not only with the great error of the Greeks regarding the stars but with an amazing and intolerable prohibition. For we say that one ought not to investigate the greatest god and the whole kosmos nor waste one's time by searching for the causes; this would not even be pious. In truth, however, the opposite is correct. Although he is an old man, the Athenian opposes what "we say" regarding a matter of such weight, for if someone believes that a branch of learning is noble as well as true, useful for the city, and altogether dear to the god, he must proclaim it: it is not sufficient that it is noble and true as well as dear to the god;

it must also be useful to the city (cf. 779e6–7). The error which practically all Greeks commit consists in thinking that such great gods as sun, moon, and other stars, in brief, the gods in heaven, never take the same path. Kleinias agrees with this statement up to a point; he strengthens his agreement with an oath: he has often in his life seen with his own eyes that some stars never travel on the same course, and as for sun and moon we all know that they always do this. Kleinias has almost sworn that the untruth is true. For in truth each of these gods always travels in one and the same way in a circle. What the Greeks say and Kleinias has confirmed with an oath is blasphemous. The young must study astronomy in order to become able always to speak piously when sacrificing and praying: what is not pleasing to the gods to hear is by this very fact harmful to the city. Since the Athenian cannot in the present context prove the truth of his assertion regarding the stars, the question whether the young should study astronomy must be left open for the time being, for if the allegedly blasphemous assertion which is arrived at without the study of astronomy were true and dear to the gods, astronomy would be superfluous and even pernicious (cf. *Timaeus* 40d3–41a5).

In speaking of mathematics the Athenian does not say that the teachers must be slaves or hired foreigners. He mentions the astronomical studies which he himself has made in his advanced years. He also does not say that girls should have the same mathematical instruction as boys. The only mathematical discipline which is presented as directly relevant for piety is astronomy, a discipline which in the *Republic* is given a lower rank than geometry.

At the end of his discussion of education the Athenian turns abruptly to hunting. Hunting occupies in the *Laws* the place which dialectics occupies in the *Republic*: there is no place in the *Laws* for the noblest branch of learning, for a branch of learning nobler than astronomy (821a8).

The subject of hunting enables or forces the Athenian to revert to what he had said on more than one occasion about the limitation of legislation and what came out perhaps most clearly in his discussion of the instruction in mathematics where legislation proved to be impossible, at least for the time being. Previously the Athenian had made a distinction between laws and admonition; now he makes a distinction between laws and something which falls naturally between admonition and laws. Furthermore, he now makes clear that the citizen deserving the highest praise is not the one who serves the laws best and obeys them to the highest degree; higher is the rank of him who obeys the written laws as well as the written praise and blame of the legislator, i.e., who obeys the legislator also in those cases where no punishment is or can be threatened and the legislator says to him only what seems to him to be noble or base. Obviously the legislator's praise and blame is more than admonition; hence it falls between admonition and law. We may assume that the man who does what is noble, even if it is not prescribed by the legislator and not followed by praise, occupies a still higher rank.

As for hunting, there is a great variety of beings which can be hunted, among them men who can be hunted in war and in friendship; one kind of hunting men in friendship brings praise and another brings blame. Generally that kind of hunting deserves praise which improves the souls of the young. Accordingly, the legislator will blame the catching of water animals, the hunting of human beings by sea, and the hunting of birds; he will praise only such hunting of four-footed animals with horses and dogs as requires constant watchfulness and exposure to serious dangers, for only such hunting will be productive of divine manliness; the young practicing this kind of hunting are truly sacred hunters. Hunting of human beings by land is only implicitly disapproved (cf. *Euthydemus* 290b5–6; Aristotle, *Politics* 1255b37–39, 1256b23–26). The law, as distinguished from the legislator's praise or blame, is naturally much more permissive.

If I am not mistaken, Kleinias addresses the Athenian as "stranger" in Book Seven more frequently than in any other book with the exception of Book One.

Book Eight

From a man's being only a plaything of god, the Athenian had inferred that everyone, man or woman, must spend his whole life playing at the most beautiful kinds of play, that education and play is the most serious thing, and that the most beautiful play consists in sacrificing, singing, and dancing with the result that one is able to make the gods gracious to him and to repel enemies and defeat them in battle (803c2–e4). It is therefore not surprising that after he has completed his discussion of education, he turns to the subject of festivals. The regulation of festivals is not entirely within the discretion of the legislator. A major part of the festivals consists of sacrifices, and only with the help of Delphic oracles can it be determined which sacrifices should be offered to which gods. The legislator does determine that one sacrifice be offered by a magistracy every day of the solar year, that there be once a month a festival in honor of one of the twelve gods after whom each of the twelve tribes is named, and that on those days there will be choral performances and Music and gymnastic contests along with the sacrifices. There must be strict separation of the festivals in honor of the chthonic gods and those in honor of the gods called heavenly; the latter are apparently not the gods in heaven who are mentioned in the discussion of astronomy (821c7) but the Olympian gods (717a6–7), yet the slight ambiguity is not likely to be accidental: the greatest god (821c2) does not wish and does wish to be named Zeus (Heraclitus fr. 32). The festivals in honor of the chthonic gods must be put in the twelfth month, the month of Pluton; warlike human beings, as the citizens of the new city are to be, must honor that god as always good to the human race: life is in no way better than death. Those who arrange these matters must be mindful of the fact that our city is the only one at the present time which disposes of all conditions of happiness and can therefore make the necessary effort to live happily; this necessarily implies that it does not commit injustice and does not suffer injustice. Committing injustice can easily be avoided, but to acquire the power of not suffering injustice is very difficult: there is no other way of acquiring that power except by becoming perfectly good (631b6–c1), and this applies equally to human beings and to cities. Does he mean that a just man unjustly killed does not suffer injustice since life is not a greater good than death? But is death also a greater good than life for the city? Be that as it may, if a city is good it will lead a life of peace, but if it is bad it will lead a life of both external and internal war. "Good" or even "perfectly good" means in this context to be able to make the gods gracious and to repel enemies and defeat them in battle. Hence one must be training for war while still living the life of peace. In fact, a city which possesses sense will take the field—the men, the women and the children—at least one day every month, paying no heed to cold or heat. There will be sham battles which imitate as closely as possible actual battles, at the same time as sacrifices. Prizes will be awarded to the victors and especially to those who have proved best in contests throughout their lives. Their praises will be sung by poets who do not have to be distinguished by poetic excellence but must be distinguished by noble deeds. The emphasis on war goes hand in hand with the demotion of poetic excellence. The provisions regarding military service and poetry apply equally to women and to men. At this point the Athenian introduces the legislator as engaging in a monologue or dialogue; one cannot well imagine the legislator acting in this manner while the instruction in mathematics was being discussed; the legislator is not even mentioned in the discussion of mathematics (cf. 818c1–3, 819e3, 822d5). The legislator arrives at the result that the citizens are to be reared as competitors in the greatest contests where they have myriads of competitors, and they must therefore prepare themselves for these contests at least as much as ordinary athletes do for their contests. As for the sham battles, one must not mind if some citizens are killed on such occasions: if some human beings die, others not inferior to them will be born to take their place. What must not be permitted to die, what must even be stimulated in a manner by the sham battles, is fear, i.e., fear of death, and this despite the fact that life is not a greater good than death, for manliness consists in dominance over fear and hence presupposes the presence of fear. The legislator will make choristry and the whole of gymnastics subservient to training for war. Nowadays this is hardly done anywhere in any way. This failure has two causes.

The first is passionate longing for wealth, which prevents men from caring for anything except for their private possessions and daily gain. This preoccupation turns men of a quiet or modest nature into traders, skippers, or menials, and the manly ones into pirates, burglars, temple robbers, warlike men, and men aspiring to tyrannical rule; the men and women of the new city are indeed to be warlike, but for them war is only a necessity (828d2, 829a7–8) and a necessity not imposed by their desire for wealth. As for the second cause, the Athenian hesitates to state it and must apparently be prodded by Kleinias to do so: the Athenian cannot stop thinking of the harm done to cities by love of gain. The second cause is the spurious regimes (democracy, oligarchy, and tyranny) in which one part lords it over the unwilling rest of the citizens and prevents the ruled from ever becoming warlike, in order to perpetuate its rule. The regime of Kleinias' city has escaped both causes. Of all sorts of regime now existing, it is the only one likely to accept the warlike education and play which has been discussed. One wonders which of the two causes has prevented Crete and Sparta from adopting the proposed scheme: was it love of gain or a defect of the regime or both? Ignorance surely was not the cause (831b6–c1). One wonders therefore furthermore whether the Athenian's hesitation to state the second cause was not due to his thinking of the defects of the Cretan and Spartan regimes.

The next subject is gymnastic contests. Not only gymnastic contests which provide a training for war, but all such contests should be instituted by the law. From this point of view the Athenian examines the various kinds of the gymnastic practices at greater length than that at which he had discussed astronomy. He then reminds his listeners briefly of what has already been laid down regarding Music by "the first legislator," i.e., the Athenian, who is not identical with the legislator used by the Athenian as a character (as especially in 829e6 and 709d10), and of what will have to be established by "the second legislators" regarding Music contests which are to accompany appropriate sacrifices.

When we survey the thematic and coherent discussions of festivals in honor of the gods, we observe that the bulk of that discussion deals with the training of the whole citizen body, male and female, for war. The thought underlying this fact is the generalized version of what we have learned in Book Seven on the necessity to soften or strengthen piety by a generous dash of manliness (814b2–5). The emphasis on superiority in war and on manliness is at variance with the Athenian's critique of the Dorian laws in Book One. But it is justified by the problem posed by piety.

Yet we must not forget for one moment the necessity of piety. (We can safely disregard in the present context the difference between *eusebeia* and *hosiotes*; cf. the synonymous use of these two terms in *Euthyphro* 5c9–d7). That necessity is brought out by the Athenian in the following manner. The equal or almost equal participation of youths and maidens in gymnastics and of course also in Music brings on a difficulty which could be overcome by the god if it were possible somehow for him to give commandments. But, in Aristotle's words, the god does not rule by giving commandments (*Eudemian Ethics* 1249b14). Hence one needs a daring human being who has an unusually high regard or willingness to "say everything" and will say what seems to be best for the city and the citizens; who therefore will establish in corrupted souls what is becoming to the whole regime, contradict the strongest desires, and be guided solely by reason, without having any human helper. The difficulty or apprehension which troubles the Athenian is this. The youths and maidens are free from the toils which do more than anything else to quench wantonness, and they are concerned all the time only with sacrifices, festivals, and choruses. (In order to bring out his apprehension as powerfully as possible, the Athenian is silent here on the strenuous military exercises to which the young people dedicate themselves; he will stress them very soon: 841a6–8.)

What will restrain the ruinous desires from which reason, attempting to become law, commands abstention? This applies of course especially to erotic desires. The danger is particularly great in Crete and Sparta, which foster sexual intercourse between males—a practice of which one may plausibly say, with a view to the conduct of beasts, that it is against nature. Above all, one must raise the question whether that practice contributes in any way to virtue: will it engender manliness in the soul of the seduced or moderation in the soul of the seducer? The answer is obviously in the negative. Hence, who will lay down a law permitting that practice? Hardly anyone who has in his intellect the true law or, what seems to be the same, reason attempting to become law (835e4–5, 836e4).

In order to establish the truth of this view on pederasty, one must consider the nature of both friendship and desire and, in particular, of the desires called erotic. There are two kinds of them and a third compounded of the first two. There is first the affection for one similar to oneself, or for one's equal in regard to virtue, and then the affection of the needy for the rich; in both cases we call the affection *eros* when it becomes passionate. Love of similars is gentle and reciprocal throughout life, perhaps because it is most natural (773b6–7), while the love of dissimilars or opposites is terrible and fierce and not often reciprocal. What disturbs one for a moment is the fact that homosexual love could seem to be love of similars and heterosexual love love of dissimilars. What the Athenian says about the character of love of dissimilars does not seem to be wholly inapplicable (if we can trust part of the literature on the subject) to heterosexual love. The difficulty to which the Athenian attends, however, concerns the third kind of love: at what does it aim? Since it is a blend of the first two kinds, it aims at opposites, the similar and the dissimilar. The man filled with the third kind of love longs on the one hand for a youth similar to him in regard to virtue and therefore forbids himself to enjoy that youth's bloom; on the other hand, his love is like the love of the needy for the rich and therefore craves satisfaction of his body's desire. The first kind of lover is not simply free from desire for the body of the beloved, but he treats that desire as subordinate; his overriding concern is with the virtue of the soul of his beloved youth; he therefore revolts at the thought of sexual intercourse with him. The second kind of lover is exclusively concerned with enjoying the body of his beloved and wholly unconcerned with the character of his beloved's soul. It goes without saying that the dissimilarity of mature men and youths is essential to all three kinds.

The Athenian raises the question whether they should forbid all three kinds of pederasty or whether they should plainly wish to permit in the city only the first kind and, if possible, forbid the two others. (The prohibition against the first kind of pederasty deserves at least a passing mention, since that kind is identical with that "corruption of the young" of which a friend and teacher of the author of the *Laws* was accused and for which he was condemned.) He addresses this question to Megillos, for he guesses that Kleinias will need quite a bit more of enchanting persuasion until he will agree; thus it comes about that for a short while Megillos is the interlocutor. But how to enact a law to this effect? The fact that pederasty is against nature and against the true law in the intellect is obviously not sufficient; we need an art, a device for this purpose. We must remember that we cannot fall back on a divine prohibition strictly understood but need instead the act of a daring human being who will say things which almost all other human beings will not dare to say (835c1–8). The device which the Athenian has in mind

is easy but at the same time of the very greatest difficulty. Its feasi-
bility is shown by the fact that most human beings, however lawless
in other respects, abstain religiously from incest and do not even
desire incestuous intercourse or anything approaching it. All desires
of this kind are quenched by a little word—the word that condemns
them as unholy, as hated by the gods. More precisely, what achieves
this effect is the fact that this little word is always and everywhere
repeated by everyone and its denial is never uttered; that little word
thus acquires the status of an unwritten law or an ancestral law
(793a9–b7). The condemnation of incest is a major theme also of
both comedy and tragedy. Megillos grants the Athenian this much,
that what is supported by a common report of mysterious origin has
some wondrous power when no one ever attempts in any way to
entertain a sentiment contrary to the law: that men never speak
against that law is not enough. Let us not forget the Dorian law of
laws. The Athenian does not seem to be perturbed by this difference.
According to him, the example of the prohibition against incest
shows that it is easy for the legislator at least to know what he has
to do when he wishes to subjugate one of the desires which to an
extraordinary degree subjugate human beings: he must consecrate
the common report condemning that desire in the eyes of all, slaves
and freemen, children, women, and the whole city. Such consecration is the device which is needed for getting accepted the universal
condemnation of pederasty, nay, of all sexual activity which does
not serve its natural purpose, the procreation of children, i.e., of all
extramarital sexual activity. Consecration of this condemnation by
a human being of extraordinary boldness takes the place of the un-
available divine prohibition. The law enjoining all these restrictions
is almost said to be according to nature. It should be mentioned
that incest, as distinguished from pederasty, is here not explicitly
said to be against nature: the conduct of beasts which bore testimony to the unnatural character of pederasty (836c1–7) is not said
to bear testimony to the unnatural character of incest (cf. also
840d3–e1). The proposed law owes its efficacy to the consecration
which subjugates every soul, fills it with fear, and thus makes it obey
the laws: the souls subjugated by sexual desire are freed through
being subjugated by fear. We have heard before that one must restrain the bad desires by these three very good things: fear, law,
and the true *logos* (783a4–7).

Despite all this, a passionate young man, full of much semen—
almost an Aristophanean figure—will vociferously protest against
the proposed law as enacting senseless and impossible rules. And

this is not an isolated case anymore. By now things have advanced to the point where a strong opposition can no longer be overcome by consecration, let alone law by itself and the true *logos*. The case is similar to that of the common meals for both sexes; common meals for men have been shown to be possible by Crete and Sparta, just as the prohibition against incest has been shown to be possible everywhere; but just as common meals for women are regarded as impossible even in Crete and Sparta, the extension of the prohibition against incest to all other kinds of improper sexual conduct is believed to be impossible everywhere. Megillos agrees and ceases therewith to be the Athenian's interlocutor; he, the oldest of the three men, was the interlocutor during the discussion of pederasty and the Athenian's device.

The Athenian attempts next to show by an argument that possesses some plausibility that the actualization of his proposal is not beyond human power. He starts from the premise that a man who has his body in good condition and is in training can more readily control his sexual desire than a man in bad bodily condition. Surely we know from hearsay of very many athletes who did not touch a woman or a boy all the time they were in training, although they were much worse educated in regard to their souls and possessed much more vigor of body than the citizens of the Athenian's and Kleinias' city. Kleinias underlines the fact that what is said of the athletes is an ancient tradition. The Athenian draws the conclusion that what the athletes could do in order to win a paltry victory, the youths of the new city will surely be able to do for the sake of the most noble victory, that victory being the victory over pleasure, over the alleged bliss of the deeds of Aphrodite; for they will be enchanted from their childhood by stories, speeches, and songs to believe that bliss consists in conquering pleasure. This is to say nothing of the effect of the fear engendered by the thought that the alleged bliss is in no way holy. Finally, in order to escape from the predicament into which they have fallen owing to the depravity of the many, the Athenian asserts that the citizens of the new city ought not to be worse than birds and many other beasts, which live chastely until the time of procreation and thereafter spend the rest of their lives piously and justly in strict heterosexual monogamy.

Yet the citizens of Kleinias' city may be corrupted by the wantonness which reigns almost everywhere else; in that case the law guardians may have to lay down a second law, a second-best law which makes an inevitable concession to depravity. The second-best law will not forbid the bad actions themselves but their being done openly rather than secretly; and it will not be a written law imposing penalties on the offenders but an unwritten law which makes the transgressions disgraceful. Those whose natures are corrupt, the men lacking self-control, will be overpowered by those who are restrained by three kinds of things: piety, love of honor, and the true *eros*. These three things are akin to the three greatest things mentioned earlier (783a5–7): fear, law and the true *logos*, as we see when we remember the relation of piety and fear as well as the fact that the unwritten law rewards with honor those who obey it to a remarkable degree. In conclusion, the Athenian states two alternative formulations of the law concerning sexual commerce, leaving it open whether what he proposes should be called one law or two laws. The alternatives are these: (1) no one should dare to touch any one of noble and free birth except his own wedded wife, generate any bastards, or have intercourse with males; (2) we should entirely abolish love for males and stigmatize it as disgraceful if someone is detected having intercourse with a woman to whom he is not wedded in holy matrimony, for instance, with his female slaves. It seems that the first alternative permits the highest kind of pederasty, whereas the second alternative forbids every kind of pederasty (cf. 837d3–7) but compensates for this severity by making a considerable concession to properly secretive intercourse with slave girls and the like. The strict prohibition against the two lower kinds of pederasty did not form part of the second-best law, "the second law," the central formulation of the Athenian's proposal. Whatever this may mean, the one law which consists of two incompatible alternatives and which therefore may be described as two laws, is laid down as law for the city. Megillos agrees; Kleinias understandably postpones his decision. The Athenian had left it open from the beginning (636c1–7) whether the subject of pederasty, i.e., of its apparently unnatural character, is to be considered in jest or in earnest.

We have now reached the end of the discussion on sex—a discussion which is in a manner a corollary of the discussion of festivals; the discussion of festivals dealt chiefly with training for war. Ares and Aphrodite are the divinities which, as it were, presided over the discussions of that part of this Book which we have considered. It would perhaps be more accurate to say that the theme of the Book as a whole is the body, for the rest of the Book is devoted to the subject of food. (The rest is definitely less dialogic than is the bulk of the Book.)

Since the new city will be located at a considerable distance from the sea and since its citizens are forbidden to engage in commerce of any kind, the legislator has to give laws only for farmers, herds-men, and beekeepers, and those whose services are indispensable for farming, herding, and beekeeping. The first place is occupied by the agricultural laws, and among them the foremost law is the pro-hibition against moving boundary stones. There is a twofold sanction for this law, first and foremost a divine one and in the second place a legal one. This law applies not only to the boundary stones sepa-rating the estates of the citizens from one another; it also forbids private citizens farming at the frontiers to move boundary stones separating the land belonging to the city from that belonging to the enemies; transgressions of the first kind will be terribly avenged by Zeus god of the tribesmen, transgressions of the second kind by Zeus god of the strangers, i.e., by two different gods. There are no legal provisions here for punishment of those who move boundary stones separating the land belonging to the city from that belonging to the enemies. What the law forbids is the voluntary moving of boundary stones. There are many other less important ways in which one can do harm to his neighbor in matters of this kind, for instance, by grazing one's cattle on a neighbor's land or by preventing his access to water, which must be properly punished by fines; in these cases there are no divine sanctions. There follow detailed regulations re-garding the harvesting of fruits. Between these regulations and those concerning the bringing home of any kind of crops and the damages which can be done in this matter, the Athenian sandwiches the law concerning the spoiling of water by means of poisoning, diverting, or theft; if someone spoils water by poisoning, he must, in addition to the payment of a fine, purify the springs or the basin of the water, and in purifying them he must naturally follow the laws of the interpreters of the Delphic laws concerning divine things. The dis-cussion of the last agricultural law gives the Athenian an occasion to observe that the innumerable details concerning judicial procedure are not worthy of the attention of the aged legislator but must be regulated by his successors in the light of the ordinances of the for-mer; after experience has shown that the regulations made by the secondary legislators are sufficient, they must remain in force per-manently.

As for craftsmen, no citizen or slave of a citizen may exercise a common craft or art; the citizen has to exercise solely the art of the citizen, and this demands his full attention. Hardly any human being can exercise two arts thoroughly. Hence also the noncitizens exercising the vulgar arts may exercise only one of them. The subject of crafts naturally leads to that of commerce. The Athenian forbids

tolls on exported and imported goods, the importation of anything
not necessary and the exportation of things that are necessary; unnecessary is, for instance, the importation of frankincense and similar foreign things for use in divine worship. To the things which it
may be necessary to import belong of course all kinds of instruments
of war, including horses; their importation may require the exportation of produce which the city possesses in abundance; permission
of such imports and exports is the business of the military commanders. Retail trade for the sake of moneymaking is not tolerated
in the whole territory belonging to the city. As for the produce of
the land, crops as well as animals, it must be divided, as it already
is more or less in Crete, into three parts, one for the citizens, one
for their slaves, and one for the craftsmen and other foreigners,
including resident aliens; the last third must be sold by the citizens.
It is in the citizen's discretion how he will distribute the first two-
thirds among the free members of his household on the one hand
and the slaves on the other. There follow regulations regarding the
dwellings and other buildings both in the country and in town. The
craftsmen are to be settled with due regard for the convenience of
the citizens. Prime concern is to be given to the temples and to the
agora. In this connection the Athenian speaks at some length of
the manner in which foreigners and craftsmen can buy what the citizens sell them through agents (foreigners or slaves). Resident aliens
are admitted if they possess a craft and remain no longer than twenty
years; they do not have to pay a residence tax. If a resident alien
has benefited the city in a remarkable way, he may try to persuade
the Council and the Assembly that he be permitted to stay beyond
the twenty years and even for life; that permission may be granted.
But such permission does not entitle his children to remain in the
country for longer than twenty years past their fifteenth birthday.

Book Nine

This is the only Book, with the exception of Book One, the first word of which is meaningful by itself, in isolation, so that it could, if need be, perform the function of a heading even in the perspective of the meanest capacities, for we are in no position to deny that such words as "These (things)" or "But" or "After" or "If" could be properly used as headings or even as book titles by writers who can afford to do so. The first word of Book One is "god"; the first word of Book Nine is *dikai* (penalties, trials). We have heard on more than one occasion of avenging gods. The chief content of Books Nine through Twelve may be said to be the penal laws.

The Athenian begins his thematic discussion of the penal law with the consideration that even the need for drawing up a penal code is in a way disgraceful for a city which is thoroughly ordered toward virtue. Yet we are not, like the ancient lawgivers, legislating for the children of gods—lawgivers, as is now said, who were themselves of divine descent and who gave laws to others of divine descent— but being humans we legislate for humans. (Minos and Lykourgos obviously did not belong to the ancient lawgivers in question.) One might say that we legislate for a city which is not best but only second-best (cf. 739d6–8). More simply, however well-ordered a city may be toward virtue, most men are by nature lukewarm toward virtue (cf. 718d7–e1). Hence we need laws which deter from crimes and provide for punishment of the criminals.

The penal legislation opens with the law regarding crimes which have to do with gods, i.e., regarding the robbing of temples. Such crimes are not only unholy but also hurtful to citizens. They will, as one may hope, never be committed by a citizen but they may often be attempted by slaves or foreigners. The law is to be preceded by a prelude which addresses a man who contemplates such a dastardly deed, pointing out to him that the evil which moves him is neither human nor divine but is an infatuation which springs up in men as the result of an ancient wrong unexpiated, and that he must guard against it by going to the rites of guilt-averting, by going as a suppliant to the shrines of the gods who turn away evil and by going to the company of men who are said in the city to be good; if all this does not quench his cursed desire, he ought to commit suicide. While the prelude is simple, the law itself is twofold. A slave or foreigner who is caught robbing a temple will receive painful and disgraceful corporal punishment and will be cast out naked beyond the borders. If a citizen is ever detected doing such a thing—having committed a grave and unspeakable crime regarding gods or parents or the city—he must be regarded as incurable, condemned to death, the least of all evils (823d4–5), and denied burial in the country; yet his children, if they shun their father's ways, will be honored and his property will not be confiscated. (The law does not presume that, as the prelude suggests, the root of the father's crime is an ancient wrong unexpiated; if it presumed this, it would also presume that the ancient curse has lost its power through the father's crime.) Confiscation of the property would be incompatible with the permanence of the lots in the same families. From this it follows incidentally that no one can be fined for any crime to an amount that would endanger the cultivation of his lot. The Athenian concludes his discussion of crimes regarding the gods with a detailed statement concerning judicial procedure in all capital cases. All citizens who have leisure are obliged to attend trials for capital crimes. Judgment cannot be passed on the same day on which the trial opens: if this had been the law in Athens, Socrates might not have been condemned (*Apology of Socrates* 37a2–b1).

The second penal law deals with the subversion of the regime. A man who enslaves the laws by making them subject to men and makes the city subject to a faction and uses violence in all this, must be regarded as the worst of all enemies of the city. A magistrate who, while not participating in a crime of this kind, yet from lack of foresight or from cowardice fails to avenge his fatherland on the plotter, is only slightly less bad than the plotter. The penalty for violent subversion is death, and the judicial procedure is the same as in the case of temple robbery perpetrated by a citizen. The Athenian adds here a provision which he had abstained from making when speaking of temple robbery: the innocent children of a man condemned to death will be sent away to their country of origin with all their property if not only their father but their grandfather and great-grandfather as well have been condemned to death. There is no hint now of an inherited curse.

The third penal law deals with the capital crime of treason; the procedure is to be the same as in the two preceding cases.

The Athenian turns next to theft, a crime which is not capital, although he has not dealt with the capital crime of murder. Or is murder in itself a crime not against the city but against the individual or his family, whereas the three capital crimes already discussed are crimes against the city? Certain it is that the law on theft applies equally to theft from individuals and theft from the city; one can steal from the city, while one cannot murder the city. The law provides that in all cases of theft the thief must pay twice the amount of the value of the stolen thing. Kleinias is displeased with the Athenian's summary suggestion that the same penalty should be affixed to all cases of theft despite the great dissimilarity among them, and in particular to thefts from sacred or profane places. The Athenian fully agrees with him; he admits that he was carried away; he was carried away apparently by his desire to speed up the discussion of penal law, a distasteful theme. Kleinias has called him back to the duty of the legislator who cannot afford to be squeamish. He remembers now his earlier comparison of all contemporary, not to say all previous, legislation to the treatment given to slaves by physicians who are slaves, as distinguished from the treatment which free men receive from physicians who are free men (720a2–e5). The physician of the latter kind converses with his patient, almost philosophizes with him, and traces his illness to its origin, while having recourse to the whole nature of bodies (cf. *Phaedrus* 270b1–e4). In the first statement the Athenian had said that the physician of the latter kind examines the free man's illness "from the origin and according to nature" (720d3): he had not spoken of "philosophizing." In fact, it is only now that he mentions "philosopher" or its derivatives for the first time in his extensive conversation with the old Dorians, who are not even tainted by philosophy. His speaking now of philosophizing cannot be explained by the subject at hand (the distinction between the vulgar and the true legislators), for he had discussed that subject before without speaking of philosophizing.

The vulgar legislator observing true legislators—men who in legislating have recourse to the whole nature of the souls (cf. 650b6–10) —would ridicule them by saying that they educate the citizens but do not give laws to them. Fortunately the three interlocutors are under no compulsion to give laws at once but can leisurely consider, regarding every regime, how both the best and the most necessary can come into being; they can leisurely consider the best on the one hand, the most necessary on the other in regard to laws (consideration of the regimes naturally precedes consideration of the laws). In other words, they can educate themselves prior to their giving laws to the citizens or prior to educating them. Kleinias realizes that the legislators who are compelled to legislate at once are like the vulgar physicians. In continuing his argument the Athenian swears "by the gods." He had done so only once before (in 720e10), immediately after he had compared the two kinds of legislators to the two kinds of physicians, when saying that the legislator proceeding "according to nature" will assign the first place to the marriage laws, i.e., not to the laws concerning the honoring of the gods. (Kleinias never uses this particular kind of oath.) In the present context, i.e., shortly after the first mention of philosophy, the Athenian's oath indicates that we are on our way to the most philosophic, the only philosophic part of the *Laws*, Book Ten, in which the existence of the gods is demonstrated, i.e., in which the problem of the gods is directly faced.

The Athenian continues his refutation of the vulgar critics of the true legislator by the consideration that the citizens will be exposed to writings by poets and others which give advice regarding the noble, the good, and the just things by teaching of what character these things are and how one must practice them. Surely the legislator too must speak on these subjects, and his writings on them must deserve the greatest attention. The writings of poets and others must be judged in the light of the legislator's writings. The educating legislator is superior to the best poets (just as the noneducating legislator, i.e., almost every legislator, is inferior to the best poets). The Athenian does not say now that, in order to deserve his exalted rank, the legislator must be superior to the other writers in knowledge of the noble, the good, and the just things, but he hints at the possibility that he and his interlocutors may fail in their quest: only if god wills will they succeed. "For we are not yet legislators but in the process of becoming legislators, and perhaps we might soon become legislators." They are not yet legislators because they do not yet know the whole nature of the souls, which one must know in order to have perfect knowledge of the noble, the good, and the just things—because they are at best lovers of wisdom (*philosophoi*) but surely not wise; they are only, as the Athenian said on a much earlier occasion, men who "in a manner long for laws" (697a7; cf. 835e4–5).

After he has thus reminded his interlocutors of what is demanded
of the true legislator and of how deficient they are in this respect,
the Athenian is in a position to state a fundamental difficulty concerning penal law; his awareness of their deficiency may have induced
him to test them by making his insufficient statements on the law on
theft. The difficulty concerns the relation of the noble things to the
just things (the good things are not immediately relevant here).
The three interlocutors and surely also the many—and of course
also the general run of legislators—are in disagreement with themselves. On the one hand, we all agree that all just things are noble.
On the other hand, we all agree that to undergo just punishment is
not noble but disgraceful (cf. Aristotle, *Rhetoric* 1366b31–33). The
Athenian here refers back to the first two capital crimes (temple
robbery and violent change of the regime), but he now defines the
second of these crimes as hostility to good laws: the attempt at violent change of a regime congenitally productive of bad laws will
everywhere be punished of course by the established regime but is
not in itself base. The Athenian is fortunately under no compulsion
to lay down a law protecting bad laws. He does not explicitly remove
the contradiction which he has pointed out. There are two ways in
which he could have done that. First, he could have questioned the
identification of the just and the noble generally, i.e., not merely
in the case of undergoing punishment. For instance, obeying bad
laws issuing from a defective regime may be just but is not for this
reason necessarily noble. But are not all laws defective, of defective
rationality, given the fact that sound reasoning and law are not
identical? Is not in all political arrangements even the best, the highest, the Leader Intellect, subservient to moderation and justice, to
virtues which are lower than the Intellect? Secondly, he could have
asserted that undergoing just punishment is noble, just as all just
things are noble (cf. *Gorgias* 476b1–e5). Undergoing just punishment would be noble if through such suffering the criminal became
better; capital punishment could be said to make a criminal better
inasmuch as it prevents him from committing further crimes and
thus degrading himself still more (cf. 854c4–5). Yet even if punishment does not make the criminal better, it may, through its deterring
effect, make others or the city better. Instead of pursuing these or
equivalent lines of thought, the Athenian asserts or reasserts that all
bad men are involuntarily bad. From this it follows that the unjust
man, being bad, is involuntarily unjust and that all crimes (unjust
acts) are committed involuntarily. This conclusion seems to be destructive of all penal law, which must attach greater penalties to

voluntary than to involuntary crimes, not to say that involuntary crimes are not crimes at all (cf. Aristotle, *Nicomachean Ethics* 1113b19–26; *Magna Moralia* 1187a11–18). The Athenian admits that he has not given any reason for his assertion that all bad men are involuntarily bad or that all crimes are involuntary. Yet he cannot treat it as true, for, he says, as if he had never heard of suspense of judgment or of Socrates, he believes it to be true and therefore it would be neither lawful nor pious to deny it (cf. *Republic* 607c7–8); hence he must correct the popular distinction between involuntary and voluntary crimes accordingly. Kleinias is willing to permit that they first correct the distinction and then (or thus) make manifest the correctness of the fundamental assertion.

The Athenian now distinguishes between doing damage and acting unjustly. If someone harms another involuntarily, he should not be said to act unjustly if involuntarily toward him, but he must be said not to act unjustly at all, regardless of how great the damage is. Generally, harming and its opposite, benefiting, have in themselves nothing to do with justice or injustice (but cf. *Republic* 335d11–12; *Crito* 49c7–9). Hence we have to be concerned only with the noble and the just things and can disregard the good things. What makes harming or benefiting either just or unjust is the just or unjust character of the doer. Accordingly, the legislator has a twofold task; in the case of damages he must provide for restoration or compensation; in the case of acts of injustice, which as such are diseases in the soul, he must provide for cure, if cure is possible. The law cures from injustice by teaching and compelling the criminal never again to dare to commit such an act voluntarily or surely much less often. The work of the most noble laws consists precisely in inducing people to hate injustice and to love justice itself or at any rate not to hate it, and they achieve this result by deeds or speeches, through pleasures or pains, generally, through rewards or punishments. As for incurables, the legislator will condemn them to death in their own interest and in the interest of the others. The Athenian indicates here the difficulty opposing the view according to which punishment ought to improve the improvable criminals. Punishment is not necessarily supposed to improve criminals through teaching only; punishment may improve also by coercion; for it is not necessary that punishment should induce the criminals to love justice; it is sufficient if it induces them not to hate it; it is supposed to induce them to hate injustice, but they may learn to hate it because of its unpleasant consequences. One also wonders whether an incurable petty thief will be punished more severely than a curable murderer.

As Kleinias observes, the Athenian has not yet cleared up the confusion regarding the voluntary and the involuntary in both crimes and damages. In order to do so, he reminds his interlocutors first of the distinction between the two affections or parts of the soul, called anger and pleasure—a distinction of which they are aware, however defective their knowledge of the nature of the soul may be. Anger and pleasure are causes of errings or crimes. A third cause is ignorance, of which there is a simple kind, the cause of minor errings, and a twofold kind, which is ignorance coupled with the opinion of wisdom, of one's having perfect knowledge of things of which one has no knowledge whatever and which, if accompanied by strength and might, is the cause of great and shockingly rude errings but if accompanied by weakness leads to puerile or senile errings deserving only the mildest of all punishments. In the case of pleasure and anger, all rightly say that one may control them or be controlled by them, but no one ever says that a man controls his ignorance or is controlled by it: the reasoning power of which ignorance is the bad condition, rules by nature anger and desire, yet does not rule ignorance but destroys it; ignorance itself cannot rule; yet it can urge a man, just as pleasure and anger can, in the opposite direction to that in which his own will draws him: man's own will is, as such, directed toward the good; he does not "will" the bad except unintentionally; vice and crime are unintentional. The Athenian is now in a position to clear up the obscurity regarding justice: the passions' tyranny in the soul, regardless of whether or not it causes damage (to others), is injustice, while what is done by virtue of the rule in the souls of the opinion of what is best, however the city or some private citizens understand the best, even if that opinion is mistaken in some point, must be said to be just; the obedience of every individual to that opinion must be said to be just and best for the whole life of man; many men do regard, though erroneously, the damage sometimes issuing from the rule of such opinions as involuntary injustice. The Athenian's remark, which is not entirely clear about "the opinion of what is best," is a reminder of the difference between law and respectable opinion on the one hand and the true *logos* on the other; for all practical purposes justice is always saddled by this unavoidable obscurity. The divorce of justice from the consideration of harming and helping (cf. 862b1–4) could be understood as a consequence of this "political" understanding of justice. For instance, giving to a man what is considered in the city to be sane and good and what belongs to him may be harmful to him. That divorce is exposed to the difficulty that the penal law affixes different degrees of harm (e.g., fines or death) to different kinds of crime according to the different degrees of harm caused by the crimes in question. In particular, penal law presupposes that death is a very great evil, and this presupposition can be questioned (828d4–5). It might therefore be preferable to understand the divorce of justice from considerations of harming and helping as following from the most noble understanding of justice as a virtue choiceworthy entirely for its own sake without any regard to its consequences, as "doing one's own work well," i.e., as successfully seeking only one's own true good, above all the true good of his soul, and hence as essentially transsocial. The most noble view of justice, which is set forth by Socrates in response to Glaukon's urging, is not set forth by the Athenian. Instead he summarizes what he had said about the three causes of errings. In the repetition, however, he no longer calls the third cause ignorance but "striving for true opinion regarding what is best": even true opinion regarding what is best, to say nothing of mere striving for it, can lead to unjust actions. He adds now a subdivision of all these errings into those committed through open violence, those committed through dark deceit, and those committed through both; punishments for the last kind must be the most severe.

The Athenian has now completed his excursus on the fundamental obscurity pertaining to penal law. He cannot be said to have shown that all vice and all crime is involuntary, unless one is willing to say that his reference to the three causes of errings which lead a man in a direction opposite to that in which his own will drags him (863e2–3) constitutes a proof of his assertion. He could be said to have proved it if he had shown that all vice and crime is ignorance, but according to what he says here ignorance is only one of the kinds (of causes) of crimes (864b1–2). Besides, if vice is ignorance, virtue is knowledge, which he denies in a very visible place (963e). Furthermore, if virtue is knowledge, almost all citizens lack genuine virtue, for they possess at best only true opinion (cf. 632c5–6; cf. 689a1–c5); they are at best, not good, but men thought by the citizens to be good (854b8): almost all men are puppets of the gods and hence all their actions are involuntary (804b3–4). This is not a satisfactory basis of penal law. We shall add that only if virtue is knowledge can just punishment be seriously reduced to education and thus be as noble as any other just thing. One might say that Plato here, as elsewhere, indicates the conditions which would have to be fulfilled if there were to be a truly gentle penal law but which cannot be fulfilled.

The Athenian returns next to the penal law itself. He refers briefly
to the three kinds of capital crimes which he had discussed, but he
speaks now not of the subversion of the regime or hostility to good
laws (860b2) but of the subversion of the present regime, which
could mean of the regime whatever it might be. He adds that if
someone commits one of these crimes from madness, disease, old
age, or puerility, he must pay for the damage he has done but shall
not be punished, except if he has killed a man and thus incurred a
pollution; in that case he must go into exile for a year. The Athenian thus effects a transition to the law on homicide. If a man kills
a fellow citizen openly and involuntarily in a public contest, in war,
or in military exercises, he only must undergo purification according
to the Delphic prescriptions. If a patient dies against the will of his
physician, the physician is pure according to law, i.e., without any
recourse to Delphic prescriptions. As for other cases of involuntary
homicide, if the killed man is a slave, the slayer must compensate
the slave's master or else he will be fined to the amount of twice the
value of the slain slave, the amount to be determined by the judges,
and besides there must be greater and more numerous purifications
than in the case of unintentional homicide in contests, the purifications to be determined in accordance with Delphic prescriptions;
if a man kills his own slave unintentionally, only purification is
required. This implies that the slave, since he is a human being,
is not simply a piece of property. If the victim is a free man, the
required purification is the same as in the case of the unintentionally
killed slave, but with this difference, that the involuntary slayer of
a free man must be mindful of the ancient story according to which
the slain free man is for some time after his death in anger at his
slayer and bent on revenge; therefore the slayer must go into exile
for a full year; if he fails to do so, the victim's nearest of kin shall
prosecute him for homicide and the penalty will be double; if the
victim's nearest of kin fails to prosecute, the pollution must be regarded as having come to that nearest of kin, and everyone may
prosecute him on that ground. (Punishment in this case serves no
educative purpose but is a concession to fears induced by ancient
stories or their underlying motives.) If the slayer is a stranger, he
must undergo perpetual exile apart from the usual purifications; if
he returns nevertheless, the penalty will be death, unless the return
is involuntary, caused for instance by shipwreck. Homicide caused
by anger would most justly be said to be in between involuntary and
voluntary homicide. But the man who kills on a sudden, without
deliberation after his anger has been aroused, and is immediately

afterward sorry for what he has done, acts less voluntarily than the man who retains his anger and takes revenge after some time; the latter deserves therefore more severe punishment than the former despite the fact that the former sometimes acts with greater ferocity than the latter. Needless to say, if a slave kills his master or any other free man, he will not be permitted to live. If a father or mother slays in anger a son or a daughter, the slayer will be exiled for three years and must perform the same purifications as the other slayers acting in anger; on return from exile, father and mother must separate and never again generate a child; whoever disobeys this law is liable to prosecution for impiety. The same rule applies *mutatis mutandis* to the slaying in anger of a spouse by a spouse or of a brother or a sister by a brother or a sister. But if one slays in anger his father or mother, if he commits a crime, that is, which includes the crimes of impiety and sacrilege, his penalty will be death, unless the victim voluntarily acquitted him of murder before he died; in that case he must undergo the purification and the other obligations imposed on the unintentional homicide; not even if one's life is threatened by his father or mother does the law permit the slaying of either in self-defense, just as it does not permit the slave to slay a free man in self-defense (cf. *Crito* 50e7–51a5).

Next come the laws regarding voluntary homicide, i.e., homicide due to yielding to pleasure, desire, and envy. (Such homicide would of course be involuntary in the strict sense since all vice and crime is involuntary.) The first place among the motives for murder is occupied by the passionate desire for the insatiable and boundless possession of wealth; next comes ambition which generates envy; thirdly the cowardly and unjust fears inducing men to do away with others who know their guilty secrets. These observations will form one part of the prelude to the law. The other part consists of the speech by which many are deeply impressed when they hear it from those who occupy themselves with these matters in the mysteries— the speech according to which vengeance on the murderer is taken in Hades and when he is born again he will suffer the penalty according to nature, i.e., he himself will die through murder. The punishment with which myth threatens the involuntary slayer is naturally much milder (865d6–e6). The law itself provides that the murderer of a fellow citizen shall be debarred from every place of lawful assembly and shall not pollute by his presence temples or any other place of meeting. In connection with his trial, it is required that there be prayers and sacrifices to those gods who are concerned that no murders be committed in cities. The convicted murderer will suffer the death penalty and be denied burial in the country. The other kinds of murder are to be dealt with *mutatis mutandis* in the same way. The most awesome and instructive example is the law concerning the most impious' murder, the murder of kinsfolk. There recourse must be had in the first place to what the murderer of this kind has to fear from the gods, i.e., to the *mythos* or *logos* or however one ought to call it, which stems from ancient priests and according to which Right, the avenger of kindred blood, has ordained that the doer necessarily suffer the same as he has done. For instance, if he has murdered his mother, he will necessarily be born again as a woman and be murdered by her children. Generally, the soul which has committed a murder of this kind must suffer a similar murder in order to be purified and to appease the wrath of the whole family. When speaking of incest, the Athenian had referred to his device which consists in consecrating a common report of mysterious origin (837e9–838a1). He employs the same device here. But while in the case of incest that device, a prelude, was not, at least not explicitly, supplemented by a law to be enforced by human beings, in the case of murder of near relatives a law of the mortal legislator is required in addition to the unwritten law. That law inflicts on the executed murderer's corpse a treatment which is proportionate to the horrid character of the crime.

Suicide, unless it is committed in pursuance of the city's sentence or under the compulsion of some extremely painful and inevitable misfortune or as a consequence of some desperate disgrace, is murder. What is to be done regarding purification in the case of suicide, god knows (cf. 835c1–4), and what he knows becomes accessible through the intermediacy of the exegetes; suicides must be buried in such a way that their memory is altogether obliterated. Murder can also be committed by beasts and lifeless things, and therefore the law provides for their punishment, which in this case naturally does not serve the purpose of improvement or deterrence but that of expiation of the family of the killed man.

After he has concluded the discussion of murder the Athenian makes a new beginning. He first states which subjects have been legislated upon already; he calls these subjects the rearing and the education of the living soul and punishment for violent deaths. If we take the marriage laws to be merely preparatory for the laws on the rearing of children, we can say that he tolerably summarizes what he has done since he began with the legislation proper, except that he now passes over in silence the laws regarding the sacred things (768d7–e3, 771a5–6, 772d5–e1; cf. 833d5–6 and 836b1).

Immediately thereafter he says, in order to introduce the next subject
of legislation, that "the rearing and education of bodies" has been
discussed and that they must now turn to the wounding and maiming
of bodies. It is hard but not impossible to say that the whole Music
education as well as the punishments for violent deaths could be
understood as forming part of the rearing and education of the
bodies, but it is simpler to say that he first mentions and contrasts
what men can do to another in order to make possible life in the
fullest sense and to destroy life, and then what they can do in order
to build up healthy bodies and to maim them. Before he turns to
his next subject, he takes up again the whole subject of legislation.
Men's laying down laws and living according to laws are indispensable if they are to differ from the most savage beasts. The reason
is this. No man's nature is sufficient for knowing what is conducive
to political life and, if knowing it, for always being able and willing
to do what is best. In the first place it is difficult to know that the
true political art must care not for the private but for the public—
for the common binds the cities together while the private tears
them asunder—and that it is to the interest of both the common
and the private if the common rather than the private is well ordered.
Secondly, if someone acquires this fundamental insight of the political art regarding the natural relation of the common to the private
and, in addition, rules supreme in the city, his mortal nature will
prevent him from acting according to that insight and urge him on
to prefer his private pleasure and ease to the common good. It is
true that a human being may be wellborn, may be by nature so
superior that he acquires true knowledge, science, and may at the
same time have supreme power in the city; in that case it would
be a grave wrong to subject him to laws, for the intellect justly rules
everything. But such good fortune can hardly be expected; therefore
one must choose the second-best, which is order and law, despite its
imperfection. The Athenian had never before stated as clearly the
natural inferiority of *nomos* to *nous* (cf. 711e8–712a3, 714a2). The
reason why he makes this statement now may well be that he turns
now to the laws regarding wounds and maims, i.e., to a part of
the penal law which falls almost entirely within the competence
of the political art as a human art, whereas the law on murder depends to a much larger extent directly or indirectly on accounts
stemming from old priests and on Delphic prescriptions.
     There is an immense variety of cases of wounding and maiming,
and therefore the legislator cannot enact adequate laws for dealing
with them; but what he cannot do, the judges who have to deal with

each case by itself can do. The question is how much the legislator should decide and how much he should leave to the decision of the judges. Generally speaking, in a city in which the judges (jurors) are well brought up, much may safely be left to their decision, while if that condition is not fulfilled, the legislator must deal with as much as possible by express law. Fortunately the Athenian legislates for a city of the first kind; he can therefore leave matters at giving outlines and typical examples for the judges to follow. A man may wound a fellow citizen while intending to kill him; such a man must stand trial for murder; but out of regard for his relatively good luck, however undeserved, and in deference to the daimon who from pity for him and his victim prevented the consummation of the murder, he will not be condemned to death but only deported to the neighboring city, and he must compensate his victim in full for the damage he has done to him. But if the criminal is a child or a slave and the victim his parent or his master, the penalty is death. The same penalty is required if a brother or a sister wounds a brother or a sister with the intention to kill. If a spouse wounds his or her spouse with the intention to kill, the penalty is not death—for spouses are not kindred by blood—but perpetual exile and loss of property. If someone wounds a fellow citizen in anger, he must compensate the victim by paying to him, according to the gravity of the wound, two, three, or four times the amount of the damage which he has done. But if a child wounds a parent in anger and the family court fails to settle the case, it is to be brought before a select group of law guardians; the penalty may be death or a heavier or a lighter sentence as the tribunal decides. In the case of involuntary woundings, only payment of the simple damage is required.

The last subject of the Book is outrage. The foremost consideration to be shared by every member of the society is that the older is greatly more revered than the younger, both amongst gods and amongst human beings who wish to be preserved and to be happy. Hence the sight of someone older suffering outrage in the city at the hands of someone younger is disgraceful and hateful to gods. One must regard anyone at least twenty years older as his father or his mother and reverence him accordingly. The same restraint must be observed regarding strangers, who as such are under the protection of the god of the strangers. If someone beats someone of his age or someone older who is childless, he who is attacked may defend himself with his bare hands. If anyone dares to assault his father or mother or one of their progenitors without fearing the wrath of the gods above or of the avengers, as they are called, beneath the earth, but as if he knew what he in no wise knows, despises the things said of old and by all, he needs some extreme deterrent. Death is not sufficient. The punishments which are most truly said to be inflicted in Hades on such offenders are more severe than death, yet they fail to deter degraded souls. Therefore they must be afflicted here, while they are still alive, with punishments which come as close as possible to the punishments in Hades. The law threatens the offender with perpetual exile from the city to another part of the country and with exclusion from all holy places; in addition, no free man may share food or drink with him or have any other such association with him: the law does not threaten the offender with death, and in particular not with an especially painful or protracted death; the city cannot act like the avengers in Hades.

Book Ten

The Athenian casts a brief glance at unlawful acts which do not, as such, lead to death, wounds, or beatings. The most important among them are due to the licenses and outrages of the young. He presents them in descending order of heinousness according to the rank of the things or beings against which or whom they are perpetrated: public temples, private shrines and graves, parents, magistrates, ordinary citizens. Robbing of temples or crimes against gods had been the first subject of penal law (853d5–6, 856b1). But robbing of temples is not the only crime against gods. In particular, one may exhibit *hybris* in regard to gods by speech as distinguished from deed. Both the wrong kind of speech and deed in regard to gods and the right kind are based on something which is neither speech nor deed but believing or thinking. No one who believes that the gods as the laws declare them are, has ever voluntarily perpetrated an impious deed or uttered a lawless speech; whoever does the one or the other either does not believe the aforesaid, or, if he believes that gods are, he believes that they do not care about human beings, or, if he believes that they care about human beings, he believes that they can easily be won over when bribed by offerings and prayers. (To believe that gods are and to believe that the gods as the laws declare them to be are, are obviously different things.) The Athenian is thus compelled or enabled to discuss what Adeimantos calls theology (*Republic* 379a5–6) within the context of the penal law, whereas Socrates discussed it within the context of prephilosophic, nay, the most rudimentary education. We have seen how much the Athenian's discussion of crimes, especially of incest, murder, and disrespect of parents is based on the belief in gods. This observation does not do full justice to his theology. After all, almost his whole teaching seems to stand or fall by the belief in gods. Almost his whole teaching is colored by piety as commonly understood, as understood, for instance, by Megillos or Kleinias, not to say by old women living in the most remote corners of Crete. Yet we have also seen that he questions piety. He surely is not, if we may borrow an expression from a distinguished contemporary student of Greek poetry, "a fundamentalist from the Bible Belt" (H. D. F. Kitto, *Poiesis*, University of California Press 1966, 213). But we must add at once that he also is not an indifferentist. He would be an indifferentist if he held the view set forth by the same author that it makes no serious difference whether one speaks of gods as Aeschylus or Sophocles does or whether one does not speak of gods as Thucydides does not (*loc. cit.*, 365). Being a philosopher, the Athenian is concerned with the truth about the gods. If, *per impossibile*, the great poets were not concerned with it, they would only confirm the extremely harsh judgment which Socrates passes on them in Book Ten of the *Republic* and which is not repeated by the Athenian.

Kleinias wonders what they should do or say to the deniers of the three fundamental points mentioned by the Athenian. The Athenian replies that they must first listen to what, as he divines, the deniers from contempt of them say to them in jest. The deniers grant that some of them do not believe in gods at all and others do not believe in gods as the three interlocutors understand them. But they appeal to the legislators to do in the present case what they had resolved on doing in all cases: before harshly threatening, they should teach and persuade by sufficient proofs that there are gods and that they are too good to be induced with gifts to act against right. As it is, the teachers said to be the best—poets, orators, soothsayers, priests, and innumerable others—do not turn most of us away from unjust deeds. Legislators who claim to be not savage but gentle can be expected to use persuasion in the first place; if they succeed, "we might perhaps obey them." The ironical deniers thus compel the nonironical legislators to prove the existence of gods. We must not forget, however, the difference between the Athenian and his interlocutors.

According to Kleinias the proof is very easy: earth, sun, stars, and the beautiful order of the seasons; besides, all men, Greeks and barbarians, hold that there are gods. He does not refer to ancient stories and hence not to gods peculiar to the Greeks. Nevertheless the Athenian replies that Kleinias and Megillos underestimate the deniers; they believe that the deniers are solely prompted by their licentiousness. What prompted them in fact is some very grievous ignorance which is thought to be the greatest good-sense. Since

Kleinias does not understand this statement, the Athenian must explain it and in the first place what he meant by the deniers' seeming
good sense or wisdom. Among "us" (Athenians and the like) there
are writings about gods which are not to be found among the Dorians
because of the excellence of their polity. The oldest of them state
how the primary nature of heaven and the other things has come
into being, and this leads them very soon to speak in great detail of
the coming-into-being of the gods and of how the gods conducted
themselves toward one another; it is not easy to blame these writings,
for they are ancient, but the Athenian cannot praise them either, for
they do not seem to conduce to the tendance and honor due to
parents; he prefers to leave the judgment to gods. But as for the
recent wise men, one must hold them responsible for the evils which
they cause and for the manner in which they cause them. To our
proof of the existence of gods, to the proof which consists in pointing to sun, moon, stars, and earth as gods and divine, the people
persuaded by the wise men of recent times reply that the heavenly
beings are earth and stone and hence incapable to care in any way
for human affairs and that all speeches to the contrary are only
resplendent disguises of this sober truth. The Athenian's report
shatters Kleinias' confidence; not only has he shown that the divinity
of the heavenly bodies is not self-evident; he has shown at the same
time that there is not that universal or almost universal agreement
regarding the existence of gods to which Kleinias had appealed.
Thereupon the Athenian takes up Kleinias' question as to what they
should say and do in regard to atheists: should they abandon the
attempt to legislate on the presupposition that there are gods? or
should they without further ado lay down laws making impiety a
criminal offense? The first alternative is manifestly impossible. The
second would require that they retreat from their resolve to provide
each important law with a prelude. But one could plead in favor of
the second alternative that in the present case the prelude will become disproportionately long: Kleinias' short and easy proof of the
existence of gods has been shown to be worthless. Kleinias protests
strongly against the Athenian's proposals: the importance of the
subject does not permit one to indulge any concern with brevity;
in one way or another our speeches regarding the gods must be
shown to possess some persuasiveness; this persuasive speech will
be the noblest and best prelude on behalf of all laws. The noblest
and best prelude to all laws which was indeed only assertoric, was
given, we recall, in Books Four and Five (723a4–8, 734e3–4). The
Athenian's reply performs two duties. He has shown the wisdom

(such as it is) of the impious; he still must show their grievous ignorance. Besides, thanks to the Athenian's powerful influence, Kleinias has become so gentle that he did not react to the impious with the appropriate indignation; the Athenian must therefore arouse his indignation against them. How can one help, he asks, speaking about the existence of gods without spirit or anger? Indeed, one cannot help being vexed with, and hating, those who impose on us the burden of proofs since they do not believe in the stories which they used to hear while infants and sucklings from their nurses and mothers of whose wisdom we have heard earlier (794e1; cf. *Republic* 377c2–5) and which they heard through their youth in prayers at sacrifices; they are oblivious of their pious parents' prayers on behalf of themselves and their children; they are oblivious of the prostrations and devotions of all Greeks and barbarians at the rising and setting of sun and moon in all kinds of misfortune and good fortune; they are oblivious of the fact that men do all these things without any suspicion that there might be no gods; they despise all this without having a single sufficient reason. How can one teach such people through gentle speech in the first place that there are gods? Yet precisely this must be done. For it must not happen that both sides to the dispute are in a state of madness at the same time —the ones owing to greed for pleasure, the others owing to indignation about the former. We see that the Athenian has aroused himself to indignation to such an extent that he now adopts the view which he had formerly rejected that the impious are prompted only by their incontinent desire for pleasure (886a8–b2; cf. 908b4–c1). All the more has it become necessary for him to demand that the impious be addressed without anger or in a disheartened manner. The address is preferably thought to be directed by the three interlocutors, with the Athenian acting as their spokesman, to a single youth who does not talk back. He is gently reminded of the inconstancy of the opinions of the young, many of which change into their opposites as time progresses; he therefore ought to refrain for the time being from passing judgment on the gravest matters; he ought to consider that he and his friends are not the first to hold that morbid opinion about the gods, but none of the people of this kind whom the Athenian has encountered who were atheists from their youth has remained an atheist till his old age, although, it is true, some have preserved till their old age the opinions that the gods do not care for human beings or that they care indeed but can easily be swayed by offerings and prayers; in the meantime he ought to inquire by himself and with others, but especially with the legislator, as to which of the alternative opinions are true, but he must not dare to become guilty of any impiety in regard to gods.

It is surely incumbent upon the legislator to teach the truth about these very things. But this means that he has to face, to refute, the arguments of the atheists: the existence of gods is not self-evident but requires an extensive and difficult speech. The men to be refuted begin, reasonably enough, by saying that all things come or have come or will come into being either by nature, or by art, or by chance. But they go on to say that the greatest and most beautiful things are the work of nature and chance, while the lesser things are the work of art. Since Kleinias does not quite understand, the Athenian explains the opinion of the opponents more fully as follows. They say that fire, water, earth, and air are all by nature and by chance; they are altogether soulless; through them earth, sun, moon, and stars have come into being; that is to say, through their aimless and compulsory motions, through their mixture, they have generated the whole heaven and whatever is in heaven and all animals and plants—not owing to intellect, not owing to some god, not owing to art, but, to repeat, by nature and chance. Art comes into being after the natural things; in contrast to the deathless elements art is mortal and stems from mortals; accordingly it produces some playthings which do not participate at all in truth but are images akin to arts like painting and music themselves; the serious arts such as medicine, agriculture, and gymnastics owe their being serious to the fact that they help nature with their power; the political art, apparently somewhat more serious than the image-making arts, has little in common with nature but much with art; in particular, all legislation is by art, not by nature, for its positings are not true. What they mean by the last assertion is this. In the first place the gods are by art, not by nature but by law; hence there are different gods for different places, as each group agreed when giving laws to itself. Secondly, what is by nature noble differs from what is noble by law or convention; as for the just things, they are in no way by nature as is shown by men's constant disagreement about them and changing of them (cf. *Minos* 316b6–c2; Xenophon, *Memorabilia* IV 4.12–14). These are the things which the young are being taught by men whom they regard as wise—private men as well as poets—who assert that right is might or victory and who draw the young to what they contend is the life by nature correct, namely, lording it over others according to truth and not being in bondage to others according to law.

Kleinias is shocked by the terrible teachings with which the Athenian has acquainted him; among other things he senses that they are destructive of the family. Without his knowing it, however, his original position was an uncomfortable compromise between the sound and the unsound view (cf. 626a3–5; cf. 690b4–8, 715a1–2); his original understanding of nature is surely not the same as that which the Athenian is going to set forth. The Athenian repeats his question as to what the legislator should do in the face of the entrenched power of the adversaries; should he threaten impious speeches and thoughts with grave if varying penalties—varying perhaps because the denial of all particular points is not equally grave or because one must consider the standing of the individual denier—without making any use of persuasion and thus taming human beings? Kleinias opts vigorously for the use of persuasion, however weak, if it is available; any legislator who is not wholly worthless must come to the assistance of the ancient law with the loudest voice by a speech to the effect that there are gods and that there is something just by nature, and he must defend law as law and art by showing that they are by nature, or at any rate are not inferior to nature, since according to the true account they are the offspring of the intellect, as the Athenian seems to him to say, and Kleinias now believes him. The belief in gods is an "ancient law" or ancestral custom or unwritten law, for it is based on a common report of mysterious origin and coeval with man: it survived the deluge when all arts and all wisdom were lost (679c3–8; cf. 793a9–c5 and 837e9–838e1). The Athenian warns the eager, perhaps over-eager, Kleinias of the difficulty and the length of the work which he demands: the speeches defending the ancient law are not the same as the ancient law. Kleinias disposes of this warning with ease, mentioning among other things that laws, and hence their preludes, remain forever and are therefore susceptible of being read and reread every so often; Megillos heartily agrees with him. The Athenian admits thereupon that one must do as Kleinias says: given the fact that the pernicious speeches have been broadcast, so to speak, among all men, the legislator's speeches defending the ancient law or the greatest laws (such as the prohibition against incest), by showing that there are gods, are indispensable.

One is tempted to say that the Dorians and hence, in particular, the new colony are in no way threatened by the new-fangled and pernicious wisdom, and that the Athenian contradicts himself by saying that the pernicious speeches have been broadcast, so to speak, among all men (cf. 886b4–5). Does he not by restating those speeches contribute to their being spread still more widely than they already are? Does he not act the part of a "corrupter of the young"? It is true that the Athenian almost contradicts himself, but this is due to his apprehension of a potential threat; the city to be founded will not be as safe as human providence can make it if the legislator does not make provisions against that threat, if the city does not possess within itself the proper protection against it; awareness of that threat will raise it to a higher level than ignorance of it would; it will be part of its qualified assimilation to Athens, which the Athenian is attempting to achieve.

The Athenian starts by asking Kleinias to repeat that, according to the adversary, fire, water, earth, and air are the first of all things and that he calls them nature, while, according to him, the soul, coming into being out of these first things, is later. Agreement having been reached on this, he concludes, swearing by Zeus, that they have discovered, as it were, some source of a mindless opinion shared by all human beings who have ever yet handled inquiries about nature. He warns Kleinias again of the difficulty confronting them: they must deal with speeches to which they are rather unaccustomed. Kleinias is undeterred: they must not avoid unaccustomed speeches if there is no other way of coming to the assistance, not so much of the ancient law, as of what the law now pronounces about the gods, by proving its correctness. The adversaries, the Athenian continues, have fallen into an error as to what the gods truly are, because they have declared that what is truly the first cause of the coming-into-being and perishing of all things is not first but has come into being later, and that what is later is earlier. For it has escaped almost all, what kind of being the soul is and what power it has—that it belongs to the first things, having come into being prior to all bodies, and governs more than anything else does all changes of bodies; if the soul is therefore more ancient than the body, the things akin to the soul will necessarily be prior to those belonging to the body, will they not? From this it would follow in particular that art and law are prior to things hard and soft or heavy and light, and of course that the greatest and primary works and actions are those of art, not to say of law. By "nature" the adversaries understand the coming-into-being connected with the first things, i.e., the first things as initiating all other things; in accordance with this usage one would have to say that the soul, and not such things as fire or air, is in an outstanding manner by nature. But to justify this, one would first have to prove the primacy of the soul. Before he begins with that proof, the Athenian utters another warning regarding the difficulty of the task; yet he suggests a new way out. He, being the youngest and most experienced of the three in such matters, will expose himself alone to the danger, that is to say, have a dialogue within the hearing of his two interlocutors with himself until the proof of the priority of the soul to the body is completed. He also calls on god's aid, for to no purpose is it more appropriate to do so with all seriousness than when one is about to demonstrate the gods' existence. He then presents himself as being asked whether all things stand still and nothing is moved or nothing stands still and everything is moved or some things are moved and others remain at rest; he replies that some things are moved and others remain at rest. Replying to further questions of the same questioner, he is brought to admit that there are eight kinds of motions; nothing is said about the things exempt from motion or change. When he adds, "except two kinds of motion," Kleinias says, "Which two?" and thus puts an end to the Athenian's monologic dialogue which was supposed to go on until the proof of the priority of the soul to the body was completed. Could the discussion of the eight kinds of motion constitute that proof? Or does the Athenian take the place of his fictitious questioner, and, what is much more important, does Kleinias take the place of the Athenian, i.e., is the reasoning which follows to be ascribed to Kleinias rather than to the Athenian? At any rate, the two other kinds of motion are the motion which can only move other things and is elicited only by the motions of other things, and the motion which can always move itself and other things; the latter is truly the change and motion of all beings, for it is prior to all other kinds of motion; it is demonstrably first in origin and strength, the alternative being an infinite regress; it is the initiating origin of all motion. To this may be added the following consideration. If, as most of the adversaries dare to say, all things were together and at rest—if motion had a beginning—only the motion that moves itself could come into being in them first. We shall say then that the originating beginning of all motions and the first motion, coming into being in things at rest and being in things in motion, the self-moving motion, is the most ancient and most powerful of all changes, while the motion originated by others and moving others is secondary. Now if we see that the self-moving motion has arisen in something bodily, we say that the thing is alive, and when we observe soul in things, we also say that they are alive. At this point the Athenian swears by Zeus, thus reminding us of the gods who had not been mentioned for some time and could be thought to have been superseded by the soul. He continues by making clear, in rather technical language, that when we speak of the soul, we mean precisely the motion which can move itself. If this is so, he concludes, are we not satisfied that the soul has been shown to be the same as the first coming-into-being and motion of all things that are, have been, and will be, and also of their opposites? Kleinias is entirely satisfied. We would then have stated correctly and decisively, most truly and most finally, that the soul has come into being prior to our body, but the body in the second place and later. Kleinias again assents. The Athenian seems to be less certain than Kleinias. He may have thought of such unresolved difficulties as these: if the soul has come into being, what is the motion or change, or its source, through which it has come into being? does it not make a difference whether one says that the soul originates all motions or whether one says that the soul is the cause of everything that is? He may have thought of the ambiguity of "soul": what is the relation of the soul which originates all motions to the human soul in particular? Or is the obfuscation of this difference required for the *metabasis* from the soul to the gods? He certainly repeats, i.e., modifies, his earlier statement according to which if the soul were prior to the body, the things "akin to the soul" or, as he now says, the things "of the soul" will necessarily have come into being prior to those belonging to the body; in the first statement he had given as examples "opinion, concern, intellect, art, and law" (892a7–b3); now he gives these examples: manners, characters, wishes, calculations, true opinions, concerns, and memories; one wonders whether the change from the singular to the plural is sufficiently explained by the impossibility or undesirability of using "intellect" (the central item in the first enumeration) in the plural; one wonders certainly whether false opinions are not also things of the soul. Or must the emergence of false opinions wait for the emergence of bodies? This is excluded by the preceding argument, which leads to the result that the soul is the cause of the good and the bad, the noble and the base, the just and the unjust things and of all the opposites (hence also of the true and false opinions). Since the soul manages, and dwells in, all things everywhere which are moved, it is necessary to say that it manages also and in particular the heaven (he does not say that it dwells also in heaven, because the soul spoken of here is also the cause of the bad, the base, and the unjust things or because it includes also the foolish soul). But, as the Athenian says, answering a question of his own for his interlocutors, this management cannot be the work of a single soul; required are at least two souls, one which is beneficent (the cause of the good, noble, and just things) and the other of the opposite character. Hence, soul drives all things in heaven, earth, and sea by its own motions—such as wishing, considering, caring, deliberating, opining correctly or falsely, joy, grief, confidence, fear, hate, love—while bringing in their train and using the secondary motions, the motions of bodies, and thus causing all changes and states of body; if it is conjoined with intellect, it leads all things to correctness and happiness; but if it associates with senselessness, it produces the opposite effects. Soul as soul, we see, has all the motions of the human soul, even though it originates all motions in heaven and earth; the primacy of the soul thus understood does not yet establish the existence of gods; but perhaps what most men understand by gods is, or approximates to, human souls, beneficial or the opposite, which possess superhuman power. Be that as it may, the Athenian continues his reasoning by raising the question which kind of soul, the one sensible and full of virtue or the other possessing neither good sense nor virtue, rules heaven and earth and the whole circuit. He answers for all three of them that if the whole motion of heaven and what it contains has a like nature as the motion, revolution, and calculations of the intellect, one must say that the best soul takes care of the whole *kosmos*; but if the whole motion proceeds in a mad and disorderly way, one must say that the bad soul is in control of the whole *kosmos*. But which nature does the motion of the intellect have? A difficult question since the intellect cannot be seen by mortal eyes. An image of the motion of the intellect is that motion which always moves in one place around the same center and in relation to the same things and in the same direction according to one plan and one order. The Athenian now repeats the question whether the best soul or the soul of the opposite character is responsible for the care and ordering of the revolution of heaven. For Kleinias there is no longer any doubt that the best soul is in charge of the whole; as he puts it, on the basis of what has been said, it would not even be pious to assert the opposite. Kleinias' answer is somewhat surprising, for when astronomy was being discussed, he shared the error of all Greeks according to which the heavenly bodies do not move uniformly; this view agreed at least partly with his own observations; the question was not settled at that time (821b3–823d1; but cf. 886a2–4). Yet at that time Kleinias' belief, based on reports of mysterious origin, in the existence of gods was in no way linked to the question of the good order of the heavenly motions; now, however, he has come to see that without an affirmative reply to that question the belief in the existence of gods would be wholly baseless; he has come to see that a negative reply would be not only wrong but not even pious. He adds only one qualification: the good soul responsible for the kosmic order may be one or more than one; after all, there is not only one god. The Athenian praises Kleinias highly for his listening to the speeches and understanding them. He then makes clear to him, taking the sun as example for all heavenly bodies, that every human being sees the body of the sun, but no one sees its soul, for no soul can be perceived by the senses but can be grasped only by the intellect or by reasoning. There are three different ways in which the soul of the sun can be thought to move its body, one of them being that the soul of the sun dwells in the sun's body as our soul dwells in our body, i.e., that the sun is a living being (*zoon*). One does not have to settle this question in order to be bound to regard the sun as a god. The same is true of the other heavenly bodies; all things are full of gods.

The proof of the existence of gods is thus completed to the entire satisfaction of Kleinias. In spite of the proof of the priority of the soul to the body one may wonder whether the existence of gods lacking bodies, being invisible, and possessing altogether permanent and unchangeable shapes (cf. *Republic* 380d1–381c10) has been established. One may further wonder whether the souls of the heavenly bodies can be assumed to be capable of such motions as fear, anger or hate, and grief. Of more immediate relevance is the status of the bad soul which is responsible for the disorder occurring within the whole, and which is not mentioned any more in the sequel. The assumption of such a soul followed from the premise that the soul is in the last analysis the cause of all things. But perhaps this premise is not tenable; in that case the soul together with something that is not soul would be in the last analysis the cause of all things. Under no circumstances can the soul or souls guided by good sense and all virtue be the cause of everything—can it or they, can the gods, be omnipotent.

After it has been established with great persuasiveness that gods are, it must next be established that they care for human affairs. Exhorting someone who believes the first point but not the second, the Athenian tells him that it is perhaps some kinship with the divine —i.e., not necessarily the preceding proof of the existence of gods— which draws him to believe in gods and to honor them, but that it is the apparent happiness of the bad and unjust which is incorrectly praised by poets and others, and glaring examples of which he may have himself observed which lead him into impiety; because of his kinship with the gods he is unwilling to blame them as responsible for such things and unable to feel disgust at the gods; he therefore sees no way out except to assert that the gods look down with contempt on human affairs and do not have care for them; to prevent his present opinion from getting still worse—could it not lead to straight atheism?—we must connect the appropriate argument with the preceding one that was directed against the atheist. He then turns to Kleinias and Megillos with the request that they should, as they had done in the preceding discussion, answer his questions on behalf of the young man who is to be cured of his errors. It is not obvious that in the preceding discussion they, or Kleinias alone, had answered on behalf of a young man (cf. 892d2–893a7). Or does it go without saying that Kleinias and Megillos never needed for themselves a demonstration of the existence of gods?

The young man was present when it was said that the gods, good in every kind of goodness, possess the care of all things, which is most appropriate to them. (We are bidden to forget what we have heard about the bad soul.) We agree that the gods possess the following kinds of goodness or virtue: moderation, the possessing of intellect, courage, and the opposite of idleness or carelessness, the last apparently taking the place of justice. The god hates idleness and carelessness. It is impossible to say that he cares only for the great things and does not care for, or neglects, the small things. For no one not lazy or indolent does this unless he believes that neglect of the small things makes no difference to the whole; he may, indeed, fail to care for great or small things without incurring any reproach if it is impossible to care for all things. At this point the Athenian demands that two men should give answers to "the three of us," the two men being the one who says that the gods can be entreated and the other being the one who says that they are neglectful of the small things; both admit of course that gods are. The first question addressed to the two men is whether they say that the gods know, see, and hear everything and that nothing of which there is perception and science can possibly escape them. Kleinias answers in the affirmative. Yet it does not go without saying that both men to whom the question was addressed would have answered in the affirmative; almost certainly the first would have but by no means the second. By conjuring up prematurely the man who believes that the gods care for human affairs but can be bribed, the Athenian has simplified matters greatly for the benefit of the good cause. According to Kleinias, the two men will also grant that the gods can do everything within the power of mortals or immortals. In addition, "the

five of us" have already agreed that the gods are good, indeed very
good. (That agreement was reached prior to the emergence of the
fifth, of the one who believes that the gods can be bribed and who
therefore cannot possibly have a high opinion of the gods' virtue.)
Idleness or indolence are now traced to cowardice and hence their
opposites to courage: the proof of providence does not require consideration of the gods' justice. After we know that the gods are
all-knowing, as powerful as possible, and of superlative goodness,
the only question that remains to be settled is whether the gods
neglect the small things because they know that there is no need at
all to care for them. (To repeat, the gods cannot be all-powerful for
the reason for which the Athenian had had recourse to the bad
soul.) The Athenian addresses his next question to one man, i.e.,
to him who asserts that the gods neglect the small things; that question prepares the insight that all mortal animals, just as the whole
heaven, are possessions of the gods and hence cannot be neglected
by them, regardless of whether they are small or large in the eyes of
the gods: while man is the animal most given to worshiping gods
and therefore, we might think, the object of the gods' particular care,
they care no less for the affairs of wolves and lambs than for human
affairs; for men too are only playthings of the gods (644d7–9,
804b3–c1). Caring for men does not require justice on the gods'
part—no property owner is called just because he diligently takes
care of his property—but it requires courage ("energy"). Furthermore, perception and power are by nature opposite to one another
in regard to ease and difficulty; it is more difficult to see and hear
small things than great, while carrying, controlling and caring for
small and few things is easier for everyone than to do the same with
or for great ones. From this the Athenian does not immediately
draw the conclusion that since the gods admittedly perceive all
things, however small, it is still easier for them to take care of them,
for they may have no reason for doing so; their being the owners
of all animal species does not necessarily induce them to take care
of every lamb, every wolf, and every human being. One has to consider the gods as makers and artisans, for the artisans necessarily
deal with individual beings or things. In other words, property
owners are not necessarily wise or infallible, but artisans, insofar as
they are artisans, are (cf. *Republic* 340d2–e4). Human artisans
never limit themselves to taking care of the whole with which they
are concerned, for instance of the whole body of the patient, or of
the great things, but through one and the same art they also take
care of the small parts of the whole. But we must not consider that

the god is inferior to mortal artificers; being most wise, willing to take care of the small things, possessing the power to do so, and being the opposite of cowardly, he certainly does take care of them. (A particularly telling example of divine care for minute details occurred in 803e4–804b4.) Kleinias fully agrees, only replacing "the god" by "gods"; the rejected opinion, he says, should in no way be considered either pious or true. The refutation of the denier of providence is herewith completed.

Yet to force him by *logoi* to admit his error is not enough; he needs in addition some enchanting *mythoi*. Accordingly, the Athenian tries to persuade the young man that he who takes care of the whole has so arranged things with a view to the preservation and goodness of the whole that also each part, so far as possible, suffers and does what is proper to it; to each of these parts rulers are appointed who are in charge of each part's suffering and action down to the minutest detail. He then addresses the young man himself, apostrophizing him "you wretch." In somewhat enigmatic language he tells him that he too is a part, however small, of the whole and therefore has been generated for the sake of the whole, and therefore that what is best in his case for the whole is best for him too. The soul whose character grows better is shifted to a better place and the worse to a worse, according to what is becoming to each of them, so that each may receive its appropriate lot. In this way he who takes care of the whole, or the rulers appointed by him, or in a word the gods, take care of all things with amazing ease. The shifting of the souls to the places most suitable to them and best for the whole occurs in an orderly manner since it occurs after death, for soul and body, while not eternal, are imperishable like the gods who are according to law. Those who have committed major wrongs go down toward the deep, to what people call Hades and the like, and mightily fear, especially in their dreams; the opposite fate is in store for those who have made the opposite choice. For this is the custom or judgment of the gods who possess Olympos, as Odysseus said to Telemachos prior to the slaying of the wicked wooers and as the Athenian says now to the childish young man who believes that the gods neglect him and hence is hardly less guilty than the wooers: neither you nor any other wretch can escape that judgment; whatever you may do, wherever you may try to hide, you will pay to the gods the due penalty, perhaps in a place more terrifying than Hades. The same is true also of those who through the perpetration of unholy deeds have in your opinion become happy and thus led you into your error, for you did not realize that those monsters through their misdeeds and punishments contribute to the gods' purpose. The gods' justice, not mentioned in the *logoi*, and especially their punitive justice is fully vindicated or at any rate powerfully asserted in the *mythoi* in which the kosmic gods, with the help of a Homeric quotation, are identified with the Olympians. Before formally concluding his argument, the Athenian apostrophizes the young man as "most courageous of all," either because he has not feared Hades and what is worse than Hades or because he has the hardihood to question the evidence of the doctrine or the general opinion. In conclusion he tells him that if he still needs further argument, he should listen to the refutation of him who says that the gods accept gifts from wrongdoers and thus can be bribed.

In establishing the third dogma, the Athenian does not infer it directly from the admitted fact that the gods possess every virtue; instead, he first lays a foundation for bringing home how unspeakably vicious the gods would be if the opponent were right. He starts from their being rulers since they manage the whole heaven perpetually. Their rulership includes, if it does not entirely consist of, the waging of a never-dying battle against the bad things, which are more numerous than the good ones, and therefore a wondrous watchfulness; in that battle we are their allies; what destroys us, what we must do battle against, is injustice and *hybris* together with folly, and what saves us is justice and moderation together with good-sense —virtues which dwell in the animate powers of the gods and of which some small trace can also plainly be seen dwelling here in us. To expect that the gods could be bribed by gifts of the wrongdoers means, therefore, to expect that the gods desert their post—that like corrupt dogs, instead of protecting the flock, they share a small part of the loot with wolves. This likeness and similar ones show forth the absurdity of the opponent's opinion. The Athenian does not elaborate the comparison—which is particularly apt since the gods are the leaders in the undying fight against the bad things—of gods who can be bribed with generals who on a campaign betray their armies and their city to the enemy; the comparison is particularly apt, for the whole ruled by the gods is characterized not only or simply by harmony and peace but by an undying battle as well. Agreeing with the Athenian, Kleinias declares that everyone who holds this pernicious opinion is most justly judged to be the worst and most impious of all impious ones. With Kleinias' (and Megillos') full approval, the Athenian finally declares that they have sufficiently demonstrated that the gods are, that they exercise care, and that they cannot be bribed.

The Athenian then apologizes for the somewhat vehement or over-zealous character of "these speeches." Although one might find that the apology applies most aptly to the *mythoi* and to the refutation of the denier of the third dogma, the context makes it certain that it is meant to apply to the whole theology.

The theology, being the prelude to the laws about impiety, is followed by those laws. Those found guilty of impiety committed by deed or speech will be imprisoned, but there will be a gradation of penalties corresponding to the gravity of the crimes. There are three prisons in the city, a common one in the market place for most cases, one near to where a special council meets at nighttime and called *sophronisterion* (the name reminds one of the *phrontisterion* in the *Clouds*), and one in the middle of the country, in a solitary and most desolate place. People become guilty of impiety for the three reasons mentioned, and each of these reasons gives rise to two kinds of impiety; there are then six classes of offenders in respect of the divine things, all requiring different degrees of punishment. Of those who do not believe at all that gods are, some have a character by nature good, hate the bad men, and through loathing injustice do not do wrong (cf. *Republic* 366c5–d1), while others are incontinent, possess powerful memories, and are quick at learning; the man of the first kind is likely to be of utter frankness of speech regarding the gods and regarding sacrifices and oaths and, by ridiculing others would perhaps make them, too, impious, if he were not punished; the other, renowned as gifted, full of craft and guile, belongs to the class of men from which come many soothsayers and jugglers, sometimes also tyrants, public speakers, and generals, plotters of private mysteries and the devices of those called sophists. Of these two types the dissembling one (the ironic one) deserves not one death or two, but the other needs admonition together with imprisonment. The same distinction into two types must be applied to the deniers of the two other dogmas. In all these cases, those led into error by folly but not possessing a bad character are to be condemned to stay in the *sophronisterion* for no less than five years, during which time no citizen may visit them except the members of the Nocturnal Council who are to take care of their improvement; if after the lapse of the five years a man of this kind is thought to have come to his senses, he will be released; if he relapses, however, he will be punished with death. Those on the other hand who, despising human beings, charm the souls of many of the living, claim to charm the souls of the dead, promise to bewitch the gods through sacrifices, prayers, and incantations, and thus from greed of money ruin private citizens and whole houses and cities, must be imprisoned in the worst of the three prisons, where no free men may approach them; after their death their corpses will be cast beyond the borders without burial; their children will be treated as orphans from the date of their father's conviction and will not be deprived by law of anything on account of the father's guilt.

Let us consider some difficulties to which this law is exposed. As for the crime of not believing in gods taken by itself, it is not clear whether a man who believes in the kosmic gods, whose existence has been demonstrated somehow, without believing in the Olympian gods, is guilty of impiety; he will be guilty of impiety if the *mythoi* supporting the second dogma are assigned the same status as the *logoi*. Furthermore, the disjunction made by the law is not complete: what happens to the atheist who is a just man and does not ridicule others because they sacrifice and pray and who to this extent is a dissembler? is it literally true of him that he deserves not one death or two, i.e., no death at all, nor imprisonment? Also, why could such an atheist not possess a good memory and be good at learning? One could say that he will become guilty if he frankly expresses his unbelief—but what if he expresses it only to sensible friends? Can one imagine Socrates denouncing him to the authorities?

The final law on this subject forbids the possession of private shrines; all divine worship must take place in the public temples (cf. 717b4–5, 885a1).

Book Eleven

This Book lacks an apparent order to a higher degree than any preceding Book. As abruptly as the Athenian had ascended to the highest subject, the gods, so abruptly does he now descend to the ordering of transactions among human beings. More precisely, immediately before taking up the subject of impiety, he had begun to speak of crimes against one's neighbor's property (884a1–3); he continues that speech now, the sanctity of property being presupposed in transactions. The sanctity of property has a solid foundation: my concern with others' respecting my property will lead me, if I have sense, to respect the property of others. The first subject taken up is others' (other families') buried treasure. Speaking in the first person singular, not as a legislator, let alone as a teacher of legislators, but as a sensible and just citizen, the Athenian gives utterance to this resolve: I would never pray to gods that I may find a treasure, nor would I, having found it, move it, nor would I contact the so-called diviners who counsel me in any case to take up what had been laid down in the earth, for my gain in substance through taking it up would be smaller than my increase in virtue and justice through not taking it up, to say nothing of the superiority of the soul to property. Not taking up treasures is one kind of "not moving the unmoved," which is generally speaking a wise and well-stated law. But one must also obey the myths which assert that taking up treasures and the like has an adverse effect on one's offspring. Disobeying the law and the myth, one disobeys also the very simple law laid down by a man in no way contemptible who said, "Do not take up what you did not lay down." The prohibition against taking up treasures is the work, then, not of one or more divine legislators, nor of the Athenian and his interlocutors, but of two human legislators who are left nameless. As for the punishment, the Athenian asks the city to abide by what the god in Delphi in each case through his oracle determines; he himself determines only the procedure and the reward for the informer (if he is a slave, he will be set free) as well as the punishment for him who failed to inform. He had not hesitated to determine the penalties to be inflicted on the different kinds of men guilty of impiety. Does he indicate by his present procedure that he would not under any circumstance entrust to Apollon or any other Olympian the determination of penalties in cases of impiety and, in particular, for holding that those gods are not, remembering perhaps Hermes' participation in lynch justice at the end of the *Clouds*? After he has opened his discussion of the laws regarding transactions with a discussion of what should be done concerning the appropriation of buried treasure, he does nothing out of the ordinary by taking up the subject of lost and found property. In that case, as goes without saying, the determination of penalties for transgressions of the law is entirely in the hands of the human legislator.

A valuable piece of property, which can easily be lost because it can run away and cleverly elude its pursuers, is a slave. At any rate, the Athenian turns next to the question of the conditions in which one may lay violent hands on a slave and a freedman. For good reasons he speaks most extensively about freedmen. Freedmen may be seized if they do not pay proper regard to their former masters. The inferiority of the freedman is preserved, among other things, by the prohibition against his becoming wealthier than his former master; any excess would become the master's property. In other respects he would have the status of a resident alien. If the substance of any of these becomes greater than that of a citizen of the third property class, he must leave the city within thirty days, taking his property with him. Transgression of this law is punished capitally. Permitting resident aliens to be equal in wealth to the wealthy citizens seems to verge on subversion of the regime.

The Athenian has now arrived at the subject of transactions proper or, more specifically, of buying and selling, a subject which he discusses at appropriate length.

He turns next to the prohibition against the giving and receiving of adulterated money and merchandise; he speaks on that subject more extensively and more emphatically than on the preceding one, prefacing the law with a prelude. Adulteration ought to be considered as belonging to the same class as lying and deception. The many wrongly say such actions can be correct provided they are performed in the right circumstances, but they fail to determine what those circumstances are. The legislator, however, cannot leave them undetermined, i.e., he must determine in which circumstances lying and kindred things are permissible. All these things are unqualifiedly forbidden in the first place if they are accompanied by perjury, and in the second place if they are done toward one's superiors, i.e., toward those who are better than oneself; generally speaking, the old are superior to the young, hence in particular the parents to their offspring, men are superior to women and children, rulers to the ruled; reverence for rulers is especially important in the case of the political rulers. This implies, but only implies, that deception of inferiors by superiors is permissible (cf. *Republic* 382c6–d4, 389b2–c7) and that the old do not in all cases enjoy the benefit of superiority. Surely no one who practices adulteration and the kindred things in the market can claim exemption from the almost universal prohibition. As for the law, it forbids him who sells anything in the market to name on one and the same day two different prices for anything he sells (this would literally be duplicity); it also forbids, of course, the sale of adulterated merchandise. The law is silent on adulterated money or coins (*nomismata*).

The subject of adulteration is plausibly followed by that of retail trade and kindred pursuits. The law on this subject is preceded not by a prelude, which as such is addressed to the citizenry, but by an advice and a reasoning which is addressed rather to legislators. By its nature, retail trade is beneficial since it renders even and commensurate to everyone's needs the essentially incommensurate and uneven wealth available in the city; this is partly achieved by the use of money. The benefit in question also requires the services of the wholesale trader, the hireling, the innkeeper, and the like; some of these pursuits are more and some are less reputable. How does it come about that trade as a whole is regarded as not noble or respectable? Even a partial improvement in this sphere would be no negligible matter and would require not a little virtue. (Cf. for this and what follows the view of Bucer, *De regno christi*, as summarized by R. H. Tawney, *Religion and the Rise of Capitalism*, III. i, Pelican Books, p. 135: "Only 'pious persons devoted to the Commonwealth more than to their own interests,' are to be allowed to engage in trade at all.") Kleinias does not understand. The Athenian therefore explains. Only a small class of human beings, by nature few and having received the most consummate rearing, are able to exercise self-control in regard to the acquisition of wealth. The many who lack that self-control have given trade its bad reputation. But if, what never ought to happen and never will, someone were to compel (it is ridiculous to say this but it should be said nevertheless) the men who are best in every way to keep inns for a time or to engage in retail trade or the like, or to compel women on the basis of some fated necessity to partake of such a mode of life, then we would see how friendly and desirable each of these activities is, and if they were carried on in an incorruptible way, they would be honored like the activities of a mother and nurse. The Athenian's explanation amounts then to this, that the activities of the retail trader and the innkeeper, which are by their nature beneficial, would in fact be beneficial if the best men and women were compelled by someone— by the legislator? by a legislator possessing tyrannical power?—to engage in them for a time; yet according to him this compulsion will never take place and ought never to take place. One may suggest that the activities in question, however beneficial and even respectable in themselves, are much below the dignity of the best men and women or that the elite of the city is needed for higher activities. Or does the Athenian bow to the prejudice of the gentlemen of the city? Or is his ridiculous proposal a deliberate caricature of Socrates' proposal that the best men and women be compelled to do the political things for a time, not as something noble but as something necessary or compulsory (*Republic* 540b1–5, 520a8 etc.)? In that case one might have to be grateful to the Athenian for the light which he sheds on Socrates' proposal by characterizing it as a falsehood which is not even noble. Yet no one can deny that it is more seemly to impose on the philosophers the duty to be kings than the duty to keep inns or to peddle. The Athenian drives home his immediately pertinent lesson by contrasting what an honest if inexperienced man would suppose if he suddenly came across an inn in a deserted and remote region in the mountains, with the sad truth. He would suppose that a lover of human beings had decided to give unselfish help to tired and hungry wayfarers exposed to winter's cold or summer's heat; but when leaving he would find himself treated like a captive enemy who is fleeced for the highest possible ransom. The legislator must provide a remedy for evils of this kind; he must be aware of the fact that he must do battle against two opposites: against wealth, which corrupts the soul of human beings with luxury, and against poverty, which through pains leads it into shamelessness. The remedy consists above all of three laws, the first forbidding trade of any kind to any of the 5,040 landowners, the second permitting retail trade only to resident aliens and foreigners, the third enjoining strict supervision of retail trade by the law guardians acting in consultation with those who are experienced in those various kinds of such trade which are indispensable to the city and therefore permitted; that supervision and consultation applies also to the fixing of prices. It could seem that the wholesale or import and export trade is silently permitted to "younger sons."

The Athenian discusses next the obligation to keep lawful agreements insofar as it applies to artificers of two kinds, the ordinary artificers and the artificers of salvation in war (the military commanders). They are sacred to gods, the former to Hephaistos and Athena, the latter to Ares and Athena. By lying concerning their craft, they would show disrespect for their divine ancestors. If an artificer of the former kind does not keep his obligation, he shows disrespect for the god who gives him his livelihood while erroneously believing that the god, being a relative, will be indulgent to him. He will be punished by the god, and secondarily a law will be enacted to suit the case. Here the law itself contains something like a prelude extolling the intrinsic dignity of art—a prelude that reminds us of the praise of the intrinsic dignity of retail trade. A second law, which determines the penalty of him who does not pay the stipulated wage to the worker at the stipulated time, is preceded by the remark that such a man dishonors Zeus, who holds the city, and Athena. As for the artificers of salvation for the whole city, i.e., the generals and other practitioners of the military art, it may suffice for us to know that those among them who are derelict in their duty do not dream of believing that they can count on the indulgence of Ares as their kinsman. While the good artificers of this kind are thus seen to be superior to the artificers proper, they are inferior in dignity to those who have proved themselves able in an outstanding manner to honor the writings of the good legislators; it is left open whether the excellent commander of an army is not equal or superior in dignity to those who are most obedient to the established laws regardless of the quality of the laws (cf. 715b7–d2, 729d4–e1).

The most important transactions or business dealings among human beings have now been more or less regulated, with the exception of what pertains to orphans and the care of orphans by their guardians; it is to this subject that the Athenian turns next. By his introductory remark he makes clear that the subjects to be dealt with in the sequel (928d5ff.) do not belong to business transactions. But it is not clear why the regulations regarding orphans are to be subsumed under business transactions. Under what then are they properly or seriously subsumed? The Athenian discusses first the great inconveniences that arise from the unlimited liberty given to men who are about to die, to dispose of their property as they wish. For most of us are in a thoughtless and enervated condition when we believe that we are about to die. Kleinias does not understand, but when the Athenian by becoming more explicit makes him understand, he reveals that he, himself an old man, favors the liberty of which the Athenian disapproves; this is the most dialogic part of this Book, which is on the whole rather undialogic. According to the Athenian, a human being on the point of dying wishes to retain his mastery over all he has and asserts his claim with anger; calling on the gods he will say that it would be terrible if he were not permitted to give what is his to whomsoever he wills and to distribute it according to the way in which different people have conducted themselves toward him, in particular when he was ill and old. The ancient legislators, frightened by this kind of speech, mistakenly gave in to it. The legislators of old were unduly indulgent to the unreasonable claims of old men—perhaps because those legislators themselves were old men. The present legislators are also old men, but one of them is the Athenian, who wins over Kleinias by addressing a prelude in his and Kleinias' name to the citizens in Kleinias' city who are about to die; the prelude is meant to persuade in the first place Kleinias himself. It rejects the claim of the testators to absolute ownership: their property and they themselves belong to their clan and still more to the city; accordingly, the legislator will lay down his laws with a view to what is best for the whole city and the clan, justly subordinating to it the wishes of the individual. The law takes care above all of the preservation of the ancestral allotment along the lines of the laws laid down in Book Five. The law entitles but does not compel the testator to leave to each of his children other than the heir of the lot any part of his property apart from the lot; the law apparently presumes that the father loves all his children, if not all of them equally. The law also provides for proper guardianship and thus begins to deal with the manifest subject of this section. The same law provides for proper guardianship in case the father dies intestate. A further law provides in great detail for the marrying of the daughters of a father who died intestate. The legislator cannot provide, as a father could and would, for husbands who by their characters and manner of life are suitable for the daughters. A further law provides for heirs in case the intestate leaves no children. In that case the family lot will be inherited by a couple consisting of the nearest male and the nearest female relative of the deceased. The law thus may compel a young man or woman to marry a repulsive member of the opposite sex. This is not the fault of the legislator, for he has to care for the well-being of the whole and can therefore not be expected to arrange everything in a way that accords with the desires of the individuals. The difficulty may remind us of a difficulty which we encountered when providence was being discussed. The present difficulty is resolved by the choice of men who act as arbitrators between the laws and those subject to the laws. These arbitrators will have to take care of all hardships of this kind and, in particular, of those threatening the happiness of orphans. In the rest of the section the Athenian speaks in the most emphatic manner possible of the sacred duty incumbent upon both the highest magistrates in charge of orphans in general and the guardians of orphans to take care of every orphan. He refers to the earlier speeches according to which the souls of the dead retain some power for some time after their death—a power through which they take care of affairs falling within the purview of men (cf. 865d5–e6). These things are true but the speeches containing them are long; one must therefore rely on, or believe in, the numerous and very ancient utterances of mysterious origin concerning matters of this kind; but one must also rely on, or believe, those who legislate that things are that way—unless the assertions in question are altogether foolish. If these things are in this manner according to nature, i.e., not merely according to *nomos*, the men whom it concerns must in the first place fear the gods above who have perceptions of the orphans' loneliness, and then the souls of the departed in whose nature it is to care lovingly for their children in an outstanding manner and who are of good will to those who honor them and of ill will to those who do not. (Observe the different manner in which the concern of the gods above and that of the dead parents is characterized.) The men whom it concerns must fear, furthermore, the souls of those who are still alive but old and of the highest distinction and who have a keen hearing and a keen sight in such matters —something which is not said of the gods above or the dead parents—and are of good will to those who are just therein but are wroth especially with those who are insolent to helpless orphans. He who is persuaded by the myth and in no way harms the orphan will not come to feel the anger of the legislator on this score, but he who disobeys will be punished twice as severely as he who harms the child whose parents are alive. It seems that the most important deterrent, apart from the law, to bad treatment of orphans and in particular to faithlessness in guardianship is the wrath of the dead parents; the guardian tempted by unlawful gain from cheating the orphan will balance that gain against what he has to fear from the dead parents; to this extent dealing with orphans comes under the heading of transactions among human beings (living or dead) or of business transactions. It is not altogether out of place to think of what Socrates indicates in the *Euthyphro* regarding prayers and sacrifices as a kind of *do ut des* between human beings and gods. As for the law regarding orphans, its principle is that the guardian must treat the orphan as if he or she were his own child, i.e., his natural child; the gulf between man's natural love of his offspring and the care for orphans is bridged by the *nomos* which is supported by the myth.

The section on orphans occupies literally the center of this Book (922a6–928d4). That this is reasonable appears if one considers the manner in which the subject is treated. The next section is devoted to serious dissensions between parents and children and between spouses as well as to dissolution of marriage by death; the discussion terminates and culminates in a powerful reminder of the duty to honor aged parents and grandparents. Under conditions specified by the Athenian, a father may publicly proclaim that his son is no longer his son according to law; in our city a man who has thus become fatherless has become by this very fact cityless, i.e., he must emigrate, for the number of 5,040 households must not be increased, and there is apparently no intermediate position in the city between people who are owners of a lot or heirs to one, and resident aliens. The law does not prevent another citizen from adopting the repudiated son, for the characters of the young naturally undergo many changes in the course of their lives; if he is not adopted within ten years, those in charge of sending out the surplus children to a colony must take care also of sons of this kind. It would seem then that in the intervening period there are people in the city who are not owners of a lot or heirs to one and yet are not resident aliens; perhaps those people are free to engage in wholesale trade, as an earlier passage (919d8–920b3) seemed to suggest. The law also provides for the legal incapacitation of a senile father; in this case there is of course no public proclamation by the son that his father is no longer his father according to law; the father only loses the right to dispose of even the smallest fraction of what is his and spends the rest of his life like a child. We have been reminded before of the fact that old age is a second childhood (646a4) as well as of the folly of old men who think that they are about to die (922b2–923a5). The provisions of the law proposed by the Athenian regarding divorce and regarding remarriage both after divorce and after the death of one of the spouses are animated by the same compassion which animated his law regarding orphans as well as by the concern for the common good, i.e., for the procreation of legitimate offspring; there is naturally no recourse to myth here. While all these provisions are indispensable in a code of good laws, they are in the context only preparatory to the Athenian's statement on the honoring of aged parents and grandparents, the only dialogic part of the present section: the part (922a6–932d8), roughly the center of the Book, which began with observations on the incompetence of the old, is fittingly concluded with a moving praise of their venerability. No god or human being having sense will ever counsel anyone to neglect parents. The subject of honoring and dishonoring parents is appropriately prefaced by this consideration regarding the worship of gods: ancient laws regarding gods have been laid down to all in a twofold manner; we honor those gods whom we see clearly (the kosmic gods); of the other gods we set up statues as images which are lifeless indeed but the worship of which, we believe, makes the living gods whom they represent feel great good-will and gratitude to us (it could seem that honoring the kosmic gods does not induce them to feel good will and gratitude); aged parents and grandparents living in one's house are as potent as a statue for procuring the Olympians' good-will and gratitude, if the owner of that kind of statue tends it properly and correctly. That this is so is shown in the first place by the efficacy of the curses of angry parents who believe that they have been dishonored by their children—for instance, Theseus believed that he had been dishonored by his son Hippolytos—for a parent's curse upon his children is more efficacious than any other curse and most justly so. If the curses of dishonored parents are then naturally hearkened to by gods, is it not obvious that the blessings of parents who are honored by their children are equally efficacious? Otherwise the gods would not be just dispensers of good things and this, we assert, would be least becoming to gods. We see now more clearly than before the difference between lifeless statues of the gods and those statues which are the aged parents and grandparents: the latter, if honored, join us in our prayers for blessings or, if dishonored, pray for the opposite, while the former are the lifeless transmitters of our worship of the gods; hence aged parents and grandparents are not merely not inferior to any other statues but superior to all. This admonition loses hardly anything of its efficacy through the fact which the Athenian in his honesty does not suppress that the prayers of parents have been hearkened to by the gods, not in all cases nor even in most but in many. For one may say that what happens in many cases happens by nature. It should be added that the present exhortation to honor one's parents is not saddled with the difficulty as to whether

one ought to honor one's progenitors more or less than one's soul
(cf. 726a3–727a3).

The Athenian suddenly turns to the subject of voluntary and
deliberate but not fatal damage caused by poison. That subject as
well as the next one (theft and robbery), belonging to penal law,
ought to have been dealt with, one could think, at the beginning of
Book Eleven at the latest; their treatment in the present context
shows that Plato had special reasons for beginning Book Eleven
with transactions among human beings and, in particular, with the
appropriation of other families' buried treasures; what these reasons
were, we believe to have discerned. There are two kinds of poisoning: one harms bodies by bodies (foods, drinks, and unguents)
according to nature; the other uses witchcraft (sorcery, incantations,
and spells), the criminals and the victims being persuaded that
people can be harmed by such means. It is not easy to know how
harming through witchcraft and all other things of this kind—is he
by any chance also thinking of curses?—naturally take place, or, if
one knew how, to persuade others of it; surely if one has no clear
knowledge of things of this kind, it is not worth while attempting
to persuade people to pay no attention to them. Nevertheless, not
only he who inflicts harm by natural poisoning but also he who
seems to be similar to him who inflicts harm, i.e., he who uses incantations and the like in the intention to harm, commits a punishable
offense; in case the actual or would-be harmer is an expert, a physician in the first case and a soothsayer in the second, the penalty is
death. Plato's openmindedness regarding witchcraft is not more remarkable than his openmindedness regarding the curses of angry
parents.

As for theft and robbery, the Athenian states in the broadest
outlines that he who causes damage to another man through theft
or robbery must pay a large compensation if the damage is great
and a small one if the damage is small and, besides, must suffer
punishment in accordance with the gravity of the defect which
caused his crime. He adds the very general remark that in the first
place the legislator and secondarily the judge must assign the just
punishment and also the just compensation; the judge must act
within the limits laid down by the legislator. "That is what we have
to do now, Megillos and Kleinias, in the most noble and best way;
we must state the right penalties and compensations for all thefts
and deeds of violence, as far as gods and sons of gods allow us to
legislate." For the members of the city and even its legislators are
not gods or sons of gods but human beings. The Athenian fails to

lay down these necessary laws. We may recall that he had begun to legislate on theft in Book Nine but that that beginning was very unsatisfactory, and as a consequence the subject was dropped (857a2–c7, 859b6–8); he does legislate on theft from temples and from the fatherland (854d1–856a9, 941b2–942a4), but he fails to legislate on common theft. In the preceding section he had discussed witchcraft or the use of spells (*goeteuein*); stealing, concealing or disguising (*kleptein*), and bewitching are kindred phenomena (cf. *Republic* 380d1–6, 413b1–c4); enchanting or disguising is no mean part of the Athenian's legislative art (664b3–c2, 665c2–5, 837e6, 903b1ff.). It could seem that he is adumbrating here the difference between himself and the ancient legislators.

The next subject is madness, especially the kind of madness that comes from a bad nature and training of spiritedness (*thymos*); the Athenian is thus led, not indeed by necessity pure and simple, but by logographic necessity to state the law regarding "evil-speaking." In what is in fact a prelude forming part of the law, he points out that from "praying against" one another and cursing one another and using bad words against one another there spring hatreds and enmities; people who do such things give in to *thymos*, a graceless thing. "In this highly colored and elaborately rhetorical passage Plato seems himself to be 'raising his voice'—perhaps on purpose to show us what sort of language it is which he deplores" (England). We may also note that he abstracts from the cases in which one of the two individuals concerned remains calm and decent. Frequently the angry outbursts lead to ridiculing of the opponent. The Athenian is thus enabled to speak and to legislate about the forbidden and the permitted kind of ridiculing, or, more particularly, of comedy. We are thus reminded of the fact that the right kind of comedy will be present in his city while the presence of tragedy in it remains uncertain. How much this fact illustrates the peculiar character of the Athenian does not need further comment. What one ought to stress is the corresponding devaluation of *thymos* (cf. 888a2–6).

From the ridiculous the Athenian turns understandably to the pitiable or lamentable; he does not turn from comedy to tragedy unless, as a jester might say, he has in mind Euripidean tragedy; for he speaks now of beggars. Generally speaking, beggars are fit to be pitied provided they are sober-minded or possess some virtue or a part of it. But in a tolerably well-ordered polity, such men, even if they are slaves, will not come to utter beggary, for, as we have learned near the beginning, if a city acquires the divine goods, it acquires by this fact also the human goods (631b6–c1); it is only by the intermediacy of a well-ordered polity that the perfectly good man does not suffer injustice (cf. 829a1–6; cf. *Apology of Socrates* 41d1–2). In the Athenian city, begging—collecting one's livelihood by ceaseless prayers—is strictly forbidden; the country must be wholly cleansed of that kind of animal, the beggar.

As if to remind us that the present overall theme is still "damages," the Athenian concludes this part by legislating on the compensation for damages caused by a man's slaves or beasts.

The last two sections of this Book are devoted to public duties or functions. The penultimate section lays down the regulations regarding witnesses, and in particular, false witnesses. The ultimate section deals with pleading and helping others to plead and, in particular, with the alleged art which claims to win lawsuits regardless of whether the actions at issue in the case are just or unjust and to do this for the payment of money. That art must never, if possible, arise in our city. But if anyone attempts to engage in that unjust practice from love of victory, the competent law court shall determine for how long a time he shall be precluded from bringing an action against anyone or helping anyone to do so; if he attempts it twice, his penalty will be death; if his motive, however, is love of money, he must leave the country forever, if he is a stranger; but if he is a citizen, his penalty will be death, because love of money is held in so high honor with him.

Book Twelve

The bulk of this Book, as distinguished from the preceding Book, is devoted to public matters, including crimes against the city, as distinguished from transactions among individuals, including crimes against individuals.

The first subject is deception of the city by ambassadors or heralds sent to other cities; men guilty of this kind of misconduct will be indicted for having committed impious acts against the law regarding embassies and commandments, which are under the protection of Hermes and Zeus; if found guilty, they will receive condign punishment. The Athenian does not determine the penalty, nor does he say which authority shall determine it. He also had not determined the penalty when discussing the first subject of Book Eleven; but there he had left the determination to the god in Delphi.

The Athenian turns next to the subject of theft and robbery; he elaborates, however, only the law regarding the theft of public property. A foreigner or slave found guilty of this crime is presumed to be curable; his penalty or fine is left to the discretion of the court. But if the culprit is a citizen and has been reared as he will have been reared in our city, he will be punished by death, since he is presumed to be incurable. The statement of the law is preceded by what is in fact a prelude which points out that none of the sons of Zeus (hence, especially not Hermes) has ever practiced theft or robbery while enjoying fraud or violence; the prelude goes on to warn the hearers against believing such tales told by poets or careless myth tellers and against inferring from them that theft and robbery are not base but things which the very gods do. Such tales are neither true nor likely, but he who commits such acts against the law is never a god or a son of a god: the legislator must know these things better than all poets. The Athenian had last spoken of gods and sons of gods in his preceding discussion, which was likewise left incomplete, concerning theft (934c5–6), where he had implied that "we" human legislators are not gods or sons of gods.

The reader who draws any inference from this does so at his own peril. But one should not worry about the inconsistency of the law laid down now with the initial statement (857b1–3), for that statement was retracted at once as inadequate.

There follow the regulations regarding military service. The most important of them is to the effect that no one must ever be without a commander (*anarchos*); this applies to both sexes, to seriousness as well as to play, to war as well as to peace; no one must grow habituated to acting alone and by himself; at all times one must look to the commander and follow his lead even in the smallest things; "anarchy" must be removed from the whole life of men, nay, of all beasts subject to human rule (cf. *Republic* 563c3–d1). The Athenian's powerful and beautiful statements could lead one to think for a moment that he is bent on establishing an armed camp rather than a city (666d11–667a1), were they not addressed to a single youth rather than to a herd, or, more generally, were it not for the important "Athenian" ingredients of his city. In elaborating the laws regarding military service he has to contend with the difficulty of distinguishing between compulsory and disgraceful loss of arms in war. For instance, if Patroklos had revived after he had lost to Hektor the arms which, as the poet says, had been given to Peleus by the gods as a dowry to Thetis, and had in this state been brought to the tent, only mean men would have abused Patroklos for the loss of the arms. But what happened to Patroklos according to this myth, i.e., according to the Athenian's variation of the Homeric story, has happened in fact to thousands and thousands whose arms did not have the distinction of those worn by Patroklos. Soldiers may lose their arms without disgrace by many kinds of mishaps. Thus the distinction between disgraceful and excusable loss of arms becomes obscured, so much so that one can easily give a good color to a disgraceful act. One must therefore make a distinction between shield flinging, which is disgraceful, and dropping one's arms, which is not, or between the coward and the unfortunate man. As for the former, it is beyond human power to inflict on him the punishment which in a manner would be most becoming, namely, his transformation into a woman; the nearest approximation to this punishment is that he be prevented for the rest of his life from risking his life in war but be condemned to live in disgrace as long as possible; an officer who uses as a soldier a man convicted of shield flinging will be fined by the auditor; the shield flinger will be fined the same amount.

No one, we have learned, must be at any time *anarchos* (not subject to a commander or magistrate). But what about the magistrates themselves? The Athenian answers this question in the next section, which is devoted to the auditors. The auditors are, and are not, magistrates; they had not been mentioned in the thematic discussion of the magistracies in Book Six; in the thematic discussion of the auditors, which is rather extensive, they are called magistrates only once. Their function is to examine, and to pass judgment on, the magistrates after the expiry of their terms of office rather than to act as magistrates; they are judges rather than magistrates simply (cf. 767a7–9). They should all be men who surpass the magistrates in virtue, divine men, admirable in regard to every virtue. As is shown in particular by the honors which they receive, they are more venerable than all magistrates, or they are the most venerable magistrates. (The discussion of the auditors thus prepares the transition from the law guardians to the true law guardians.) They are the ones who alone can secure the unity of the polity in the midst of the multiplicity of the magistracies and thus the preservation of the polity. Their selection must be in accordance with their surpassing importance. It must be of surpassing solemnity. Every year after the summer solstice the whole city must assemble in the precinct that is common to the sun-god and Apollon and must present to the god three male citizens, fifty years old or older; each citizen must propose that man whom he believes to be best in every respect; he cannot, of course, propose himself. The three nominated men who receive the most votes are elected; if the three elected men each receive the same number of votes, their order of rank will be determined by lot; the three elected men, i.e., the three best men, are then presented to the sun-god and are dedicated by the city according to the ancient law as its first-fruit to Apollon and the sun-god in common. The three auditors annually elected will form part of the whole body of auditors; seventy-five is the age limit for them. They reside in the precinct of Apollon and the sun-god. Appeal from their judgment on magistrates to the appropriate law court is possible; the auditors themselves may be prosecuted if their judgment has been found to be unjust by the judges. The Athenian speaks at considerable length of the surpassing honors to be given to the auditors both while they are alive and after their death. Among other things, they all are to be priests of Apollon and the sun-god, and he who has been adjudged first of those appointed in every year is to be the high priest for that year. While in the election of ordinary priests the lot is decisive, it plays only a very subordinate role in the election of the auditors. (Thirty-six lines out of the 106 which are devoted to the auditors are devoted to their honors; 11 out of these 36 lines are devoted to the honors they receive while they are alive, and 25 to the honors they receive at their burial and in their graves. The contrast between the detailed provisions regarding the burial of auditors and the perfunctory statement of the *Republic*—465e1–3— on the burial of the subphilosophic rulers is noteworthy.) If an auditor proves unworthy of his high office, he will be deprived of it and of all the honors going with it.

While in the election of the judges who are to form the highest court for all civil suits the electors are required to take an oath (767c4–d4; cf. 755c8–d2), the Athenian was silent on oaths in the section on the auditors. He thus prepared the discussion of the subsequent section. Rhadamanthys, being the son of a god and legislating for a community the majority of whom were sons of gods, put the litigants in a case on their oath about their assertions, and thus secured a speedy and safe settlement. He could do this since he had perceived that the human beings of his time believed that gods manifestly are (for were they not manifestly themselves the sons of gods?). But Rhadamanthys' device is no longer appropriate in our time, in which the three fundamental theologoumena set forth in Book Ten are no longer universally or even generally believed in. Human opinions about gods having changed, the laws also must change. We have been made witnesses to the change of human opinion about gods since we were compelled to accept the Athenian's critique of the divine legislations of Crete and Sparta. Remembering this fact we are entitled to think that the change from Rhadamanthys' time to the Athenian's time is not altogether a change for the worse; it is the change that makes philosophy possible and hence necessary. The Athenian acts here on what he had said in his account of human life in the olden times, i.e., after the Flood (679b3–e5). Laws laid down by means of the intellect will not permit the litigants to take oaths; otherwise the city will be filled with perjurers. But judges must take oaths when about to pronounce judgment, and electors too must take oaths.

Just as in the section on auditors nothing was said about oaths, which became the subject of the subsequent section, in the section on oaths nothing was said about penalties for false oaths, while penalties for certain kinds of offense against the city became the subject of the subsequent section. The kinds of offense in question do not call for whipping, imprisonment, or death. One wonders in

retrospect whether the penalty for perjury is whipping, imprisonment, or death or something still more terrifying and degrading. (Cf.
937b7–c5.)

The next subject is intercourse with foreigners either by citizens
going abroad or by admission of foreigners into the city; the section
devoted to this subject is the only one in Book Twelve (with the
obvious exception of the final section devoted to the Nocturnal
Council) which is not wholly undialogic: Kleinias at one point in
it raises a question. Intercourse with foreigners causes a great danger
to well-ordered cities, for it may lead to innovations; the cities
which are not well-ordered, i.e., most cities, are not exposed to that
danger: they cannot get worse than they are. To prohibit altogether
the reception of men from other cities and the traveling of our own
citizens is not possible; furthermore, expulsion of foreigners (as the
Spartans practice it) is incompatible with good reputation among
others, and such reputation must never be scorned. For however
much the many are deficient in being virtuous, to the same degree
they can judge other men; there is some divine power of guessing
well even in bad men so that very many of those who are altogether
bad distinguish well in their speeches and opinions the better men
from the worse. This being so, most cities are rightly exhorted to be
concerned with good repute with the many, with their "image," as
the contemporary vulgarians say. Of course, the most important
thing is to be truly good and to seek good repute solely through
this and there is every reason for hoping that our new Cretan city
will gain for itself the most resplendent and best reputation in regard
to virtue. Taking into consideration the requirements of preserving
the virtuous city and of a decent respect for the opinion of the many,
we shall make the following arrangements regarding intercourse with
foreigners. No one younger than forty will be permitted under any
circumstances to go abroad except on military expeditions; no one
will be permitted to go abroad on his own, as distinguished from
being sent out by the city as herald, ambassador, or *theoros* (spectator) of one kind or another. Of special importance are the embassies sent to the Panhellenic sacrifices and games; they must consist
of the cream of the city; on their return they will teach the young
that the political institutions of the other cities are inferior to those
of our city. Furthermore, the city ought to send out spectators of the
following kind, namely, citizens who wish to behold the affairs of
other human beings at some greater leisure than going abroad on
missions for the city would permit; the citizens in question must
have the permission of the law guardians for their travel. A city

cannot be perfectly civil without such knowledge of good and bad
human beings as is acquired by intercourse with foreigners, nor can the
laws be preserved by [no]* more than mere habit, which is obviously
insufficient without such intercourse. Divine men, conversing with
whom is eminently valuable for the understanding and the improvement of the law of one's city, arise no less in badly ordered cities
than in well-ordered ones. Of course, a spectator of this kind must
be incorruptible. He must be over fifty years old and not older than
sixty. He must be a man of high repute militarily and otherwise.
He may stay abroad for as long as ten years, if he wishes. On his
return he must report to the Nocturnal Council; the Athenian describes its composition here for the first time, without, however,
using its official title (cf. 908a4, 909a3–4). Most noteworthy is the
fact that half of those attending the meetings of that Council are
young men between thirty and forty years old. The members of the
Council always converse about laws of their own city as well as
about anything remarkable they hear of laws elsewhere; they converse of course also about subjects of learning that have a bearing
on the clearer understanding of laws. As soon as he has returned,
the spectator will communicate to the Council whatever he has seen
or heard of foreign customs, including those of education, and what
he has thought out himself. If through his travels he has become a
much better man, he will receive honors during his life and after his
death; but if he has become corrupted, he may not associate with
anyone young or older, for pretending to have become wise he will
corrupt others; if he does not comply with this restriction to a strictly
private life, i.e., if he is found guilty of meddling in any matter of
education and the laws, he will be punished by death. In spite of the
profound differences between the Athenian's city on the one hand
and Crete and Sparta on the other, some equivalent of the Dorian
law of laws is preserved. The concluding part of the present section
is devoted to the admission of strangers. The Athenian speaks of
four classes of strangers who can be admitted with the proper safe-
guards. The fourth and most noteworthy class consists of the rare
men who correspond to our spectators of other cities' laws. In order
to be admitted to our city, a man of this kind must be at least fifty
years old and he must claim that he wants to view something noble,
superior in beauty to anything to be found in other cities or to
exhibit to another city something of that kind. Anyone of this kind

*["No" inserted.—J.C.]

may go unbidden to the doors of the wealthy and wise, being himself both wealthy and wise: he will both teach and learn. (One wonders whether the spectators from the Athenian's city travel at their own expense and therefore whether they must not be wealthy in the literal sense.) He will depart as friend from friend, honored with gifts and fitting honors. It would be a great understatement to say that the Athenian stranger meets these conditions. He mentions in passing that strangers admitted to the city may be of the female sex. He concludes the section with strong disapproval of the inhospitality of the Egyptians (and the Spartans).

After having devoted seven sections to public matters (including crimes against the city), the Athenian devotes five very brief sections chiefly to private law or crimes against individuals (953e5–955b7); he then devotes seven sections, i.e., the rest of the Book, again to public matters. By assigning the relatively trivial center of the Book to private matters, he forces us to wonder whether the private is in the last analysis in the service of the public, or whether the public is essentially in the service of the private since it is designed to protect (cf. 920d7–e3) and to foster (666d10–e6) the private. The central subject of the last section of the first "public" part is the spectator of foreign cities and laws who reports his findings to the Nocturnal Council; the subject of the last section of the final "public" part is the Nocturnal Council.

The first section of the final "public" part makes it a capital offense for a citizen to make peace with an enemy with whom the city is at war (as Dikaiopolis does in Aristophanes' *Acharnians*) and to wage a war against friends of the city.

The second section makes it a capital offense for citizens to accept gifts for their services to the fatherland. No distinction in this respect between beneficial and harmful services should be made, for it is not easy to know what is beneficial or not and, even if one does know, to abide by that knowledge: knowledge and abiding by one's knowledge, knowledge and virtue, are different things; for very many who are very bad have knowledge of the good (950b5–c2).

The next section regulates mandatory contributions to the public treasury. Neither in this nor in the next section is anything said about penalties.

The next section, the central section of the final "public" part, deals with votive offerings and other gifts to the gods. Votive offerings of gold, silver, ivory, iron, and bronze are not desirable. The most divine gifts are birds (cf. *Phaedo* 118b7–8) and paintings which a single painter could complete in a single day.

After speaking of the gifts to the gods, the Athenian can claim with some justice that the political order proper—the division of the whole city into parts, i.e., above all both the clear separation of citizens from noncitizens and the division of the citizen body into the four property classes—and all the most important transactions have been stated, for he does not now limit the transactions to transactions among human beings (cf. 913a1–2 and 922a6–8). What remains to be done is to regulate judicial procedure. The Athenian had spoken of this subject before; his present statement partly repeats and partly supplements his first statement and thus fulfills the promise which he had made at the end of the first statement (768c3–8). In a second statement he had said that many details are not worthy of the attention of an aged legislator and should be determined by his young successors (846a8–c8); he now repeats this second statement also. But now, after he has discussed indigenous and foreign spectators, he adds that, as regards the courts' dealing with matters touching the city directly, the law guardians must borrow ordinances laid down by respectable men in other cities and improve on them, if need be; accordingly he refers here implicitly to the Nocturnal Council (957c1). The reference here to the respectable legislators in other cities (which are presumably less well-ordered than our city is) is not unnaturally accompanied by the Athenian's being silent now on the necessity that every citizen participate in the judicial process (767e9–768b3). He thus prepares a reassertion of the divine and admirable character of the laws if they are correct and therefore reveal their kinship with the intellect, and renewed praise of the superiority of the legislator's writings to the writings or speeches of poets and others: the legislator's writings must supply the good judge with the sole standard of judgment. In agreement with all this, the Athenian here designates the whole of virtue as justice, or rather the whole of vice as injustice.

We have now reached the end of the legislation except for the law regarding the end of the whole polity, of the whole of political life, which is death (632c1–4). The legislator must concern himself with the proper burial of those who have led a law-abiding life or at least have not lost through heinous crimes the right to be buried. The law regarding burial concludes the legislation just as the law concerning marriage—the proximate condition of the birth of children—opens it. What sacred law prescribes regarding burial with a view to the gods below and the gods here must be learned from the interpreters. The human legislator is competent to forbid the use for burial places of any places which earth, being our mother, by her nature wishes to give sustenance for human beings. It is likewise incumbent on the human legislator to assert the following things: the soul is altogether different from the body; what makes each of us alive while he is alive is nothing but the soul, the body being only a semblance which attends each of us; when men have died, their bodies are finely said to be mere shades; what each of us truly is— that which is given the name of being an immortal soul—goes away to other gods to give an account of its life here, as the ancestral law declares. These assertions guide the regulations regarding burial and mourning. Within the limits determined by the law, the inequality of the citizens regarding property is permitted to extend to the expenses for their funerals.

The legislation would now have been completed if it were sufficient to establish the legal order without having taken care of its complete and lasting safeguarding. Kleinias agrees to this proposition but does not quite see what the Athenian is aiming at with it: is not such safeguarding assured by the chorus of Dionysos, by the provisions for the upbringing of every new generation by what almost amounts to a prohibition against change, at least of the fundamental laws, and, last but not least, by the auditors? The Athenian finds his thought nobly expressed by the names which the men of the past have given to the three Fates, especially to the third, whom they called Atropos. Socrates had referred to the three Fates near the end of the *Republic* in a very different context: the myth of Er. The Athenian refers to them in an entirely nonmythical context. The laws, he says, still lack the power, agreeing with nature, of irreversibility. In reply to Kleinias' eager question as to what might supply salvation, a stable foundation to the regime and the laws of the new city, he refers to what he had said about the Nocturnal Council; he repeats his earlier statement (951d5–e5) about its composition, i.e., he changes it somewhat. Kleinias does not notice the change. The Athenian goes on to say that the Nocturnal Council must be cast out as a perfect anchor for the whole city. He promises that, in explaining what this means, he will not omit anything as far as zeal is concerned. But obviously there are reasons other than lack of zeal which may cause or justify omissions. Each thing, we are told, has its proper savior for all its operations, as in an animal the soul and the head, the virtue of both of which supplies salvation to the animal. Virtue accrues to the soul above all through the intellect, to the head above all through sight and hearing. Generally speaking, intellect combined with the most noble sense perceptions and the union into one of the intellect and sense perception would most justly be called the salvation of each operation. What the Athenian is aiming at with this statement is not at all clear: all animals with the exception of man lack intellect, and yet intellect is said to be needed for the salvation of every animal; is the distinction between man and the other animals to be blurred? And is it to be blurred in order to underline as strongly as possible the indispensable contribution of sense perceptions which are common to all animals and, we may add, of other things common to animals to the salvation of man and the city? The Athenian passes over this difficulty for the time being and speaks in the immediate sequel only of man or, more precisely, of the arts. In every art the intellect in combination with sense perception deals with a peculiar thing, i.e., aims at a peculiar target; for instance, in a ship the pilot and the sailors, fusing their sense perceptions with the piloting intellect, save themselves and whatever belongs to the ship. The intellect is particularly concerned with the target which, as target of this kind, is not perceived by the senses. If the settlement of the country is to be complete, the settlement must include in the first place an ingredient which knows the aim of the political art and then in which manner it may attain that aim, and which of the laws in the first place and then which of the human beings advises it nobly or basely; without it the city will lack intellect and sense perception and hence will act haphazardly in everything. That part or pursuit of the city which provides the desired safeguard, the desired fusion of intellect and sense perception, is the Nocturnal Council, as Kleinias guesses. That Council must possess every virtue, i.e., every virtue of the soul and of the head. Accordingly, it must above all not be confused by a multiplicity of targets but look at a single target only and, as it were, shoot all its arrows at that very target. From this we understand the confusion reigning in the cities. In every city the legislator looks at a different target, as if there could be different targets for the political art, which is one, or as if there could be a medicine the target of which were not health. The target at which legislation ordinarily aims, and with a view to which it delimits the just things, is either the rule of some without any regard to their virtue, or wealth without any regard to freedom from foreign domination, or a zealously sought life of freedom, or a combination of two targets such as freedom and mastery over other cities, or—and this is the target of those who believe themselves to be most wise—all targets mentioned and all others of the same kind without one of them being singled out as the authoritative end.

At this point Kleinias comes, as it were, to the Athenian's help: our end has been correctly determined a long time ago; for we said that our whole legislation must look to one end, that end being virtue; it is true that virtue consists of four virtues, but the intellect is the leader of them all, and to the intellect all other things and the three other virtues must look. The Athenian praises Kleinias for the most noble manner in which he follows, for it is irrelevant in the present context and for the present purpose that the difference between good-sense—one of the four virtues—and intellect be considered and stressed. (Cf. 688b2–3 where the leader of the whole virtue is called "good-sense and intellect and opinion": as little as opinion is the same as good-sense or intellect, so little is good-sense the same as intellect; in some men the leader of virtue is good-sense, in others it is true opinion—632c5–6—in still others simply opinion regarding some image of virtue.) The Athenian goes on to draw Kleinias' attention to a point which apparently has not been settled "a long time ago." There is a multiplicity of intellects like the piloting, the medical, and the strategic intellect, each aiming at a single end: let us address the political intellect (the statesman's intellect), which might claim to be superior to all rivals, and ask it as if it were a human being what the single end is at which it aims. Neither the political intellect nor the two interlocutors can answer that question; as it seems, the answer is not that the single end in question is virtue. For however important legislation may be, the statesman's art is not exhausted by it; hence the fact that the end of legislation is virtue does not prove that the end of the political art is virtue. This may have been the reason why Kleinias was not able to answer the question concerning the single end of the political art; the Athenian sees the difficulty elsewhere. Perhaps it would be more correct to say that he has a different notion of what the political art is about (cf. 650b6–10). Even if, and precisely if, the end of the political art as a whole is virtue, and all virtues must look to one and the same Leader Intellect, there remains a difficulty not discussed hitherto: there are four kinds of virtue, each of them being one, for otherwise they would not altogether be four; yet all four kinds are one inasmuch as each of them is "virtue." It is not difficult to say how the four virtues, or at any rate how courage and good-sense, differ from one another, but it is no longer easy to say how they are one. Since Kleinias does not understand, the Athenian proposes that one of them should ask questions and the other should answer them. Kleinias again fails to understand: how can questioning and

answering as such be helpful? The Athenian tells him therefore to
address to him the twofold question regarding the unity and duality
of courage and good-sense, and he tells him what he, the Athenian,
will answer to the second question, which is, as we have heard, the
easier of the two: courage differs from good-sense because it has to
do with fear, of which the beasts also partake, and the beasts, just
as very young children, partake of courage, for the courageous soul
arises by nature and without *logos*; but a soul having good-sense
and intellect can never arise without *logos*. Having answered the
question regarding the difference, the Athenian asks Kleinias to tell
him how the two virtues are one and the same, despite their being
two. Kleinias, who did not and could not answer the easier of the
two questions, naturally cannot and does not answer the more difficult one. It would be disgraceful to believe that the Athenian plays
a cruel game with him or holds him up to ridicule, but he does what
he does in order to throw light on the Nocturnal Council, for men
of Kleinias' kind will form no insignificant part of it: many members
of that Council will lack the ability to raise and answer the most
important questions; they will lack the true art of raising questions
and answering them, the true art of conversing (*dialektikē*).

The statement on the a-rational or subrational character of courage is not altogether surprising; the Athenian had spoken in the
same vein on moderation (710a3–b5; cf. also 897b8–c1). The reason why he now singles out courage is not merely that he wishes to
link the end of the conversation with its beginning, with the critiques
of the Dorian overestimation of courage (630c2–3), but also that
from a political point of view courage can be said to be more indispensable than moderation: moderation in and by itself does not
deserve honor (696d4–e2). When Socrates describes the nature of
the guardians in the *Republic*, he says that they must be courageous
like noble puppies (374e6–375a9); he does not speak there of their
having to be moderate. In any case, it makes sense to say that the
city needs some kind of virtue which is subrational, some animal
virtue. For the city—and hence the target at which the political art
aims—is not simply one but complex, consisting of very different
parts. It suffices perhaps to think of the profound difference between
demos and non-*demos* and the necessity, following from this difference, of diluting true proportionate equality which for us is always
the political right, with that equality which gives everyone the same
(734e6–735a4, 757b1–758a2, 759b6). One may also think of the
fact that the common good has a ceiling (the genuine virtue of all
citizens who are capable of it) and a flooring (survival), and that

these two ends may make opposite demands on the statesman (cf.
709a). To come back to the main point, each virtue is one and all
four virtues are one, not in spite of, but because of the amazing
differences between the virtues and within each virtue, for all these
differences can only be understood in the light of, they all flow from,
the unity of virtue; virtue as virtue, at least as human virtue (cf.
900e1–9) consists of both the *logos* and the subrational (653b1–6).
Virtue (and each virtue) is necessarily accompanied by images of it
(655b4–5); it necessarily shades off into these images; hence there
cannot be knowledge of what virtue is without knowledge of that
multiplicity: one cannot know what courage is without giving due
weight to the animal courage so strongly stressed by the Athenian.

After the Athenian has asked Kleinias to make clear the unity of
the four virtues, he does not wait for his answer but goes on to ask
him whether it is sufficient, in the cases of all things which have a
name and also a *logos*, to know the name only, or whether it is not
disgraceful for a man of any account to be ignorant of all such
things (names, *logoi* etc.) in regard to matters of surpassing greatness and beauty. Kleinias is inclined to agree. He definitely answers
in the negative when the Athenian asks him whether there are
greater subjects for the legislator, for the law guardian, and for anyone who regards himself as of outstanding virtue or is judged to be
such by the competent authority, than the four virtues. The Athenian
draws the conclusion that the interpreters, the teachers, and the
legislators must be able to teach to a higher degree the others, both
those merely lacking knowledge and those in need of punishment
what power vice as well as virtue has; they surely must be better
men and better teachers of virtue than alien poets and would-be
educators of the young. He doubtless has in mind the members of
the Nocturnal Council, although his allusion to its composition differs considerably from his two earlier allusions. That composition
cannot help remaining somewhat obscure, just as the relation of the
Council to the magistracies. The obscurity is due to the impossibility
of assigning to the wise as wise their proper place and status in a
politically viable form. For the city, lacking the head and senses,
cannot have wisdom or good-sense as the man of good-sense can;
it can only resemble the latter. The city itself may be compared to
the trunk of the body: the head, i.e., what resembles the head,
namely, the Nocturnal Council, does not belong to the city itself,
to the true city (cf. *Republic* 372e6–7). Surely the members of the
Nocturnal Council need a more precise education than the citizens
as citizens. That higher and, indeed, highest education must enable

one to look from the many and dissimilar things to the one—the one *idea*—to see everything in its light and to order everything with a view to it: the precise knowledge of the virtues, which is, as it seems, the highest function of the Nocturnal Council, consists above all in grasping the unity of virtue. Kleinias does not see the supremacy of this approach, but he trusts the Athenian and therefore agrees. Thereupon the Athenian draws the conclusion that we must compel, as it seems, also the guardians of our divine regime to see precisely in the first place what the one and the same thing in the four virtues (courage, moderation, justice, good-sense) is which we justly call by the one name "virtue." The required knowledge includes knowing whether virtue is by nature one or a whole or both or perhaps something different. Without the required knowledge, i.e., if we are unable to say whether virtue is many or four or one, we are not adequately equipped in regard to virtue. The Athenian gives Kleinias a last opportunity to escape from the most arduous task. But, swearing by the god of strangers, Kleinias refuses to take the easy way out. The Athenian, however, refuses to say now how they can contrive the achievement of the goal; Kleinias is left wondering whether the contrivance is possible. The Athenian, we see, has now abandoned the sub-Socratic level on which he had argued throughout the conversation; he has postponed that abandonment as long as he could: until the very end.

The Athenian next indicates two further subjects of study; of the first he speaks with extreme brevity while of the second he speaks rather extensively. The central subject is the noble (beautiful) and the good. We hear that it is necessary for our guardians to know how and in what manner the noble and the good are one or, to borrow the expression used shortly before (965c2), to know the one *idea* of the noble on the one hand and of the good on the other. Nothing is said about the relation of the noble and the good to virtue except that it is clearly implied that "the noble and the good" and "virtue" are not identical. Nor is anything said about the relation of the *idea* of the noble and that of the good. The men who are to be truly guardians of the laws must truly know what pertains to the truth of all serious subjects and must be able both to expound that knowledge in speech and to conform to it in their actions; they must therefore be able to discern the speeches and deeds which are noble according to nature and those which are not.

The third and final subject of study which the Athenian mentions concerns the being and power of the gods; it surely belongs to the serious subjects; it is one of the most noble subjects; the Athenian

does not say that it is the most noble subject, superior in nobility
to virtue and the idea of the good (cf. 964b3–7, 965c1–6, 890b6–
c1). The relation of the third subject to the first two is left in becoming obscurity. While the large majority of the citizens must be
permitted to follow merely what the laws tell them regarding the
gods, the true guardians must make every effort to acquire full
assurance, full proof: no one may be elected guardian of the law who
merely believes in the gods as the laws declare them to be and because the laws declare them to be (cf. 885d4–5, 890a6–7, b6–7,
891e1–2, 904a9). Kleinias agrees without hesitation. But when the
Athenian asks him whether we know that there are two things which
lead to assurance regarding gods—two things which we have discussed earlier—Kleinias does not know to which things he refers.
The Athenian reminds him or rather tells him that the two things
in question are these: the soul is the most ancient and divine of all
the things whose motion, bringing in its train coming-into-being, has
provided ever flowing being; and the orderliness of the local change
of the stars and all other things which are ruled by the intellect who
thus regulates the whole. Astronomy, then, far from leading to atheism as the many suspect, has precisely the opposite effect if it is
properly studied. There was indeed a time when the study of the
stars was not guided by the awareness of the priority of the soul
and hence of intellect to body, and thus led to atheism; at that time
the poets abused those who philosophized by comparing them to
howling bitches. (The terrible error of those men does not deprive
them of the title or honor due to men who philosophize.)

The Athenian concludes his statement on the third subject of
study to which the true guardians of the law, the members of the
Nocturnal Council, must devote themselves by saying that no mortal
human being can possibly ever become firmly god-revering if he has
not grasped the two things now stated: (1) the soul, while being
immortal, is the oldest of all things which partake of generation and
rules over all bodies; and (2) the intellect in the stars. It follows
from this grave statement that the grasp of the first two subjects of
study, i.e., of the ideas of the virtues and of virtue and of the ideas
of the noble and of the good, does not by itself lead to the habit of
god-revering or of piety. Hence it could seem that the third study,
in itself bi-partite, is the highest of the three. In the first place it is
mentioned at the end, and the end seems to be the best (cf. 627d11–
628a5). Besides, the virtues are the good dispositions of the soul
(cf. 653b1–6), and the soul, while akin to the ideas, is for this
reason not an idea (*Phaedo* 79d9–e5, 80b1–3; *Republic* 490b1–4).

Furthermore, from the virtues one is more directly led to their leader, the intellect, than to the ideas, and the intellect is the ground of the kosmic order, within which and through which virtue is possible (cf. *Gorgias* 507d6–508a8). Yet apart from the fact that considerations such as these would lead to the result, unacceptable to most people, that there are no ideas of the virtues, the Athenian does not say or indicate anything to the effect that the third subject of study is higher in rank than the first two, or even equal in rank to them. We are then forced to conclude that the ideas retain in the *Laws*, if in a properly subdued or muted manner, the status which they occupy, say, in the *Republic*.

Firmly established piety requires full assurance, full proof of the first theologoumenon which was in a manner proved in Book Ten. In the recent restatement it is less than clear whether each star possesses intellect and hence is a god (cf. 899b3–c1). It is clear that, according to the final statement, firmly established piety does not require full proof of the second and third theologoumena, which are also in a manner proved in Book Ten. Nor does the final statement even allude to the Olympian gods. In this respect the difference between the Nocturnal Council and the auditors is especially noteworthy. The members of the Nocturnal Council are not as such, as the auditors are, dedicated to Apollon or, for that matter, to any other Olympian, nor are they as such, as the auditors are, priests of Apollon or, for that matter, of any other Olympian; nor do they receive, as the auditors do, surpassing honors during life and especially after death. (A comparison of the three statements on the composition of the Nocturnal Council—951d4–e5, 961a1–c2, 964b8–9 —is instructive.)

The members of the Nocturnal Council must have taken hold of the subjects of learning which necessarily precede astronomy, they must use their knowledge for the pursuits and customary practices related to character, and they must be able to give an account of whatever is susceptible of an account. They must also have acquired the common virtues, i.e., the virtues which every citizen can acquire and which are presupposed rather than supplied by the highest kinds of study; those virtues do not include piety, for the piety of the citizen is replaced by that piety which alone is firm and which comes only from the study of the soul and of the intellect regulating the whole. Only the members of the Nocturnal Council can be truly rulers, or magistrates, of the whole city. The Athenian raises next the question, whether they should add to all the laws previously laid down this further law which provides for the legal establishment of the Nocturnal Council of magistrates. Kleinias answers in the affirmative, although he has a certain awareness of the difficulty. The Athenian thereupon declares his eagerness to assist, for he possesses very long experience in "such matters" and has given much thought to them. Yet he regards the attempt to legislate regarding "such matters" as premature: first the Council itself must be set up. It seems that the Council cannot be simply subject to the legislator as the other magistracies are. The setting up of the Council requires in its turn extensive preparations. To mention only the central point, it is not easy to find out what subjects the members of the Nocturnal Council ought to learn; nor is it easy, if another man has found out, to become his pupil. The Athenian thus adumbrates the fundamental difficulty regarding the Nocturnal Council: are all its members men each of whom can acquire within his soul science of the subjects in question? Are its members potential or actual philosophers? A glance at Kleinias is sufficient to make one see the pertinence of the question. The heterogeneous composition of the Council makes it impossible to give a simple answer. Hence the Athenian cannot, as Socrates in the *Republic* can, determine the subjects of study and the time to be allotted to each.

"This being so, what ought to be done, stranger?" Kleinias asks most appropriately. The Athenian begins his reply by pointing out how dangerous their undertaking is: the attempt to establish the Nocturnal Council may lead to total victory or total defeat for their attempt to found a city; if the attempt to establish the Nocturnal Council fails, the whole enterprise fails. The Athenian is willing to share in the risk by expounding his opinions about education and rearing, a subject raised just now and not for the first time. (He does not retract his refusal to become a member of the new city: 753a5–8.) The risk itself is of incomparable greatness: by correctly establishing and ordering the city Kleinias will achieve highest glory or will never escape the reputation of being the most courageous of his successors, for he has no predecessors and his successors are only his imitators. If this divine council—earlier (965d9–10) the regime had been called divine—comes into being, we must hand the city over to it. (The divine Council or the divine Assembly is obviously different from the Assembly of all citizens—cf. e.g. 764a3 —which one is tempted to call the human Assembly, the Assembly *tout court*; while the divine Assembly is the grand theme of the final section of the *Laws*, the other Assembly is never thematically discussed in the work; surely the city cannot be handed over to the human Assembly. Can the two Assemblies thrive together in one and the same city?) So to speak, none of the legislators of the present day, despite or because of their inadequacy (962d6–e9), will quarrel with this. Thus there will be accomplished in waking what shortly before we treated in our speech as a dream. The members of the divine Council must be carefully selected, properly educated, and, after the completion of their education, settled in the akropolis of the country; then they will be guardians the like of whom we have never seen before in our lives in regard to excellence of guardianship.

Megillos, who has not said a word for a long time (891b7), is so much impressed by the glorious prospect which the Athenian has conjured up that he turns to "dear Kleinias" with unusual liveliness and tells him that one must either abandon the settlement of the city or not let the Athenian stranger go: he must be made a participant in the settlement of the city by means of beseeching and contrivances of all kinds. Kleinias fully agrees but adds that Megillos too must help. With Megillos' "I shall help" the dialogue ends. The Athenian "naturally" does not respond.